Testimonies from Wellstone Action Participants Who Have Won the Wellstone Way

Winning Your Election the Wellstone Way provides a refreshing look at how to run an election in a grassroots people-powered way—just as the great Senator Paul Wellstone did—and **win**.
▸ Representative Tim Walz (MN-01)

As a teacher, coach, and neighborhood activist, I didn't spend my career planning to run for office—but I knew that I had the experience to lead my community in the Arizona Senate. Camp Wellstone gave me valuable skills that helped me run an organized, energizing campaign. *Winning Your Election the Wellstone Way* makes those skills available to progressive candidates and campaign managers throughout the country.
▸ State Senator Paula Aboud, Tucson, Arizona

Once I made the decision to run for office, I felt like I had pointed my skis down a steep mountain: it was thrilling and challenging, and everything went very fast. Wellstone Action's expertise and training gave me and my campaign the critical skills and confidence we needed to win. *Winning Your Election the Wellstone Way* is a must for emerging leaders who have decided to step up for their community and run for office.
▸ Angelique Espinoza, elected to city council in Boulder, Colorado

I was fortunate to attend Camp Wellstone while preparing for my first campaign. Not only did I learn important skills that significantly contributed to my winning the election to the Raleigh city council, but I also created a valuable network of friends and politically active folks, and we continue to support each other. I often refer back to the lessons learned at Camp Wellstone. EVERYTHING they teach you is valuable—pay close attention to everything they say!
▸ Rodger Koopman, elected to city council in Raleigh, North Carolina

A new generation of candidates has helped to shepherd in the rising progressive movement, but each of them needs a highly skilled campaign manager. *Winning Your Election the Wellstone Way* is a crucial reference tool for campaign managers on races big and small. Like Wellstone Action's trainings, this book offers an opportunity to learn tried-and-true tactics from campaign veterans.
▸ Nicholl Caruso, Wisconsin state director for Progressive Majority

Winning Your Election the Wellstone Way

Winning
Your Election
the Wellstone Way

*A Comprehensive Guide
for Candidates and
Campaign Workers*

Jeff Blodgett AND Bill Lofy

WITH BEN GOLDFARB
ERIK PETERSON
AND SUJATA TEJWANI

University of Minnesota Press
MINNEAPOLIS • LONDON

Published by the University of Minnesota Press
111 Third Avenue South, Suite 290
Minneapolis, MN 55401-2520
http://www.upress.umn.edu

Library of Congress Cataloging-in-Publication Data

Blodgett, Jeff, 1961–
    Winning your election the Wellstone way : a comprehensive guide for candidates and campaign workers / Jeff Blodgett and Bill Lofy ; with Ben Goldfarb, Erik Peterson, and Sujata Tejwani.
       p.   cm.
    Includes index.
    ISBN 978-0-8166-5333-1 (pb : alk. paper)
    1. Political campaigns—United States.   2. Campaign management—United States.
  3. Wellstone, Paul David.   I. Lofy, Bill.   II. Title.
    JK2281.B62 2008
    324.70973—dc22
                                      2008011082

Printed in the United States of America on acid-free paper

The University of Minnesota is an equal-opportunity educator and employer.

16 15 14 13 12 11 10 09 08   10 9 8 7 6 5 4 3 2 1

CONTENTS

About This Book

JEFF BLODGETT

In the fall of 2005, Wellstone Action published our first book, *Politics the Wellstone Way: How to Elect Progressive Candidates and Win on Issues*. The idea was to take the body of material that we taught and handed out in our trainings and compile it into a book to reach a broader audience. Our ambitions for the book were modest: in addition to using the book at our trainings, we hoped to reach a group of people who believe in progressive politics and want to get involved in politics but don't know how. Two years later, after seventeen thousand copies of the book had been sold and readers started asking when the next one would be published, we knew we had created something worth replicating.

Winning Your Election the Wellstone Way is a logical outgrowth of *Politics the Wellstone Way*. As Wellstone Action grew during the past two years, the individuals we have trained have gone out and organized, run for office, and worked for candidates. As they expanded their set of experiences and understanding of how to engage in effective political action, we expanded the scope of our trainings. We began to offer advanced campaign management trainings and created a training curriculum geared toward people who want to pursue a career in campaign management. It didn't take long for it to become clear that a more comprehensive book was needed.

That's why we wrote this book. *Winning Your Election the Wellstone Way* is a comprehensive guide for people running for office and for those helping them. It draws on the examples and real experience of many recent successful candidates and campaigns small and large. It is a book designed to help you learn from people who have been there and have been successful. If you're looking for a detailed overview of what it takes to run for office and win, this book is written for you.

When we held our first political action training in 2003, none of us imagined that by 2008 Wellstone Action would have trained more than fourteen thousand candidates, campaign workers, students, progressive activists, and others. More than five years after the plane crash that took Paul Wellstone's life, his model of political organizing endures, and Wellstone Action has become a national center of training and leadership development. The foundation of our trainings is the political approach to organizing that Wellstone practiced successfully as a community organizer, political candidate, and U.S. senator. It's an approach to political change that combines three components: organizing in communities on an ongoing basis, electing progressive candidates, and developing leaders who articulate a new vision for our country and work to implement a change agenda. While this book focuses on just the electoral component, we believe the progressive movement needs all three to ultimately succeed with political and social change.

Wellstone Action was created in the wake of tragedy. The plane crash that killed Wellstone also took his wife, Sheila; their daughter, Marcia; three talented campaign aides; and the two pilots. It was a devastating loss for the country and for those who worked closely with Paul and Sheila. But instead of mourning what could have been, Mark and David Wellstone, the surviving sons, enlisted the help and advice of their father's friends and colleagues to continue what Paul did best—motivate and inspire future leaders.

Wellstone Action is a nonprofit whose mission is to teach effective political action skills and train people to build their capacity and become better advocates, organizers, candidates, campaign workers, and citizen activists. To those of us who worked closely with him—I did for more than twenty-five years, as a student at Carleton College and later as the manager of all three of his campaigns for U.S. Senate—we're sure this is what Paul would want us to be doing.

Wellstone Action's results have been extraordinarily rewarding. In addition to holding trainings in thirty-nine states (and counting), we have grown as a center of political training and leader development. Wellstone Action runs eight training programs:

> ▶ *Camp Wellstone* is the centerpiece of our training offerings. This well-traveled three-day training, designed for candidates, campaign workers, and issue advocates, teaches the nuts and bolts of winning electoral and issue campaigns.

- ► *Advanced Campaign Management School* is an intensive five-day training for experienced campaign workers who are looking to be campaign managers and senior staff on electoral campaigns.

- ► *Campus Camp Wellstone* is specifically aimed at college students getting started in progressive political activism.

- ► The Sheila Wellstone Institute uses a unique advocacy training, called *Camp Sheila Wellstone,* for people involved in the movement to end domestic and sexual violence.

- ► Our two-day *Voter Engagement School* is held in partnership with organizations working to build political power in communities of color and other underrepresented constituencies.

- ► Our *Labor Training* work is with leaders, rank and file, and staff of labor organizations that are working to build internal and external political capacity and leadership.

- ► *Wellstone Organizing Fellows* is a program to develop new political organizers in communities of color.

- ► We hold *Custom Trainings* with like-minded organizations that are working to build their political power.

One motivation that underlies all of our training is our desire to see new waves of leaders—champions of the issues we care about who are grounded in our communities—stepping forward to run for office at all levels. So we also partner with national networks that focus on developing good candidates for office: Progressive Majority, EMILY's List, the White House Project, Emerge, and many local efforts. We help candidates in our trainings find these networks and take advantage of what they have to offer. If you are in one of Progressive Majority's targeted states, for example, you may be able to join their candidate Farm Team and receive ongoing advice, resources, and assistance from experienced and knowledgeable Progressive Majority staff. If you are a pro-choice Democratic woman, you might be able to take advantage of the great trainings by EMILY's List, benefit from their trained staffers, or become one of their targeted races. These candidate development groups are a key part of the effort to reclaim our politics.

At Wellstone Action we've gathered together the best and most current campaign practitioner-trainers who teach the set of core competencies for candidates and campaign workers involved in running winning campaigns. We're constantly looking for current best practices by studying recent races and learning from successful candidates and campaign workers and by staying involved in campaigns ourselves. We've accumulated a wealth of knowledge, information, case studies, and stories about how to win elections, and we pass it on to others.

One difficulty we found in writing this book was deciding what scale of campaign to target. What might be critically important to a large-scale campaign—management systems for a staff of thirty or more campaign workers, for example—isn't relevant to a town council race managed by a part-time volunteer. Yet while scale does make a big difference when discussing campaigns, there are many fundamentals, strategic imperatives, and tactics that are common across the size of campaigns. In the end, each campaign is about effectively communicating a message to voters and managing and maximizing the three resources of time, people, and money in a way that helps you win your election. For example, even if you're not running a television advertising campaign, the principles of using paid media apply to nearly every campaign.

What keeps us going in this work is Paul Wellstone's model of persistence. He never stood still. He was always organizing, always advocating, and always empowering other people to become their own leaders. Paul's relentless drive and optimistic outlook on the future inspires our work, and we hope that, even in an indirect way, it will inspire you to seek opportunities to make a difference in your community, whether that means running for office, managing a campaign, or volunteering your time to a campaign.

We also hope you will view your work as part of a broader, long-term progressive movement. We have a lot of work ahead of us, and it will take decades to get it done. So, good luck on your campaign, and if you have a chance, join us for one of our trainings. We plan on sticking around for a while and hope you do, too.

CHAPTER 1

Running to Win: Qualities of Good Candidates and Managers

Since 2003, Wellstone Action has trained thousands of candidates and campaign workers, providing both philosophical and practical advice for how to run progressive campaigns and win. Participants in our training programs have gone on to win races for mayor, city council, state legislature, sheriff, school board, secretary of state, Congress, and other positions. We've trained candidates, campaign managers, press secretaries, field directors, volunteer coordinators, and finance directors for campaigns in thirty-eight states. These individuals come from widely diverse backgrounds. Some are from rural areas, others from urban centers. Some needed clear and specific guidance for every step of the campaign, while others take some suggestions, ignore others, and create their own style of campaigning. As we tell our training participants, campaigns are not one-size-fits-all undertakings. The successful progressive campaigns we've been involved with have varying messages, employ different strategies, use different tactics for communicating with voters, and have their own style and tone.

Despite their differences, there are two things that all of these candidates and campaign workers share: a progressive political outlook and a desire to win. We will not spend a lot of time in this book talking about what it means to be a progressive. Our focus instead is on skills, strategies, and tactics that help candidates and their campaign workers win elections. But we write this book because we are progressives who want to see our values brought into the public and political realm. Values such as a belief in economic justice and equality of opportunity, the primacy of educating our children and supporting families, and making sure we *progress* as a country to the point where good physical and mental health care is not just a privilege for some. We believe homes should be safe places for women and children and should be free of violence. We believe our role in the world needs to be one of leading in matters of peace and justice, instead of sowing disaster for years to come, as we have been doing in the first part of this century. We believe, as Paul Wellstone would say, that we move our country forward in this new global economy by focusing as a country on the goals of a good education, good health care, and good jobs for all Americans. And that "we all do better when we all do better."

We'll leave the rest of the definition of what it means to be a progressive to you and others. This book is about the other thing we hope you share: a desire to win. We want to win not for the sake of winning but because winning is how we actually move our communities, states, and country in a more progressive direction. In other words, we work to attain *power* to make the change we seek in this world. Sometimes the concept of power makes progressives uneasy; after all, most of us have grown accustomed to fighting the people and interests that control power in our communities and in our country. We're used to railing against the misuse and abuse of power. We've seen too clearly the corrupting influence that power can have on those who control it. But as Harry Shearer asks: "If absolute power corrupts absolutely, does absolute powerlessness make you pure?"

Power is neither a good nor a bad; it's neutral. Look at the Latin root of the word power, *potere:* "to be able to." That is, power enables one to achieve things. Martin Luther King Jr. used to say that power is simply the ability to achieve a purpose; whether it is good or bad depends on the purpose. Used the right way, power can improve people's lives and positively change the state of our nation. We should not be afraid of power. On the contrary, we should pursue it ethically, aggressively, and skillfully. We're not interested in selling out our values, but we do like to win.

A story from one successful progressive candidate, Green Bay City Council Member Celestine Jeffries, illustrates why we emphasize power as our ultimate goal. Jeffries, who had grown concerned that her neighborhood had fallen on hard times, began pushing for greater accountability for rogue landlords who let their properties fall into disrepair. Then in 2005, an advisory committee of the city council proposed eliminating the inspections department of city hall and putting the duties under control of the fire department, which Jeffries felt would severely weaken the inspection process. "So I went to a meeting of the city council and I spoke out very strongly against this proposal," she told us. She left feeling that she had spoken too forcefully and hadn't shown enough restraint. At a meeting a couple weeks later, she saw the mayor and approached him. "I apologized for losing my cool," she said. "And he responded with words I'll never forget. He said, 'Celestine, you know what you need? You need more power.' I was floored, absolutely floored." She took the mayor's advice to heart and launched a campaign for city council, winning 57 percent of the vote and becoming the first African American ever to serve on the Green Bay City Council. As the mayor who encouraged Jeffries knew, winning is about gaining power and using it to empower others.

So how do ethical, caring, and passionate progressives stay true to their values and beliefs and win an election at the same time? In other words, how do you win elections the right way? We believe it is possible to stay true to who you are and win your campaign. We believe you can articulate a message about values and employ strategies that both galvanize a strong grassroots base *and* appeal to undecided voters, and throughout this book we will give examples of campaigns that have won this way. This book zeroes in on the skills required to run these kinds of campaigns in a winning way.

Ultimately, we at Wellstone Action do our work (and wrote this book) because we believe that at this point in time for our country and the world, we need many new people stepping forward to run for office and assume roles of leadership. More than ever before, we need new waves of quality leaders at all levels. At Wellstone Action we are hardly alone in our commitment to building the progressive movement through electoral victories. A large and growing network of progressive organizations has formed in the past few years with a focus on developing progressive candidates and campaign workers to win elections across the country. These groups, including the White House Project, Progressive Majority, Center for Progressive Leadership, and EMILY's List, to name just a few, are doing great work to mobilize a broad network of progressive candidates and activists committed to winning elections.

A consistent theme of all these organizations is the need for each of us to consider running for office. It's not easy to be a candidate, and for those of you who advocate and organize from the outside, don't misunderstand: yours is also critical work. But without people willing to run for office themselves, we remain on the outside and without certain power. Some of our urgency comes from losing Paul Wellstone's voice on the national stage just when we needed it the most. But we know Wellstone would be saying, "Don't mourn, organize." And for Wellstone, organizing meant bringing communities together to realize their power, fighting for the issues, and stepping forward to run for and win elective office. So we honor those who have taken the plunge and decided to be candidates, and we encourage more progressives to consider making the same decision.

The advice we provide in this book is aimed at both candidates and campaign workers. While some of the specific information about candidates and the decision to run for office is not directly relevant to campaign workers, we present to both audiences anyway, because not only is it good information for campaign workers to know, it is also the type of advice that good campaign workers will give to their bosses. Likewise, we talk in detail about the role of campaign staff and volunteers. While this isn't aimed at candidates, it's good background information for candidates to have, provided that candidates understand that their role is not to manage the campaign—their role is to raise money and speak directly to voters.

The Need for Total Commitment

Running for office requires having a total desire for holding the office you are seeking. Running for office, says State Senator Patricia Torres Ray of Minnesota, "requires a genuine commitment to the candidacy. You have to demonstrate that you really want to be in that office. Sometimes people run for office because they want to run for something else. I think people have to be genuine about wanting this and letting people know that this is what they want to do and why." Voters know passion when they see it in candidates. Another successful candidate said, "People recognize that passion and they can sense when you are genuine."

Passion not only makes you a more genuine candidate—it can give you confidence. "My advice to anyone running for office is to be very clear about why it is you want to do it," said Andrew Gillum, who became the youngest member of the Tallahassee City Commission in 2005 after running an aggressive grassroots campaign. "When it gets tough, that will be the one source of strength to rely on. You need a way to articulate to yourself and to others exactly why you want to have this job. If you can do that, you'll be able to renew yourself throughout the campaign even when others can't." It helps to write this down very early in the campaign with a narrative answer to the questions: "Why do I want to do this job?" and "Why am I the best candidate?" Too often this very basic answer goes unexamined and unarticulated. The wordsmiths and messaging all come later and are informed and grounded from this core.

Commitment extends not only to your passion for holding office, but also to the amount of time it takes to run a winning race. Ask yourself: Am I really prepared to put in the work a campaign requires? Is my family ready? Kathy Hartman, a newly elected county commissioner in Jefferson County, Colorado, told us, "I wish I had taken more seriously the advice of the people who told me how much time this would take out of my life. I had been warned ahead of time about some of the time requirements, but I just didn't take it seriously enough. As early as April, I was working forty hours a week on the campaign, and I had a day job! My days started at five in the morning and ended at eleven at night." Another successful candidate, State Representative Steve Simon in Minnesota, told us that one of the most important things for new candidates to know is that you have to "be willing to work really, really hard. There's no escaping the fact that it's just a lot of time. You can't fool yourself into thinking it's not." So the decision to run for office or work on a campaign should not be taken lightly. Give it the time and thought it deserves. Ask yourself and your loved ones some key questions: Will your family support your decision? Is there a realistic path for winning? What are the issues that might force decisions that could cost you an election? Are you prepared to raise the money? Are you prepared to work harder than you have on anything in your life? Are you prepared to be a public person from now on, even when you may not be "working"? Are there people in your life you can really count on to succeed? For campaign workers, the questions are similar: Is the candidate someone I believe in? Do I have the time, energy, and inclination to devote twelve to fifteen hours a day, six and sometimes seven days a week, to this campaign? Do I have the support of my family and loved ones? Will I receive both the support I need to do the job and the authority to control the key campaign management decisions?

We strongly recommend that you as the candidate and your campaign workers—whether you are deciding to run or have already announced your candidacy—seek out advice from as many people as possible. You will find during the campaign that people like to give you advice. (In fact, sometimes they give you more than you want!) Take them up on it. Even if you don't use the suggestions people give you, the fact that you are asking them signals that you respect their opinions and will make them more likely to support your campaign. One of the biggest mistakes of new candidates and campaign workers is the impulse to "fake it" and pretend they know more than they really do. So make a list of people who are experienced and respected in the political community. Even if you don't know them well, ask them to meet face-to-face so you can get their suggestions on how to run and win. Not only will most people agree to such a meeting, they will also be flattered. "I was like a sponge at the beginning of the race," one candidate told us. "I had a breakfast meeting almost every day, asking the same questions of different people—How much will this cost? How good are my chances? What are my potential opponents up to?—and I realized that I was quickly creating a buzz about my candidacy. These people liked to feel that their opinions mattered, and I gave them a little ego boost by sitting down with them and asking their advice."

If you do decide you are ready to run, remember that while you are working hard, you also need to take care of the things in your life that are most important. "As busy as I was, one of the best decisions I made was to pick a time every week that was family time and make it sacred," said Commissioner Hartman of Colorado. "No matter what anyone said, I wouldn't let them touch that time. There are always important events to attend, and there are a lot of things that people will tell you that you need to do, but you really need to protect your family time." Taking care of yourself is good for your family, but also for your campaign. Tired candidates make mistakes: they misspeak in public appearances and interviews, lose their temper in front of volunteers or voters, deliver lackluster speeches, and deflate the energy from campaign events. Many candidates and campaign workers told us that one of the most important qualities that make a good candidate is the ability to deal with the roller coaster that is a campaign. There will be good days and bad days, but the candidate is always on, is always under scrutiny, and is the one who sets the tone for the campaign. As one successful candidate told us, "When you're on the campaign trail, you always have to be precise." Staying healthy and well rested helps a candidate stay focused and disciplined.

The decision to run for office or work on a campaign is deeply personal; no one can make the decision for you. But once the decision is made, the next challenge is to be the best candidate and run the best campaign possible. It starts by being authentic.

The Best Candidates Are Authentic

Of all the characteristics that define good political candidates, we believe authenticity is at the top of the list. In fact, evidence from the past several election cycles strongly suggests that voters are attracted to candidates who convey a certain authenticity. Voters are looking for candidates who understand their lives, seem real, and are running for the right reasons and not just for their own self-aggrandizement. As Al Quinlan, a Democratic strategist, puts it: "Voters choose a candidate more and more based on who that person is, not just what they say they will do. It is a gut reaction based on how a candidate presents him- or herself. Do they only talk about their ten-point plan on education or do they also share how hard it is to spend time with their kids? Trust is a two-way street: in our personal lives and in politics. If people trust that you respect them and are honest, then they will support you even if they disagree with you on certain issues."

We asked dozens of candidates and campaign workers to tell us what they think makes for a good candidate. Almost to the person, they talked about authenticity in one way or another.

- ► "Don't ever feel bad about standing up for what you think is right."

- ► "The most important thing for me was to convey a message that I myself believed in. I think I was successful because I was able to have the confidence in myself to say 'This is me' and authentically relate to a broad audience."

- ► "You have to be able to connect with the audience. You feel it; it's an emotional thing that you can't fake. You have to have a voice that is authentic."

- ► "People had to believe that I was real."

Everyone is an authentic person of course, so why do some candidates come across as more authentic than others? Because they have effectively conveyed to voters some things about themselves, their story, their values, and the experiences that inform their worldview. It is difficult, if not impossible, for candidates without an ability to articulate what drives their interest in politics to be seen as authentic. That's just common sense. Think about it: if you meet someone new, what are the characteristics that make you want to get to know the person better? It's not complicated—they are engaging and interesting. They share your values or understand your experience even if you come from different backgrounds. They are good listeners and are responsive. In short, you like and trust them. That's also true of political candidates. Quinlan expresses it this way: "The dimensions and qualities that make up the authentic candidate are no more complex than those lessons some of us learned from our parents: tell people about your life, be decisive and don't run away from an honest debate, stick to your principles, and make sure that you always say what you mean and mean what you say."

Sounds pretty straightforward, right? In many ways, it is. But political campaigns have a way of either turning candidates into people they are not or instilling an overwhelming fear, caution, and carefulness that holds candidates back from revealing their true selves. You don't need to look far to find evidence of this phenomenon in candidates of all political persuasions. After all, how often do we hear people characterize candidates as self-serving and phony politicians? But being authentic is more than just appearing "not fake." It requires intentional effort to let voters get to know a candidate.

Consider former governor and presidential candidate Howard Dean. In the early stages of the 2004 presidential contest, Dean ran a smart, strategic campaign for president that defied conventional wisdom. Here was a candidate who was not afraid to stand up for his beliefs, particularly his strong opposition to the war in Iraq. He inspired thousands of young people to participate in politics, and he utilized the Internet to expand and harness his base of support, raise money, and communicate his message to voters. But by the night of the Iowa caucuses, his campaign had run out of steam. Many analysts point to Dean's inability to connect with voters beyond the initial excitement about his candidacy. Dean himself acknowledged that he fell short when it came to revealing more about himself as a person. Roger Simon, in *U.S. News and World Report* (July 19, 2004), analyzed the Dean loss in Iowa:

> More than any other candidate, Dean resisted emphasizing his "story," his human dimension. Bill Clinton had shown the power of having a story—abusive father, high-stepping mother, drug-addicted half brother—so that people could have something to identify with. By 2004, the telling of a human story had become an essential part of almost every stump speech: Gephardt talked about how he had grown up poor in Saint Louis, Edwards talked about working in the textile mills with people who had "lint in their hair and grease on their faces," and Kerry, of course, talked about Vietnam. But Howard Dean often failed even to tell crowds that he had been a practicing physician. ("You should tell people you're a doctor," a supporter in South Carolina upbraided him after one of his speeches. "In the South, we *like* our doctors.") . . . After his campaign was over, Dean admitted that his failure to make a more human connection with

voters hurt him. When his opponents raised questions about his temperament, he said, the voters didn't have a positive image to counterbalance that. "I think the temperament issue, which also was untrue, did hurt because people didn't know me that well," Dean told *U.S. News*. "It was written about so much that, you know, some people came to believe it." But couldn't Dean have fought that by telling a more personal story, by selling himself to voters as a human being? "It's true, it's true," Dean replied. "You know, maybe I should have done that."

The point is not to single out Howard Dean (he was authentic about being forthright and outspoken about his views) but to say that as simple as it sounds, being an authentic candidate doesn't always come easy. This is particularly ironic since his early breakthrough in New Hampshire was in part the result of a deliberate strategy by his campaign to have campaign workers use their personal stories to recruit other potential supporters at house parties. Dean focused so much on empowering the voters who were supporting him ("You have the power!") that it came at the expense of telling his own story: why his life and his values made him run.

This also means avoiding a trap that progressives often seem to fall into: using the rhetoric of public programs, plans, and policies instead of communicating in the plain language about the values that underlie those programs, plans, and policies. Al Quinlan writes about the progressive proclivity for the language of government: "Our troubles actually stem from something very positive. We believe that government is good. We believe that with the right ideas we can change people's lives and the country for the better. Government is about policies, issues, solving problems, and responsible leadership." Linguist Geoffrey Nunberg also writes about this problem in *American Prospect* (March 2004, "Speech Impediments") and suggests "a new progressive rhetoric, one free of the technocratic jargon for which Democrats have had a lamentable penchant in the past. Phrases like 'unfunded mandates' and 'single payer' may be accurate, but at the cost of coming across as opaque to the Great Unwonky who make up most of the electorate." Or as Paul Wellstone wrote: "Too many progressives make the mistake of believing people are galvanized around ten-point programs. They are not! People respond according to their sense of right and wrong. They respond to a leadership of values."

This does not mean, of course, that issues are not important. Rather, it means that, as a candidate, you should talk about issues at the level of values, using the words that people use every day. It means that instead of focusing on your detailed plans on your key issues, you should tell voters why you care about an issue and what informs your positions on important issues. Health care, good jobs, education, and the environment are moral issues. Nunberg suggests that progressives recapture the "moral values" high ground by not being afraid to speak (in plain language) about our values: "a fair day's pay for a fair day's work," "many hands make light work" (particularly in the war on terrorism), "pick up after yourself" (when it comes to corporate responsibility for pollution), and so on.

Polls show that the American public embraces a progressive issue agenda: support for making health care more accessible and affordable, raising wages for working people, investing more in educational opportunities for children of all backgrounds, curbing the influence of money in politics, and changing America's reckless, unilateral foreign policy. But recent national elections have shown that important groups of voters don't always vote on these issues—instead they have gravitated toward the candidate they saw as having stronger or consistent values.

A related dimension of authenticity has to do with giving voters a sense of your core convictions. What are the things that are most important to you? What are you passionate about? Where do you draw your lines in the sand? What are you prepared to lose an election over? Knowing the answers to these questions means first knowing yourself, so spending time reflecting on your personal convictions is a good exercise early in the process of preparing your run.

There are many examples of "conviction politicians"—leaders who stand firm on strongly held beliefs and values, particularly even when those convictions clash with public opinion or the views of key groups of voters and organized interests. At these times, conviction politicians show the courage of their convictions by saying to voters: "You may not agree with me always on every issue, but you will always know where I stand, and I will always do what I think is right." Often voters appreciate this quality in their leaders, will overlook particular disagreements on issues, and will reward candidates for their courage by voting for them.

Our favorite example of this type of conviction politics is Paul Wellstone. While he took some big political risks by standing by his beliefs even when they weren't popular, voters rewarded Wellstone because they like to see courage in their leaders. In the end, voters knew that when it counted, he was on their side and would fight for them. Wellstone's vote against President Bush's Iraq War Resolution one month before election day—one of only twenty-three and the only senator in a contested reelection race to vote that way—stands out as a powerful example of conviction politics. Not only was it the right thing to do, but voters also rewarded him for his courage: his poll numbers jumped up after the vote.

Another dimension of authenticity has to do with the voters' sense of your motivation for running for office. Do voters think you are in it for the right reasons, or are you more about getting ahead for yourself? A great example of telling your story and conveying authentic motivation is Tim Walz, a candidate for Congress in 2006 in Minnesota's First District. Walz, a high school teacher who had never run for elective office, decided to take on a popular six-term incumbent. The district, which encompasses much of southeast Minnesota, is traditionally conservative, and the conservative incumbent was widely expected to win reelection. But Walz ran a campaign that highlighted his real experience and commitment to his community as his qualifications for serving the First District in Congress. A longtime National Guardsman who served in Afghanistan, Walz was a popular high school teacher and football coach who believed that because of his life experience he could do a better job in Congress than the incumbent. He appealed to voters with a great "authentic" message: "I sure never prepared my life around a run for Congress, but my life has prepared me well. My experience as a public school classroom teacher (and son of a teacher) has taught me the importance of investing in our children and investing in our communities. My military service has taught me the importance of giving back to our country and keeping our commitment to those who serve. Authentic experiences are what have prepared me to serve in Congress." Voters responded to this grounded, humble message, and Walz came from behind to win a hard-fought election that gained national media attention. One voter summed up the positive feelings about Walz that put him over the top: "He seems like a genuine person with a passion to do something right."

Strategy Must Accompany Authenticity

Authenticity alone doesn't win elections. In the end, campaigns are also about the voters—their concerns and circumstances—and if you can't connect with voters around what drives them, then all the authenticity and conviction in the world will not help you win a majority vote. This is where strategy comes in, making conscious choices about what to emphasize considering your convictions, values, viewpoints, and issues. As political writer Marc Cooper suggests, "The trick of effective politics is precisely to unite people with different views, values, and families around programs, candidates, and campaigns on which they can reach some consensus, however minimal."

A winning campaign makes choices about the best argument for your candidacy and provides voters with a clear choice between you and your opponent. You can't talk about every item you feel strongly about, nor can you win elections by *only* standing firm on unpopular ideas. It is about more than just what you think; it is about communicating and connecting with voters. Good strategy can be found in places where the candidate's values and experiences overlap with the values and experiences of large numbers of voters. This is the "sweet spot" where real connections can be made with voters. Ultimately this "gap" between a candidate's values and experiences and those of voters is bridged by trust.

How you present yourself matters to voters. That choice must reflect your personality, background, and political philosophy, but it's one that has to be made deliberately. Examples of winning candidates include those who chose to run as reformers, with a goal of cleaning up politics and the way politicians do business. Another candidate emphasized her credentials as a community organizer and ran a campaign built on her broad-based support in the community. Other approaches include running a campaign emphasizing your progressive credentials in a district with a high progressive performance or running as an "accomplisher" who delivers results and gets things done without regard for party or political ideology.

There is also the populist economic approach, one that we have seen work for statewide candidates all across the country. These progressives reach across ideological fault lines on social issues and unite majorities around an economic agenda. Populists focus on the concentration of corporate and economic power and its encroachment into our government and into our lives. They give voice to lower- and middle-class voters and their concerns around their family's economic security. An economic populist agenda focuses on economic opportunity, curbing big power, education, health care, and jobs. These are the issues that have the most impact on people's lives, both directly and indirectly. As Paul Wellstone put it, "If you want real national security, lower crime, and an economy that works for everyone, not just the richest corporations in the world, focus on a good education, good health care, and a good job." Wellstone advocated for average Minnesotans rather than the interests of big business—a message popular with undecided voters as well as with Wellstone's base.

You don't hear many in Washington suggest that a populist agenda can be a winning policy. Indeed, as the writer and progressive activist Jeff Faux has pointed out, "People who consider themselves liberals are outraged when the maids and gardeners who work in their gated communities want to bargain collectively for a raise. In the '90s a Democratic president would frequently appear on the front pages of the *New York Times* shedding tears as he felt the pain of poor and disadvantaged children and then go to Washington and sign off on a pinch-penny budget that was far below what was needed to deal with their problems." Yet recent elections offer evidence that some Democrats are moving away from a corporatist approach to politics. Candidates like Jon Tester in Montana and Sherrod Brown in Ohio demonstrate the success that can result from speaking directly to the economic insecurities facing Americans today. At a time when job security continues to deteriorate, wages stagnate, health care costs rise, and opportunities for young people dry up, voters are looking for candidates who understand what they are going through and will give them a voice in their government.

Other Qualities of Successful Candidates

There is never just one thing you can point to to explain a winning candidacy. There is a package of candidate qualities that usually come together to win races. We describe some of them here and on the pages that follow.

A Commitment to Grassroots Organizing

We have found time and again that successful progressive campaigns harness the power of a base of active, committed, and excited supporters. We believe in applying the principles and sensibilities of community organizing to electoral campaigns. This means that the candidate first builds a base of support and then uses those supporters to continue expanding the base and reaching out to new voters. It places a heavy emphasis on direct voter contact through intensive field organizing and voter targeting. Winning the Wellstone way is all about running a campaign that is built from the grassroots, involves a broad and diverse base of supporters, and connects with a majority of voters around the concerns and circumstances of their lives.

Depth and Breadth of Relationships

Politics, like organizing, is all about relationships. The best candidates come to a campaign with a base of supporters. They are grounded in communities, constituencies, or issues and have been leaders of some kind in their communities already. Mark Ritchie from Minnesota is a great example. A community organizer for more than two decades before his successful run for secretary of state of Minnesota, Ritchie knew that he had to rely on his long-standing connections across the state if he was going to win his party's nomination and go on to win the general election. "The fact that I had spent my life in organizing means I built relationships over time, and it also meant that I knew that relationships are the basis of really, well, everything. I'd show up at an event in rural Minnesota, and I'd see a farmer I had met twenty years ago. I really worked those connections. I had a life of work, a big extended family, so to speak, and I asked for their help."

Raising the Resources It Takes to Win

While we find the dominance of money in elections to be a destructive force in our democracy (and a tough issue that good progressive candidates should tackle once in office), the fact remains that if we want to build power by winning elected office, candidates must make sure they raise the money to fully fund the kind of campaign that it takes to win their office. In our many interviews with successful (and unsuccessful) candidates, one consistent piece of advice we hear can be summed up by one of our winning Camp Wellstone graduates: "Get the money!" The reality is that money matters if we want to win. In the chapter on fundraising strategies and tactics, we'll talk about how to break down the fundraising challenge into manageable chunks and how to set up the systems that help you raise the resources. We also examine grassroots fundraising strategies by cultivating small donors, getting people to give multiple times, and weaving fundraising into your organizing strategies. Successful candidates learn that campaigns are mostly about "The Ask": asking for people's votes, time, and money. If you are confident as a candidate and are in it to win, you need to get over any fear of asking your supporters to help you fund your campaign.

Hard Work

As much as we like to win, sometimes there are good reasons why campaigns lose. Maybe the campaign message didn't resonate or wrong decisions on strategy were made. Some campaigns just get outworked. In fact, in some close races, it is the campaign that works the hardest that usually wins. Good candidates and their teams work hard, put in the hours raising money or knocking on doors, get up early and stay up late, and put other things off until after Election Day. So often we hear losing opponents (both progressive and conservative) explain their losses by saying, "We simply got outhustled." You can't win every election, but you really don't want to lose because you didn't work hard enough. One caveat to this: as a candidate you must also get regular rest so that you are always the best public person you can be when out campaigning.

Discipline

Along with hard work comes discipline, or staying focused on a plan, strategy, and timetable. A campaign goes one of two ways: you either run your own race or have it run by your opponent. Your opponent runs you if you don't have or follow a plan, if you stay reactive instead of proactive, or if you go off on unstrategic tangents. This is particularly important around message delivery. Breaking through with voters in this busy, noisy world we live in is one of the single biggest challenges all candidates face today. Conciseness, frequency, and repetition are all techniques to allow you to be heard by voters. Saying something different all the time means voters have a hard time hearing anything from you. That is what message discipline is all about. Well-run, disciplined campaigns are ones that make intentional and strategic decisions to do certain things and follow a certain direction and then effectively implement those decisions during the course of the election.

Qualities of Good Campaign Managers and Campaign Workers

When we ask successful candidates and campaign managers to name the reasons they won, one common response is, "I had a great team working with me," or "I found good people I could trust to do the work while I stayed focused on being the candidate." Winning campaigns are never solitary endeavors; every campaign needs a manager along with a team of people who keep focused on the goals, work the plan, and help the candidate be at his or her best every day. A well-functioning team, with a person in charge, operates with clearly defined jobs, measurable goals, and a problem-solving attitude. Unresolved personality conflicts, gossiping, infighting, and personal agendas are the sure signs of a losing campaign.

We've gathered a lot of stories, both good and bad, about progressive campaigns over the last couple of election cycles. Here's a particularly bad (and not atypical) one about a dysfunctional campaign:

> The personal egos of the senior campaign staff got in the way of the business of campaigning. The candidate was fortunate to have a senior staff who was very experienced and skilled, but each of those staff members had their own ideas about how every aspect of the campaign should be run, and there were daily disagreements over the smallest of details. This made it almost impossible to formulate or stick to an overarching campaign strategy, which all campaigns need for cohesiveness and direction. . . . The personal egos and inability to compromise or communicate effectively was a major weakness of this campaign; the ramifications of this were felt throughout every aspect of the campaign.

How can a campaign avoid a situation like this? With a good campaign manager, firmly in control, who can balance the need to communicate internally while maintaining efficient decision making. It's also up to the rest of the campaign team to do their part. Campaigns are anything but a normal work environment and thus are not for everyone. You work long hours under stress and deadlines; there are no elaborate work rules and personnel policies; you are thrown together with others and have to quickly learn to work together; you are not always paid well (or at all). And yet, people are expected to be flexible and do whatever job they are asked to do.

Many of the qualities that make for a good candidate similarly make for a good campaign manager: discipline, hard work, strategic vision, the ability to connect with people, and commitment to a set of core values. But campaign workers have a unique role on a campaign. On one hand, it is the campaign manager and staff who effectively run the campaign. Starting with the campaign manager and moving down, the campaign workers set strategy, identify voters, recruit volunteers, make phone calls, canvass targeted neighborhoods, and raise money. Although it's the candidate's name on the ballot, the campaign workers are responsible for ensuring the campaign's success. On the other hand, campaign workers should never forget that they work for someone else. While they may share the candidate's vision for the future and believe strongly in the candidate's message, ultimately that vision and message are the candidate's and the candidate's alone. So working on a campaign requires putting aside your own agenda or desire for advancement and simply working hard to get your candidate elected. You might run the campaign, but in the end it's not your campaign but the candidate's.

Whether there is trust or not between a campaign manager and a candidate can be the difference between winning and losing. Experienced campaign manager Matt Filner describes trust as "the rudder that guides the campaign through the rough spots." And inevitably, there will be rough spots in the campaign, times when the candidate and the campaign manager need to hold things together. Elizabeth Glidden, a successful city council candidate, said that new candidates need people who believe in them, and that starts with the campaign manager. "You need someone who believes in you, because you need to believe in yourself. Voters are not going to believe in you if you don't believe in yourself." Secretary of State Mark Ritchie described what real trust looks like between a candidate and a campaign manager: "My campaign manager could tell me what to do, and I would do it. He had a way of explaining things to me that really worked. It wasn't 100 percent of the time—sometimes we disagreed—but he knew what we needed to do. The bottom line was that I didn't run this campaign. I wasn't 'handled,' but my campaign manager ran this campaign, and that's the way it needed to be."

One of the key functions of the campaign manager is to give direct, honest advice to the candidate. "I think a candidate needs to surround herself with people who can be critical," State Representative Steve Simon of Minnesota told us. "My campaign manager was a real straight shooter. We'd leave an event and I'd ask him how I did, and I always knew he'd be honest. In a very low-key, professional way, he would say, 'average to below average,' or 'you didn't really connect there.'" Another candidate told us: "I made it very clear to my campaign manager that she would be doing me no favors if she simply agreed with everything I said or told me I was doing a great job even when she didn't believe it. I had so few people I could count on for objective advice that without her ability to give me her honest opinion, I would have been surrounded only by people who were telling me what a great job I was doing." Sometimes, however, candidates mostly hear about what they're doing wrong. Another Minnesota candidate, State Auditor Rebecca Otto, told us, "You have to be open to critique and be able to adjust, but you really need to take that advice from people you trust, like your campaign manager. Everyone will tell you what to do, and sometimes people will tell you all the things you're doing wrong. If you take advice from everyone, you will lose your way. Don't get freaked out by all the noise and the doubters." This point is almost more important for candidates because it is the candidate who sets the tone for encouraging directness. Don't shoot the messenger; instead listen and take things to heart.

Good campaign managers keep the campaign running smoothly, but they don't need to be experts in every aspect of the campaign. The sign of a good campaign manager is someone who knows what they don't know and seeks out the people who can help on those areas. One candidate told us he was nervous about having to hire a young and relatively inexperienced organizer as his campaign manager because of budget reasons, but the young manager actually used that to his advantage. "I didn't have much money to spend, which required me to hire someone young, but we overcame that because I introduced him to people who have a lot of experience and told him to use them as a resource. He constantly checked in with people who knew more than he did about running a campaign. He knew what he didn't know, and he called on these experienced managers to become his mentors, which they did." Indeed, we have found that behind a good campaign manager is a circle of mentors and contacts that the manager relies on during the course of a campaign.

It's critical that your campaign understand that the candidate should never also be the campaign manager, either explicitly or by action. That's right, the candidate should *never* try to run his or her own campaign. It's pretty simple: a candidate needs to focus on voters, while the campaign manager needs to run the campaign. The candidate should not spend her time on the minutiae of running a campaign. She should not balance the checkbook, run staff meetings, debate office equipment to purchase, or otherwise waste any opportunity she has to speak directly to voters or raise funds. Even if the campaign manager is part time or a volunteer, that person needs to be someone other than the candidate.

It's also usually a poor choice to have your spouse or close relative run your campaign. If the campaign manager cannot speak honestly and directly to the candidate and the candidate cannot fire the manager if something goes dreadfully wrong, then the wrong person is running the campaign. Having a spouse manage a campaign can be problematic.

Consider the experience that Kathy Hartman had in her race for county commissioner in Colorado. "One of the reasons I won is that my opponent's campaign manager was his wife," Hartman told us. "That meant everything was personal. For example, we criticized my opponent for taking money from a developer after he took a controversial vote on an issue. His campaign totally overreacted to the attack, which was stupid. We ended up getting three media stories out of this, and it got even worse for him. Because he was so upset, he claimed he had never met this developer in his life. Turned out we had records to prove that he had. So he not only got dragged into responding to our attack, he said things that weren't true and that we could prove weren't true."

There are exceptions to the rule about spouses as campaign managers. We know of campaigns that have gone very well with the spouse at the helm, and in very small local races, having a spouse as a campaign manager may be the only option. One candidate for city council told us that while she initially opposed the idea of her husband managing her campaign, he was also the most experienced and committed person who was willing to do the job (and do it for free!). They created a great working relationship, and she relied on him to both run the daily operations of the campaign and also give her clear, honest, and sometimes tough advice. For most candidates, that's a role better left to someone who is not immediate family, but we recognize that every candidate has to make the decision that works best.

Regardless of who manages the campaign, the other staff need to understand their roles, define a set of objectives, and go out and achieve them. If you are a campaign worker, you will likely hear some variation of this mantra from your campaign manager: "Your job is to get to work, help implement the plan, not complain, not say 'But that's not my job,' and just put your head down and get it done." That might sound a little harsh, but campaigns are not places you should work if you need constant affirmation from your superiors. Yet the best campaigns are not run as military command-and-control structures, just as they are not run by consensus. There should be an openness to sharing ideas, to disagreement and debate, and to creativity. After all, if we ourselves cannot figure out how to make this happen in our own organizations, how do we expect it to happen elsewhere? Having said this, once a campaign decision is made, the time for debate and second-guessing passes and it becomes time to get the job done—the job of winning the race. The environment of a campaign is too intense, the pace is too fast, and the stakes are too high for campaign workers to worry about bruised egos. Ultimately, you are there for the candidate (another reason it's important to choose your candidate wisely), not yourself.

CHAPTER 2

Writing a Campaign Plan and Laying Out a Path to Victory

WALK INTO THE OFFICE of a political campaign in October and you will likely witness a hurricane of activity. Amid piles of campaign literature, phone scripts, and empty pizza boxes, you'll see stressed-out campaign workers and overworked volunteers. The candidate rushes into the office and then heads out a few minutes later for another campaign event. It can seem like chaos. And yet, if the campaign is run well, the chaos is more likely a campaign in high gear implementing the final parts of a deliberate, strategic plan. Campaigns are frenzied affairs, particularly in the final weeks, but the difference between a campaign that effectively manages the frenzy and one that is overwhelmed by it often comes down to planning.

The scarce campaign resources of people, money, and time are the reason we plan. There is never enough of any of the three. Volunteers are hard to recruit and maintain, and you can never have too many. Money, as anyone who has run for office or managed a campaign knows, takes work to raise and is easy to spend. In addition, some states require campaigns to operate under tight spending limits. And time—perhaps the most important of the three—is finite, no matter how early you start planning and working. The plan answers the question: "How do I manage people, money, and time to win my election?" We see planning as a process, a series of questions you ask yourself at the beginning of the race; the written answers to these questions is your plan. Plans clarify the choices you need to make at the beginning of the race and provide a structure for implementing them. Having a plan and sticking to it is the difference between running your own race and having it run for you either by your opponent or by external events.

Plans are also tools for management and accountability. Matt Filner, the director of Progressive Majority Minnesota who has written dozens of campaign plans, calls the plan a "buy-in document" for the campaign, both for the candidate and for the team. "When the campaign gets rough, you need to make decisions that reflect a strategic statement of your values and your approach, and that's what your plan is." The plan should be written in a way that allows the candidate to measure progress and hold people accountable to decisions and jobs. A plan also helps with fundraising and volunteer recruitment. Donors want to give to campaigns that can demonstrate how they will spend money wisely. Volunteers want to join campaigns that will take advantage of their skills and commitment. People join the campaign when they have a sense that the candidate has a plan to win and that they have a role in it.

The process of planning can also help build trust between the candidate and his or her team. The plan establishes a contract of sorts between the candidate and the campaign manager. This is particularly important when the campaign hits a difficult period. After all, candidates justifiably get nervous when they don't know if all the work is getting done. It's their name at the top of the ticket, it's their campaign, and it's their future. But as we said in the previous chapter, a candidate trying to be both the candidate and the campaign manager is a recipe for disaster. As a candidate, you need to trust your campaign team to implement the work. If a plan is written down and you have good people around you to implement it, it can help build the trust one needs to step away from the day-to-day. In this way, the planning process actually allows you to get to a place where you can focus on being the best candidate possible.

The strongest comments we heard about the importance of planning came from experienced campaigners who wished they had planned better from the start. Consider the example of Andrew Gillum, the successful candidate for city commission in Tallahassee. Gillum was a twenty-three-year-old college student at Florida A&M University when he decided to run, and although he had served as president of his university's student council, it was his first run for nonstudent office. The odds were against him. Five other candidates were in the race by the time Gillum announced his candidacy, and several were well-known and well-respected community leaders with access to wealthy donors. Not only was Gillum unknown to many voters in his district, he also got started late and filed for his candidacy on the last day possible.

Gillum had some aspects of a plan. "First, I knew that when you have six people running, everyone has to carve out their piece," Gillum told us. "My strategy was to start with the people I knew and who knew me: students, progressive activists, African Americans. We then implemented a deliberate strategy of banking votes. We pulled down the voter log in the county. We pulled any name of anyone who was registered in certain parts of the city where I was known. In the process, we built our grassroots campaign bigger and bigger every day."

Gillum worked hard and won his race, but it was not always smooth along the way. Because he hadn't developed a well-articulated plan that covered all aspects of the campaign, Gillum and his volunteers often found themselves improvising. "We came up with harebrained ideas as we moved about the campaign," Gillum said. "The plan grew out of suggestions and thoughts that came from my friends and volunteers." If there is a single area that Gillum wishes he had spent more time planning, it was fundraising. "I wish I would have had much more training in fundraising, both high donor and low donor. As I had to get out to a larger audience, it was not possible to touch everyone, so I had to have some way to get up on the radio or on TV to reach those people."

Andrew Gillum's example is typical of many candidates, especially those running for the first time. Candidates may have an idea of what they would like to do, and they might have some of the right tactics to get there. But better to take time at the start to think the campaign through, figure out what it takes to win, decide on a strategy, and figure out how to use time, people, and money, and how to raise that money. And then put the work plan on paper.

Where to Begin

Sometimes a plan doesn't get written because people are just too busy and it's hard to carve out the time for planning. But activity doesn't automatically equal progress. Don't get caught in the trap of having too much to do with no time to plot out exactly how you are going to win the campaign. A plan that is not written down on paper is no plan at all. There is no way anyone else can use it or follow it if it remains in the campaign manager's head or yours.

If you're having a hard time getting started on the planning process, we suggest bringing together your circle of trusted campaign advisers. If you have a campaign manager, that person can help lead this discussion. This should not be a big group of people, nor does it need to be all the people who are involved on a daily basis during the campaign. You're just getting started, so these are people you have brought together to give you advice and to brainstorm with you. In the most general sense, you can begin the conversation by asking a series of questions:

- What are the chances of winning this race?
- What base of supporters do we bring to the race?
- Who are key people we need at the start of the campaign?
- What do we know about the district and its voters?
- Who votes and where do they live?
- Who is our likely opponent?
- How much is it likely to cost and where does the money come from?
- Who are our likely donors?
- How are we going to research the opponent and our candidate?
- What are the filing requirements and deadlines?
- What's the timeline with the important dates of the campaign?

The answers to these questions will help you form a general strategy for winning. Now you have a better sense of whom to target as your voters. You may have a list of people you can call for campaign contributions. You begin to identify the scope of work for a campaign manager, whether that person is paid or a volunteer. You review any decisions or incidents that could hurt you in the campaign. Above all, you are starting to get your arms around the components of a campaign plan. You might not have all the answers to every question in detail, but you're getting a good start.

Write the Plan

Now it's time to write the plan. A campaign can be naturally organized into parts, so when you start writing a plan, you want to break it into sections, starting with a section on background and basic information. The best way to begin writing a campaign plan is to rewrite an old plan, using the categories and framework from it as a takeoff point. We rarely start the planning process with a blank piece of paper. Take out an old plan and use its structure to facilitate a systematic thinking through of how to put together the components of time, people, and money to win.

Background Section

One of the earliest steps in assembling the material necessary for planning is pulling together a series of basic data: past election results, voter file, maps of the district, who is likely to run, past amounts typically raised. You should know everything about the laws, rules, regulations, and timelines that govern the race. That includes knowing about contribution limits; spending limits (if any); reporting requirements; important dates such as filing, reporting, and primary dates; requirements in the off year (if any); disclosure requirements; limits on party contributions and activities; and the rules and regulations regarding contact and coordination with other organizations, including corporations, PACs, 501(c)(3)s, 501(c)(4)s, and 527s. The laws will be dramatically different in statewide, state legislative, national, and local races. For example, some states have laws that allow campaigns to spend a certain amount of money in the off year and another amount in the election year (say, $30,000 in the off year and $250,000 in the election year). That's important information to know; it means that if the campaign starts in the off year, you can spend a total of $280,000, but if you wait until the election year, you only have $250,000 total. These types of laws can play a pivotal role in the campaign. Find out everything you can about your restrictions and opportunities with regard to campaign finance law.

Strategy to Win

Every plan should spell out in a concise manner your strategy for winning the race. For example, in a state legislative race in a contested primary, the strategy for winning might be something like this: Consolidate your geographical base and your ideological base of environmentalists, plus former anti-incumbent voters. The key persuasion universe will be found among labor and identified likely swing primary voters. This statement is necessarily broad—there is a whole plan to detail out later—but such a statement serves a very important purpose in the planning process. It acts as a hypothesis that guides a series of other questions asked when putting together a targeting, message, media, and fundraising plan. It also serves to answer the question often asked during a campaign by donors and especially by ideological issue groups (e.g., labor): How are you going to win? Your strategy statement evolves out of the general discussion above and then is tested against available data (e.g., targeting) as the planning process develops. It is necessarily a dynamic process; targeting and a larger strategic overview and understanding of the race go hand in hand and develop more deeply in tandem.

Targeting

We like to start our plans with the targeting strategy. In this section, you answer: What is the likely voter turnout and how many votes does it take to win (the win number)? Where do you find the voters you need to win? Where are the most likely base voters? Which voters are most likely and least likely to vote? Who are the most likely swing voters? What are the demographics of your district and how will you utilize that information in your campaign? Do you need to bring new voters into the process to win? Which voters are not likely to vote for you at all, so you can narrow your universe and preserve resources? The answers to these questions are specific numbers and lists of names. A targeting plan both evolves out of the more general overall discussion above and informs it.

Message Strategy

You start this section by finishing the sentence "I am running for office because . . ." Eventually, this sentence becomes a paragraph, and then a page, but this requires a process of message development. That means answering questions such as these:

- ▸ Why are you running? What are your core political values and what are the sources of those values?
- ▸ Who are your audiences, what do you know about them, and what do you want them to do?
- ▸ What is your opponent saying about you? What are you saying about your opponent?
- ▸ What research do you need?

▸ Can you boil down your message to one minute?

▸ Can you integrate your message across your voter contact, paid and earned media, and fundraising?

Self-research and Opponent Research

This section contains a concise summary of what you need to know about you and your opponent. What is the public record of each candidate? What are your weaknesses? What is in your personal, professional, family, or financial past that would make a damaging news headline if the press knew about it? (Always assume they will!) What is inconsistent between what you say and what you've done in the past? What about the opponent? What are the issues on which he is most vulnerable? Where can you find hypocrisy between rhetoric and action? What are her strengths? If you or your opponent has a voting record, what is your plan for carefully researching that record? This research, again, helps inform your overall strategy, like decisions about where there may be political opportunities to go after a specific constituency.

District Research

Research the district, seat, or ward you are seeking to represent: What are the past election results? How have Democrats, Republicans, and third party candidates fared in the past? How much money have past candidates raised and spent? What constituencies live in the district?

Field

The field plan typically consists of four components: base building, direct voter contact, visibility, and getting out the vote.

BASE BUILDING

In this section you will determine which base communities need to be brought into the campaign, how that relationship will be structured, and who will be responsible. There will also likely be discussion of what communities or constituencies need outreach or a more deliberate process of relationship building.

DIRECT VOTER CONTACT

Plan how you will find and communicate with the voters you need to win. Through targeting you will have identified a pool of voters; the direct contact section is about taking the campaign directly to those voters with a series of layered conversations. This involves voter identification and persuasion, determining the overall number and schedule of voter contacts, and laying out a plan for door-knocking, phoning, direct mail, and building the volunteer operation necessary to contact voters. The campaign model we describe in these pages relies heavily on a grassroots organizing strategy.

VISIBILITY

Visibility takes many different forms, most of which come under the rubric of the field plan. At one level visibility includes lawn signs, bumper stickers, and so on. But it also includes a description of major field events and a strategy for having a presence at community events like parades and county fairs.

GETTING OUT THE VOTE

This section describes your plan for mobilizing your supporters to get out and vote. Most early campaign plans do not elaborately detail a get-out-the-vote (GOTV) plan, which is fine; there will be time to do that as Election Day approaches. Yet it is still important to include getting out the vote in your plan and make it more detailed as the campaign develops. At a minimum this should include the estimated target number of supporters you wish to turn out and the general means for turning them out—phone canvassing, mail, and the number of contacts you estimate for each. This will allow at least rudimentary budgeting early on in the process and will avoid the too frequent phenomenon of leaving GOTV thinking and budget until it's too late.

Voter Contact through Paid Media

Paid media is another way of communicating with voters. Some campaigns will rely heavily on paid media, while others will use them very little. How are you going to dominate one medium of paid media? Will you spend the bulk of your paid media budget on direct mail? Radio ads? Television ads?

Internet ads? Newspaper ads? How much will it cost to hire media consultants, and is it worth it? Will you do cable or network TV?

Fundraising and Budgeting

Budgeting and fundraising go hand in hand and are intimately connected with the overall plan. A common mistake is to let fundraising drive the campaign process rather than seeing it as the disciplinarian of the planning process. The campaign's strategy to win and the overall win number drive both the budget and fundraising goals. The first question should never be "How much do I think I can raise?" Instead, it should be "How much is necessary to win?" Once this has been determined, then the question switches to "How can I raise this money?" Of course, this changes somewhat when operating in races that have strict spending caps. How are you going to raise the money necessary to win? Who are your most likely donors? What's your plan for reaching them? How much money will you get from phone calls, events, or mail solicitations? How many large, medium, and small donors do you have? Where do these donors come from? The budgeting and fundraising components of the planning process are dynamic. If there is no realistic way to raise the money that you think is necessary, sometimes painful choices need to be made.

Staff Roles and Responsibilities

What are the campaign functions and what staff will be needed and responsible for them? Who will be paid and who will be volunteer? What are the systems for handling scheduling requests, managing data, running a direct voter contact program, and implementing the other campaign functions? What is the infrastructure of the campaign, and how are the key decisions made?

Technology, Administration, and Systems

What technology does the campaign need? The right technology setup, aligned to the scale of your race, is critical: database, Web site, network, and telecommunications infrastructure. The key here is always to go back to the win number and decide if technology will get you closer to it. Technology should be your friend, not a source of frustration. Keep it simple and focused on what is necessary. Complex systems usually break down, almost always at the most inopportune time.

Timeline

When thinking about timing, there are two important concepts to keep in mind. The first is that all campaigns should follow a natural flow that starts with organizing your closest supporters, building your base, and then moving out to a more general electorate. The second major concept in timing is to start with Election Day (whether it is the first Tuesday in November or when early voting, voting by mail, or absentee voting begins) and work backward. The timeline has the major dates, but all activities of the plan have implementation dates next to them.

Those are the key components of the plan. Now let's turn to a preview of the roles and responsibilities on a campaign team.

Creating the Team

Regardless of the size of the campaign, the basic functions remain the same. The campaign manager oversees either a volunteer or paid staff that is responsible for a variety of tasks. On a large campaign, like a race for governor or Congress, the manager directs a team of a dozen staffers or more. On smaller campaigns, this might be an all-volunteer team and it might consist of people who fill one or more of these functions:

> ▶ **Field.** The field director is in charge of implementing the direct voter contact plan: writing a field plan, overseeing the identifying and persuasion of voters, creating a campaign presence at community events, directing the canvassing and phoning operations, and managing all other aspects of the campaign's direct voter contact work, including a staff of paid or volunteer field organizers in larger campaigns.

> ▶ **Volunteers.** The field director also oversees the volunteer program. Good campaigns have lots of volunteers. Lots of volunteers are a great thing if they have clearly defined work projects, feel welcome

at the campaign headquarters, and know that their presence is valued. The only way to make sure volunteers are treated well and that the campaign is maximizing volunteer resources is to assign one person to coordinate the volunteer activities. That person is responsible for welcoming volunteers to the office, training them in whatever they are working on, answering their questions, and establishing a sense of teamwork and common purpose.

▶ **Communications.** The communications director is, in addition to the candidate, the public face of the campaign. She is responsible for communicating the campaign's message to the media and the general public. The communications director usually serves as the campaign's spokesperson and uses relationships with reporters to place news stories and create earned media opportunities for the campaign. The communications director also ensures that field and fundraising communication, direct mail, campaign e-mails, and the Web site are consistently delivering the appropriate message. Generally all public campaign materials, from press releases to the Web site to canvass literature, will be approved by the communications director to ensure message discipline.

▶ **Finance/fundraising.** Every campaign needs to raise money, whether it's two thousand dollars or two million. Finding a good fundraiser makes raising money a less daunting and more manageable task. In the chapter on fundraising we spend significant time on the right way to raise money. The finance director must work closely with the campaign manager to ensure that the budget remains realistic and to identify trouble long before it might hit.

▶ **Scheduling.** The scheduler is one of the most underappreciated roles in a campaign. Few things are more important than the candidate's time and how it is managed. The scheduler works with the campaign manager to weigh scheduling requests with targeting data to determine where the candidate's time is best spent. A scheduler should have attention to detail, a sense of humor, and patience. He'll need all of these qualities, especially in the final hectic months of the campaign, as requests pile up and everyone seems to want some of the candidate's valuable time.

▸ **Research.** We talk in later chapters about the role of research in a campaign and the importance of knowing the potential strengths and vulnerabilities of both the candidate and his or her opponents. The campaign should have a volunteer or staff member who focuses on self-research and opposition research. On small campaigns, this role is often filled by the person in charge of communications. Larger campaigns should have a full-time research director and even supporting research staff.

▸ **Administration/operations.** Most campaigns are legally required to have a treasurer. This is a crucial position of responsibility, so the treasurer must be chosen wisely. The treasurer is responsible for all compliance activities—filing fundraising reports, overseeing the financial statements, signing the checks—and is often the person whose name is required to be on campaign materials ("Paid for by Jackson for Governor, Susan Lee, Treasurer," for example). An operations director makes sure all paperwork and filings are done correctly and on time; manages the office, technology, and supplies; and ensures that the day-to-day ship runs smoothly.

▸ **Online organizer.** Depending on the size of the campaign, this role is often filled by the person in charge of communications, but larger campaigns should have a full-time director in charge of online organizing and how it integrates with the rest of the campaign—in particular fundraising, volunteer recruitment, base building, and communications.

▸ **Technology/database.** In a modern campaign, even a small one, someone needs to be in charge of maintaining the Web site, the database, and campaign electronic communications.

▸ **Legal counsel.** Campaigns of every size must have legal counsel to advise them on the legal rules and regulations surrounding their run for office; this person should have the experience and knowledge of the relevant campaign laws to make sure the campaign operates within the law. This is generally a volunteer, but depending on the law locally, it may have to be reported as in-kind contribution.

▸ **Policy.** Larger campaigns may have a policy director who is responsible for developing campaign positions on issues, drafting responses to candidate questionnaires from interest groups and organizations, fact-checking public communication that includes policy positions or statements, assisting with debate and press event preparation, and briefing the candidate on important issues that develop. This person is often an attorney or someone with a significant amount of legislative experience and ability to do research very quickly.

▸ **Political.** A political department is the hub of external relationships for the campaign and is responsible for outreach to important constituencies. A political director ensures that the campaign is thus building and managing its base, including geographic, issue, and demographic constituencies.

CHAPTER 3

Creating a Message and Delivering It to Your Audience

THE WORD "MESSAGE" seems to mean something different for everyone. For some, message is a sound bite or a slogan. To others, it connotes spin and propaganda. Still others view message as something that progressives have not been adept at delivering. When we asked participants in our trainings to describe what message means to them, we heard from one person that "it means manipulating the media and misleading voters." Another said, "To me, a message is the way we explain our value system." Progressives seem to have ambivalent feelings about message and how to incorporate a message into our campaigns. On the one hand, we understand the importance of effectively communicating a message, but on the other hand we have all witnessed the manipulation of political messaging that happens in an age of sound bite politics.

It's our view that many progressives don't understand the importance of messaging and therefore aren't very good at it. Conservatives consistently beat us when it comes to delivering a clear message to voters. While we try to educate the public about our policy agenda, conservatives speak about the values they share with voters. While we explain to voters why they should care about our latest ten-point plan, conservatives stick to broad vision and themes and avoid policy minutiae. Progressives have a tendency to think that if voters had all the facts, they'd vote for us. Rather than concentrating on the specifics of plans and programs, conservatives often focus on the values that voters already know intrinsically and connect their agenda with these broadly held values. It's pretty clear who has come out ahead in this debate. With some exceptions (most notably Bill Clinton in 1992 and 1996 and congressional Democrats in 2006), conservatives have handed progressives a sustained electoral thumping in the past few decades on the federal level.

There are two ways progressives can respond to this reality. One is to complain and blame others: the problem isn't our message, it's that the media are biased and don't allow us to deliver our message fairly. Or the problem is that conservatives are essentially cheating by not telling the whole story and manipulating voters. Or the people to blame are the voters themselves, who are too lazy, tuned out, uninformed, and uncaring to respond to a progressive message. Here's another excuse: we're at a disadvantage because our message is more complicated; the other side simplifies it down to lower taxes and smaller government, and our argument is more nuanced.

The other response is to understand the role and importance of message strategy and master the practice of it. Sure, the media are biased. One need only turn on a TV and scroll through the channels to see that Americans are not getting the full story when they watch the evening news. At a time when conservatives have their own national television network and the radio airwaves are filled with the rants of right-wing ideologues, we do have an obligation to focus attention on the increasing dominance of conservatives in the press. It is also true that the conservative messages that we hear are simplistic, often rely on fear to make an impact, and do manipulate public opinion. But these should not be excuses for not doing our job better. Nor should we assume that because our message isn't resonating, it's somehow the fault of our intended audience, that they are just not sophisticated enough to understand it. In addition to being wrong, that assumption is elitist and insulting and surely not a way to win the hearts, or the minds, of voters.

The good news is that progressive campaigns *can* develop and communicate effective messages that connect with voters and help win elections. There are great examples of effective progressive messaging in races all across the country, from school board to U.S. Senate. While each message of a successful campaign is unique, they share several traits. They focus on a specific audience of voters. They treat message as a conversation between the campaign and that audience. The messages are credible and convey the authenticity of the candidate. They are relevant to people's lives. They are short, clear, and concise. They present voters with a clear choice and a contrast with the opponent (or opponents). And they are repeated constantly throughout the campaign in a disciplined, focused way.

Message as a Conversation

Progressives need to think about message as a conversation between the campaign and the voters. Conversations are the way people communicate, and whether a conversation is taking place at a front door or through paid media, make sure it has the qualities of a good conversation. What are we looking for when we sit down with someone we don't know very well or we meet a person at a party or at work and start chatting? For most people, a good conversation is one that touches a shared set of interests and values. After all, it's not very interesting to talk to someone whose interests don't intersect with yours. A good conversation is engaging; both sides listen to one another, are open to hearing a different point of view, and respect that point of view even if they disagree with it. Good conversations are often story based, when participants share their own stories and link them with others. Good conversations often lead to action, whether that action is as simple as someone changing his or her mind or as dramatic as a person going out and volunteering in support of a cause. Above all, what most people are looking for in a conversation is a sense that the person they are speaking with is real, not fake or phony or arrogant. We want to be treated with respect, not pandered to or manipulated. And we want to know that we are at a minimum understood, that our values are respected and, at best, shared by the person we are speaking with. We don't like feeling condescended to or lectured; the best conversations are with our peers, not between student and teacher or between adult and child.

All of the characteristics of a good conversation should apply to political message delivery. As in a conversation, it is not just *what* is said in a political message—the content of the message—that matters. It is also *who* delivers the message—whether the messenger is credible and believable—that moves voters. And it is *how* that message is developed and delivered that can make the difference between merely having a solid message and actually ensuring that an audience hears and embraces that message.

But before dealing with the issues of content, messenger, and delivery, step one of developing message is to clearly identify the audience.

Identifying and Getting to Know Your Audience

Your campaign's audience may seem obvious; you are trying to get as many voters to support you as possible. But that doesn't mean every voter is part of your audience. Some voters will never support your campaign no matter what you do or say. Others might be open to persuasion, depending on how you craft your message. Others will be inclined not only to support your campaign but also to actively work on its behalf if they hear an inspiring message. In our chapter on targeting, we discuss how your campaign can use different information to identify and target specific audiences needed to win an election. This same targeting data should be used to inform your message decisions. We'll save a detailed discussion of targeting for the next chapter, but the key thing to remember is that the first question your campaign should ask when developing a message is "Who is our audience?" There may be multiple audiences over the course of the campaign; if you have a primary, you shouldn't be focusing on general election voters a year out from a campaign, for example. You may consider your base audience different from your persuadable audience. Not knowing your audience is like blindly trying to convince a stranger to support your campaign without knowing anything about the voter's background, preferences, or history of voting.

Sometimes you will have more than one message on a campaign. That doesn't mean you have messages that contradict each other, but that you have different audiences that respond differently to a message at different times of the campaign. There are also messages that are aimed at mobilizing the base and messages aimed at swing voters. A good example is Wellstone in 1996. Wellstone's campaign had two messages that reinforced each other. The first was an organizing message: "We're the number one target for defeat by the other side because Paul's been fighting hard for you and standing up for our shared values." That was a message to our base supporters; we needed them to understand that this was not going to be an easy election and that they could not become complacent. The overall campaign message was, "You always know where Paul Wellstone stands, and he won't stop fighting for working families and children." The two messages complemented one another, but were tailored for different audiences. To an undecided general election voter, the fact that the Republicans made Wellstone a top target was irrelevant, but it was a great way to fire up the base. The second message accurately summed up Wellstone's work as a senator, but omitted the partisan contrast for the broader audience.

Identifying your audience is only the first step; now you need to get to know them. Knowing your audience means conducting informal research by listening to voters at the doors and on the phones and creating "feedback loops" with volunteers that allow them to tell the campaign what they're hearing in the community and at people's doors. Every campaign that actually talks with voters at their doors or on the phones can test its messages. Try out different messages or phrases and debrief your volunteers when they come back in from the field. A few hundred responses and you have a pretty good idea of whether or not your message is resonating. Formal research is also available; even if you don't have enough money to do a poll, there are a lot of polls out there, both public and from other campaigns, that contain a wealth of information about voter attitudes. Try to get your hands on as much polling data as possible by asking your informal networks and, if possible, talking to people in your party organization who might have access to polling data.

Content: What Makes for an Effective Message?

Crafting a good message is a long and sometimes difficult process. Even the most simple and straightforward messages require time, energy, creativity, and testing to produce. Effective messages are concise, relevant to voters, and contrasting.

Concise

At a time when Americans are bombarded with different messages in the media every day, campaigns have only a small window of opportunity in which to gain people's attention. People lead busy lives; between working, taking care of children, and paying the bills, most Americans don't have time to focus on politics at all, and they certainly don't have time to delve into policy details. That can be supremely frustrating for you as a candidate and your campaign team. After all, you are dedicating almost every waking moment to the campaign. You understand how high the stakes are and how important it is that people grasp the choice before them. But unless your campaign can adjust to the reality of having to make your message short and concise, you will largely be having a conversation with yourself, not voters.

The truth is that those of us who care passionately about politics—who write and read books on how to win elections, for example—are not normal. Unlike the vast majority of Americans, we follow politics closely. We read the newspaper every day or almost every day. We watch the television news. We frequently visit political blogs and Web sites. We vote in every election, from local races to the presidency. We could probably tell you the names of a majority of members of the president's cabinet. In short, we're a little weird. Most people, even those who are relatively well informed and stay current on political news, are not nearly as engaged in the political process as we are. They draw their opinions mostly from impressions, not from a diligent review of the candidates' positions on issues. They usually vote with their gut, rather than with a litmus test on policies.

So you don't have much time to make the case to voters. That means you should be able to deliver your core message in as few words as possible. We always recommend that candidates boil their messages down to one sentence, one paragraph, and one page. This helps you articulate the five-second version of your message, but also gives you material for longer opportunities to deliver your message. Ultimately, you're going to need both a long version of your message and a short version. As one candidate told us, "You have to be ready—really ready—for that League of Women's Voters debate when you're going to get one minute for a closing statement. You will also get requests from newspapers that are putting out an election edition and need you to say in fifty words or less why you are the best candidate for the job." Fifty words isn't much of a chance to make a nuanced argument. To give you perspective, this entire paragraph is 169 words.

Here are some examples of concise messages that have worked in recent elections:

- ▸ America needs a new direction.
- ▸ I am running for office to get the government off your back.
- ▸ I was raised to respect my elders and take care of them, and to take care of our children. That's what I'll take to the legislature.
- ▸ We're going to build a bridge to the twenty-first century.
- ▸ I am nobody's senator but yours.

Some of these messages probably sound familiar. In the 2006 midterm elections, the first message, "America needs a new direction," was pretty much all a progressive candidate needed to say and voters understood what she meant. That does not necessarily translate into a victory, but that short, succinct message was easily understood, easy to repeat over and over, and easy for Americans to agree with. But don't confuse a slogan for a message. While a message can often be boiled down to a few words, a slogan is just empty words when not backed up with values, authenticity, and a connection to voters' concerns.

To help craft your message into a concise statement, we suggest you spend time thinking about how to complete this sentence: "I am running for office because . . ." There are a couple reasons why this is a good exercise. The first and most obvious is that you will get asked, "Why are you running for office?" repeatedly throughout the campaign, and you should be able to give the same answer, without hesitation, every time it's asked. The second is that it helps clarify your core reason for running and gives you an opportunity to try it out while the campaign is still in the early stages. For example, suppose the first message you come up with is this: "I am running for county commissioner because I have a detailed plan to reform the contracting system for wastewater treatment processes, as well as the permitting procedures and development review board's internal review process, to ensure public input and an end to the regulatory lapses that have resulted in environmental degradation and poor public services for taxpayers." By the time your audience wakes up from the nap you just induced, they will have written you off entirely. Another way to make the same point but in a language your audience understands might be to say: "I am running for county commissioner because our county's families, our traditions, and our small-town values are being undermined by big city developers who care more about profits than our quality of life."

You probably know the KISS principle: Keep it short and simple. When in doubt, cut words. If you think your message is too long, it probably is. In fact, chances are that if you think your message is too short . . . it's still too long! If you make your message long, complex, and full of policy details, you will lose your audience. Keep it short and simple, and people will listen.

Relevant to Voters

If your message is concise, people are more likely to pay attention. However, you may have the shortest and most concise message in the world, but it won't make a difference if it is not relevant to people's lives. Remember our discussion in the first chapter about finding the sweet spot with voters—the intersection between the candidate's experiences and values and the voters' experiences and values—when thinking about how to make your message relevant to their lives. Is your campaign message about what's important to you, or is it focused on what's important to voters?

Here's an example that illustrates the importance of making a message relevant to your audience: health care. Roughly 50 million Americans, about 15 percent of the population, lack health insurance. This is embarrassing. The United States is alone in the industrialized world in allowing so many of its citizens to lack basic health care coverage. So how can we develop a message about health care that focuses on ending this disparity but that resonates with our intended audience? One option is to focus on the uninsured, as many advocacy groups and progressive activists have done. The message is simple: "It's time to cover the uninsured." That is a concise, simple message that is undeniably true.

It is also, in our view, a message that risks sounding irrelevant to many voters. Think about it. If 15 percent of Americans lack health insurance, that means 85 percent of Americans have health insurance, and 90 percent of voters have health insurance. However, a significant portion of those Americans are underinsured and nearly everyone in that group has been facing double digit increases in their health care premiums for the past decade, as well as an increasingly hostile insurance industry, ready to decline coverage at every turn. A majority of Americans are barely able to keep the insurance they have, and millions live in fear of losing their health insurance through job loss or injury. Still many voters fear radical change, for they fear such change will put what they do have at risk. So when you say that we have to cover the uninsured, what will the majority of people who already have insurance think about that message? To them, "cover the uninsured" means they will help subsidize the uninsured. Americans are generous, but when they can barely provide coverage for their own families, their generosity has its limits, and in their experience it will be them, not the better off, who will pay the bill.

But what if you focused not on covering the uninsured but on the benefits of universal health care coverage for people who already have insurance? What if the message was this: "What we need is health care that we can all count on when we need it." Or another possibility, depending on the target audience, might be: "Too many of us are paying way too much for health insurance, and every year it gets worse. When people lose their health insurance, we all pay. By making health care universal and available for everyone, we can save money and guarantee that none of us will fear losing our health insurance." This variation on the message does nothing to compromise your position on the issue—you still believe in covering the uninsured—but you are meeting voters on their terms. And best of all, the message is factually correct: it's true that universal health care will bring costs down. Right now, people with insurance subsidize the uninsured every day, when they go to emergency rooms instead of seeking preventive treatment. The message has moved from an abstract notion about doing the right thing to an emphasis on the economic insecurities shared by the vast majority of voters.

Contrasting

Elections work best when they are about clear choices for voters. Particularly when you are running against an incumbent, you want voters to understand the difference between you and your opponent. That reality can give rise to negative campaigning, as campaigns resort to personal and misleading attacks against opponents. But it can also lead to an important debate over core principles that helps inform voters. We have seen too many examples of over-the-top attack politics in the past few elections, but pointing out differences on issues is a critical aspect to a message strategy. Elections are about choices, after all, and a winning message must acknowledge that choice, either implicitly or explicitly.

Paul Wellstone made good use of contrast in his campaign messages. As an outspoken progressive, he used contrast both to energize his base supporters and to appeal to swing voters. In his signature campaign message, he drew a clear contrast with his opponent without having to mention his name: "It's true that the pharmaceutical companies, the tobacco companies, the oil companies, and the Enrons of this world don't like me very much, but they already have great representation in Washington. It's the rest of the people that need it. I represent the people of Minnesota." The message tapped into a broader theme that Wellstone was on the side of regular Minnesotans while his opponent represented the interests of big business. As much as people distrust big government, Minnesotans also distrust corporate control of our daily lives. It wasn't just Wellstone's base that loved this message (although it was essential to Wellstone's success that his supporters were so enthusiastic about him that they volunteered day and night to get him elected); it was that undecided voters liked it, too.

While everyone has a different definition of "negative" campaigning, contrast should not be confused with going negative. Using contrast is simply a way to let voters understand the choice in front of them. It is a choice of values, background, and vision for the future. Every campaign has a goal of taking advantage of every opportunity to deliver the message, and presenting a clear contrast between you and your opponent is one way to achieve that goal. This is especially critical when you are challenging an incumbent. In this case, as the challenger, you need to present the case as to why voters should fire the incumbent. People are not fired simply because a better candidate for the job appears; it is because they have failed at their job. If a challenger can't make this case, it will be very hard to win.

The Messenger

Good messages are only as effective as the person delivering the message. Your campaign can come up with a brilliant message that is clear and concise, resonates with your intended audience, and addresses what's on voters' minds. But if the person delivering that message lacks credibility or is not believable, the message will be ineffective. We agree with a conclusion reached by David Axelrod, a campaign consultant who argues that the problem with the progressive message in general, particularly in the past two election cycles, is not that the messages themselves were ineffective, but that they did not fit with the candidates delivering those messages. "Unless a message authentically reflects the messenger, it's likely to fail," Axelrod explains. We think effective messengers share two qualities: they are compelling and credible.

Compelling

Everyone has a story to tell. Whether it is a formative experience from the past, a unique background, or an unlikely path to political activism, good candidates tell voters about the experiences that shaped their past and inform their present views. Campaigns should not shy away from talking about personal stories but should embrace those stories. We believe an important shift is occurring in progressive American politics right now. It is a shift away from a political strategy of selling policies to voters. Instead, an increasing number of progressive candidates are successfully selling leadership to voters. This shift represents a sea change in the traditional progressive model. Where once we tried to get elected on the strength of our programs and ten-point plans, we are now focused on the strength of our candidates' leadership qualities, backgrounds, and, yes, personalities. This is not a debasement of politics; instead it focuses politics back on the core values and human relationships that build trust. Sometimes progressives dismiss as shallow the concept that voters would vote for a particular candidate (even one who counters their own self-interest) because they could see themselves going out for a beer with that candidate. Yet who do we go out for drinks with? Our friends. People we like. People we trust and think we will have a good time with. This is all about trust and building some form of relational bond between voter and candidate, one that transcends any specific issue position.

This shift is good news for progressive politics. It signals new opportunities for candidates who might not have spent years climbing the political ladder but whose life experiences make them more prepared to hold elected office than their opponents. We introduced you earlier to Andrew Gillum, a member of the Tallahassee City Commission who ran for that position fresh out of college. By traditional measures, Gillum had no business running for office: his experience was limited to serving as the president of his university's student body, and as an African American student activist he had witnessed how little respect students received from the city's elected officials. "I decided to run for city commission because I felt that someone who looked like me, with my background, deserved to be represented. I was young, new, and undaunted by the process. Elderly people saw me as their grandson, middle-aged people saw me as their son, and younger women saw me as a potential boyfriend! More than policies, we were selling leadership and a personality. That's something people don't get very much in the political process."

Don't be afraid, in other words, to tell your story. Where did you learn the values you bring to the campaign? How did your family background lead you to where you are today? Talk about the things that give you hope and the challenges that make you fearful for the future. If you have kids and a spouse, how do they affect you as a candidate for office?

Emphasizing the personal does not need to come at the expense of issues and policy; the campaign still needs to clearly articulate the candidate's positions on issues and approach to policy. But in the end, voters are looking for candidates they can trust. The campaign's goal is to find every window of opportunity to communicate its message. Personal stories are memorable, allow voters to get to know a candidate, and above all, create opportunities for the candidate to build trust with his or her constituents. These personal stories only work, however, if the messenger is credible.

Credible

Chances are pretty good that you have seen those television commercials for Trident gum, the ads that talk about all the dentists who recommend Trident for their patients. Do you remember the tagline they use with those ads? They say, "Four out of five dentists recommend sugarless gum for their patients who chew gum." Think about that statement. If four out of five dentists recommend sugarless gum *for their patients who chew gum,* then what is the fifth dentist recommending? Sugared gum? The statement is absurd, yet Trident has used that tagline for years in its advertisements. Obviously it works. Why? Because dentists are experts, they have credibility when it comes to taking care of our teeth. The reason this is an effective ad is the same reason that someone standing in front of a science class in a lab coat is more believable than a similar person standing in front of a classroom in shorts and sneakers. Credibility of the messenger counts when it comes to influencing voters, just as it does for consumers.

Think back to the 2004 presidential election. Why were the Swift Boat Veterans' attack ads against John Kerry so effective? There are a lot of reasons, but one of the main ones is that the ads were delivered not by politicians but by actual veterans who had served with Kerry in Vietnam. Since Kerry already had his own credibility problems ("I voted for the $87 billion before I voted against it."), he created an opening for an attack that proved devastating to his campaign. Never mind the fact that many of the claims made in the ads were demonstrably false; they were believable because they presented credible messengers.

Or consider one of the epochal moments in the presidency of George W. Bush. In the midst of the Hurricane Katrina disaster, the president, whose credibility had begun a precipitous decline because of his handling of the war in Iraq, uttered eight words that will be forever remembered as a symbol of his presidency. Speaking to his director of federal emergency management, Michael Brown, whose previous experience included a stint as the head of the Arabian Horse Breeders Association, the president assured him, "Brownie, you're doing a heck of a job." The statement cemented Bush's reputation for making pronouncements that had little grounding in reality. After accepting such statements for the better part of Bush's first term in office (in part because of his effectiveness at conveying a willingness to stand up for what he believed in), the American public had finally had enough. Bush was mocked for being out of touch with the reality on the ground in New Orleans, and his response to the tragedy was roundly panned.

How does the importance of credibility translate to a campaign? For starters, it suggests that candidates should focus on their strengths and not try to be someone they are not. We have seen a lot of good potential candidates tell us that they decided not to run for office because they felt they didn't have enough experience with policy issues to be effective. They might not have been a part of all the debates or have a deep understanding of every issue. But when pushed, they reveal that they do, in fact, understand the issues as well as anyone, even if it's from a different perspective. For example, you might be a candidate running for school board for the first time. While you might not have a mastery of budgets or education policy, you probably bring experiences to the campaign that will serve your constituents well. Rather than lead with policy details, you could begin by sharing your own experience with the public school system, whether that was an experience you gained from having children in the schools or from going through the schools yourself as a kid. We heard from one such candidate, who told us she used her lack of policy experience to her advantage by delivering a straightforward message about her values: "I might not know everything there is to know about writing a school budget, but I know what it's like for my kids to be students at our schools, and I know what it's like to be a parent who wants the best for her kids. I'm running for school board because I believe we can do better for all of our kids." The point is that experience is more than just a government résumé or expertise in the minutiae of any particular public policy. Voters are interested in issues, but they are likely as baffled by the complexity of most public policies as the rest of us. What they are more interested in is how the candidate will approach the issue or problem. How do they perceive the candidate's character? Will the candidate represent voters' interests? Will he or she empathize with their predicament or perspective? Will the candidate tell the truth? And if the answers are yes, a candidate has a much greater chance to win trust and votes.

How to Deliver the Message: The More Personal, the Better

By now you have heard us say this more than once, but it bears repeating throughout the book: the best way to deliver a message is through direct, personal voter contact. In this chapter, we have covered the "what" (content) and the "who" (messenger). Much of the rest of this book is about the "how"— how can a campaign with limited resources target its voters? How can the campaign messengers, including not only the candidate but also campaign staff and volunteers going door to door, move the most voters through personal conversations? While these tasks require a robust field operation and political outreach program, it is worth pointing out the spectrum of message delivery options available to a campaign. In order of importance, these options include the following:

▸ **One-on-one conversations with voters on their doorsteps or in their workplaces.** For local races, this means a candidate is out knocking on doors every evening, speaking directly to voters and delivering the campaign message. For bigger races, volunteers and campaign staff are surrogates for the candidate. To be effective, the campaign's message must be fully integrated into its field operation. Volunteers should be well briefed and practiced in delivering the message (they don't need to know the nuance of every issue, just have a clear understanding of the core message).

▸ **Community events.** Having a presence at all key community events is important not just for the campaign's visibility, but also because it gives you an opportunity to deliver a message in person. Finding opportunities to speak one-on-one with voters is the primary function of a field operation. While a conversation at the door is ideal, a conversation at a community gathering is also highly effective.

▸ **House parties.** In both large and small races, house parties are a particularly effective way to combine personal contact with the candidate, volunteer recruitment (and fundraising), and base building.

▸ **Phones.** Phoning has a bad reputation because a lot of people dislike making phone calls and even more people dislike getting a political call while they are eating dinner. But used right, phones are a great way of having direct contact with voters, and in many circumstances (locked buildings, difficult geography, etc.) they are the best way to have a personal conversation with a targeted voter.

▸ **Paid media.** In large races, having a personal conversation with every targeted voter is impossible. Paid media—television, radio, newspaper ads, and direct mail—are a way to deliver, unfiltered, the campaign's message to its audience.

▸ **Earned media.** Using the press to deliver your message is far more affordable than using paid media, but the disadvantage is that your message goes through the filter of a media outlet. Nonetheless, campaigns that build relationships with reporters and use the media effectively often successfully rely on earned media as a main source of communicating the campaign's message.

In later chapters, we spend significant time describing both field and communications tactics for direct voter contact.

Developing the Message

At the start of the campaign, we suggest that the campaign team, led by the campaign manager but with the active involvement of the candidate, spend time with a small group of trusted advisers to brainstorm message ideas. This is an opportunity for the team to throw all ideas, even ones that might sound silly or unlikely, on the table for discussion. With these ideas written down in the form of a long list of messages—whether they are one sentence or one paragraph—a process of elimination can begin. Each message can then be evaluated, with the audience in mind, to determine whether the message will resonate with voters.

Until now, our discussion of message has focused on the conversation your campaign is having with voters. But of course this is not the only conversation that is taking place. Your opponent is also carrying on a conversation while at the same time trying to interrupt your conversation. Some campaigns struggle with message and get distracted by opponents because they don't have a clear picture of what the other candidate is saying about herself, nor are they able to anticipate what attacks the opponent will make on any given day.

One way to take the mystery out of the message process is to use a tool called the Tully message box, named after Democratic strategist Paul Tully. The message box is a simple diagram that lays out the four core messages being delivered by the two campaigns: what we are saying about ourselves, what we are saying about our opponent, what the opponent is saying about himself, and what the opponent is saying about us.

In addition to helping clarify what you say, the message box helps you play an effective defense. It gives a clear idea of where your opponent will attack you, how you can respond, and how you can move the conversation back to your message. You want to present voters with a clear, contrasting choice, and a message box helps articulate that choice. A message box also helps a campaign stay disciplined and "on message" by clarifying the core arguments in the campaign.

To give you an idea of how to use a message box, let's use as an example the 2004 presidential election. In that campaign, Senator John Kerry tried to unseat President Bush by arguing that Bush had been an ineffective president and that he, Kerry, had a plan for getting the country back on track. Bush, in the words of Democratic consultant David Axelrod, relied on "figuring out how to make [his] stubbornness into a political virtue." He contrasted his unwavering positions with Kerry's tendency to change his views depending on the political climate.

Why is the message box useful? Because while it doesn't necessarily tell you who is going to win the message argument, it clarifies how you can preempt your opponent's arguments and seek opportunities to exploit your opponent's weaknesses. In the case of Bush and Kerry, the message box reveals a clear difference between the two candidates. While Kerry focuses on convincing voters that he will be a more effective president, Bush focuses more on character. The Bush campaign was highly effective in defining Kerry as a weak and indecisive leader whose views change. Kerry, of course, gave the Bush campaign plenty of fodder to make this attack, but never made a compelling argument about why voters should no longer trust Bush to lead the nation. In the end, the campaign came down to an argument between effectiveness versus character. In most elections, character will win.

Electoral campaigns can also draw lessons from issue-based campaigns about effective messaging. Let's look at the Chicago "Big Box" ordinance that was passed and vetoed in 2006. This ordinance would require very large "big box" retailers like Wal-Mart and Target to pay workers a minimum wage of $9.25 per hour with benefits, which would rise to $10.00 per hour plus benefits by 2010. Working to pass the ordinance was a coalition of thirty labor unions, community groups, and religious leaders. Opposing the ordinance was a coalition of business groups, large retailers, and religious leaders. Also opposing the ordinance and threatening to veto anything that passed was Mayor Daley, who had never had to veto any bill in his seventeen years in office. The challenge, then, was passing a big-box ordinance in the face of the mayor's opposition and the opposition of the world's largest and wealthiest corporation, Wal-Mart.

To set the stage, Wal-Mart had come to the city a few years earlier looking for city subsidies and was refused. They then came back with a revamped

Message Box

What we are saying about ourselves	What they are saying about themselves
What we are saying about them	What they are saying about us

Message Box: Bush/Kerry 2004

Kerry on Kerry: I have a plan.	Bush on Bush: I'm a strong leader and won't waver from my beliefs.
Kerry on Bush: He's screwed everything up and doesn't know what he's doing.	Bush on Kerry: He's a flip-flopper.

"Big Box" Message Box

We need good jobs, not poverty jobs.	We're bringing jobs to poor Chicago communities.
We can pay more, and when they don't they hurt the whole community.	They're antibusiness and pushing "Chicago" jobs to the suburbs.

A message box is a tool for clarifying the core arguments of the campaign. It doesn't tell you who will win the argument, but it helps you anticipate what to expect from your opponent and how your campaign can continually stay on message. The message box should be frequently referenced by your campaign manager and communications team.

strategy to target low-income neighborhoods and promised to build ten to twenty stores in neighborhoods that were desperate for jobs and economic development. Both sides developed powerful messages. Proponents wanted to make this a community issue, not a union issue, so they framed the debate as "good jobs versus poverty jobs." They could have taken many other strategies that progressive groups have taken regarding Wal-Mart: for example, that Wal-Mart is an evil company that exploits workers and hurts third world countries through sweatshop labor (the "shame" campaign). Other focuses of some campaigns are hiring practices, discrimination, failure to follow wage and labor laws, environmental degradation, or antiunion practices. The ordinance itself contained many provisions to address these issues, including "free speech" provisions that would have required access for charitable activities and theoretically union organizers. None of these became the message focus because they did not have the broad value-based appeal of other messages. Consider the campaign's intended audience. Many of the low-income residents shopped at Wal-Mart (as do many Americans). To connect with a "Wal-Mart is evil" message, they would have had to see themselves as doing something wrong by shopping there. Instead, proponents focused not on stopping the big-box retailers from coming, but on pointing out that big-box retailers could afford to pay better wages and, when they did come, they should pay a living wage. The city should focus on creating well-paying jobs in these neighborhoods, not poverty wages.

Opponents wanted to divide and conquer the proponents and frame the debate as "unions versus community" or "antibusiness/antidevelopment versus jobs" or "poor neighborhoods versus wealthy neighborhoods" (and an insidious undertone was racial: "poorer communities of color versus wealthier and suburban white communities"). They focused on the ordinance as a "job killer" and an elitist attempt to drive jobs away from poorer neighborhoods to the suburbs.

Both sides did their message work well. Alderman Joe Moore, the sponsor of the ordinance, spoke on message on National Public Radio's *POV* show, saying: "The principle underlying this [ordinance] is that nobody should work a full day's work and not be able to get out of poverty. A job should lift someone out of poverty, not keep someone in it. . . . And so the effort of this ordinance is to try to affect that and provide for the ten thousand Chicagoans who work in big-box retailers a wage by which they can support their families and lift themselves out of poverty." Proponents succeeded in passing the ordinance by a narrow, presumably veto-proof margin. But in the end the mayor vetoed it and sustained his veto by swinging three aldermen to switch their vote. In his veto statement, he again was strictly on message: "I understand and share a desire to ensure that everyone who works in the city of Chicago earns a decent wage. But I do not believe this ordinance, well intentioned as it may be, would achieve that end. Rather, I believe it would drive jobs and businesses from our city, penalizing neighborhoods that need additional economic activity the most."

This is an example of both sides of the campaign developing powerful messages and finding deep resonance with their intended audience around those messages.

Message Discipline

Having a great message is useful only if that message is delivered repeatedly. As we mentioned before, voters are bombarded with messages every day. The way to break through to voters is to "stay on message"—that is, repeat the message over and over again. As one former governor told us, "The key thing I learned in my campaigns was that you have to say something eight hundred or more times if you want it to stick. I got so sick of saying the same thing over and over again, but I came to understand that unless I was saying it, no one would listen. By about the eight hundredth time, people started hearing what I was saying." A campaign's job is to repeat the message constantly, every day. The staff and volunteers should be repeating the message in their sleep by the end of the campaign.

Campaign workers also have a responsibility to keep the candidate on message, by making his or her job as easy as possible and preparing the candidate for every event or interview. We spoke with a campaign manager who told us that despite a well-organized campaign that ultimately won in the fall, they did not do a good enough job of maintaining message discipline with the candidate. "A weakness of our campaign was that staff did not always do their utmost to keep our candidate on message," he said. "Knowing what kind of group you're speaking to and which comments should not be said to them are vital components of good campaign speeches. Doing a better job at this aspect of the campaign would have prevented a couple of verbal gaffes from occurring, which proved to be minor setbacks for the campaign."

There is a phenomenon in political campaigns known as "winning the argument, losing the campaign." Your opponent will always be poking, prodding, and goading you to debate in the "zone" of a campaign where they know they will ultimately win, no matter how strong your argument is on its academic merits. For example, many progressive candidates get furious when conservatives try to stake out national security or probusiness issues as their own. We know that we've got fundamentally better ideas about keeping people safe or developing healthy local businesses. But our inclination to argue these points ad infinitum and prove we're right can be a dangerous one. The reality is that many voters simply don't have the time or desire to tune in and learn the nuance of difference on every particular issue.

If you engage in protracted debates in "zones" that are not core to your winning strategy, the choice presented to voters will be about something that puts you at a distinct disadvantage. Elections can't be about everything. They are often about whatever the candidates spend most of their time talking about. This is what people mean by "controlling the terms of debate." Your job is to make sure that you don't get lured into arguments in which you ultimately lose even if you think you're going to win in the short term. Moreover, you need to remember that your opponent is human, too, and is susceptible to spending time talking about issues where *you* ultimately win no matter what is said.

Having message discipline doesn't mean that you shouldn't respond to an inaccurate characterization of your position or try to neutralize an issue that your opponent is trying to use to advantage. However, you're winning when you're successfully bringing the campaign back to what *you* want to talk about, defining the choice to voters on *your* terms, no matter where an opponent or outside forces are trying to take you.

Message discipline also requires settling on the right message and sticking with it. Consider this example of a messaging challenge that took place in Vermont. In the spring of 2007, the Vermont legislature passed a comprehensive bill that addressed climate change by establishing a state utility that residents could enlist to help make homes and businesses more energy efficient. The bill, one of the most far-reaching ever passed by a state legislature, was fiercely opposed by the conservative governor and the business lobby, who argued against its source of funding (a tax on nuclear power) and suggested that there wasn't much that a small state like Vermont could do about global warming anyway. When the governor vetoed the bill, supporters began a campaign to persuade the legislature to override the veto.

One of the core questions supporters of the bill faced was "What is our message?" To some, the message should have been about the environment, while others advocated for a focus on the economic savings that would result from the bill. Still others wanted to focus on the parts of the bill that would create jobs. The bottom line was that all of these messages were effective, depending on the audience. A clear majority of Vermonters had expressed an interest in taking significant action against global warming. On the other hand, the bill's supporters could point to powerful evidence that the legislation would end up saving hundreds, perhaps thousands, of dollars for people who took advantage of the efficiency program. The jobs argument was also persuasive; the state was desperate for new jobs in a growing industry, and the bill presented an opportunity to create a new green industry in the state.

The supporters of the bill had good message content, but when they settled on one message—that it is time to back up our words with action and fight global climate change—they found that they weren't gaining much traction. The reason? They had misidentified their audience. In this case, their audience was not just the general public, although the public certainly played an important role. Their immediate audience was the group of legislators who had originally voted no on the bill and whose votes supporters needed in order to override the veto. These legislators, many of whom came from conservative areas in which an environmental message fell flat, were not moved by the climate change argument. So supporters of the bill changed tactics and began focusing instead on the cost savings. They reminded Vermonters of how much they were paying for heat in the winter and how up to half the heat produced in their homes was wasted because of inefficiencies. They talked specifically about how much money they could save on their monthly energy bills if they took advantage of this new utility. It was a better message, but by the time supporters settled on it, a frame had been set: the bill was about a tax, not about Vermonters' energy bills. In the end, the veto override fell short. With message delivery, you usually get only one shot to make an argument to the public, and it's very difficult to start over with a new argument.

Case Study: Klobuchar for Senate, 2006

To tie these principles together in a real example of a progressive candidate who communicated a winning message, let's look at the 2006 U.S. Senate race in Minnesota. How did Amy Klobuchar, a county district attorney without any legislative experience, turn one of the country's most competitive Senate races against a conservative three-term congressman into a twenty-point landslide victory? How did she become the first woman elected senator in her state's history while defying partisan electoral history and winning over voters in traditionally conservative areas?

Klobuchar's historic win began with a statewide grassroots campaign that engaged thousands of people at a high level, traveled countless miles by car and foot to spend time in each of her state's 87 counties (parades, coffee shops, VFW halls, and bean feeds galore), and raised the financial resources she needed. A favorable political environment ensured that she had a legitimate chance to win, but something else helped account for her overwhelming success: an ability to communicate clearly the way her life experience informed her politics, the values she shared with voters, and the trust people could have in her to do what was right—no matter how hard it might be. In short, people knew that Amy Klobuchar was on Minnesota's side—on *their* side—and wouldn't be led astray when they sent her off to Washington to do their business.

To illustrate how Klobuchar talked about who she was and where she came from, here's an excerpt from the speech she gave to the state Democratic-Farmer-Labor Party convention:

> My grandpa worked fifteen hundred feet underground in the Zenith mine on the Iron Range. A few months ago I was at Vertin's Cafe in Ely, and this guy came up to me, he stood up, and he said, "You know, my dad worked on your grandpa's crew," and he got tears in his eyes and he said, "You know, when your grandpa led his crew into those mines, he didn't stand up at the top and radio down, he always went first, he went with the guys and he was never afraid." My grandpa taught me that you work hard, you stand up for what you believe in and you do your work without fear or favor.

This personal story of being the granddaughter of an iron ore miner from rural Minnesota told voters a lot that they needed to know about her. She had deep roots in the state, was in touch with the struggles of working people, and had a clear set of values that went back several generations. In short, she knew where she (and her listeners) came from. From that same speech, here's how Klobuchar talked about her work as a chief prosecutor:

> When I became chief prosecutor I could not believe what would happen when we would have cases with wealthy, well-connected people; the courtroom was packed with their friends. When we prosecuted

someone who was poor or middle class, they're lucky if their mom can take the day off work to stand behind them in that courtroom. *I figure my job is to even the playing field no matter where someone comes from, to do my job without fear or favor* . . . and I think we need a little bit more of that in Washington, D.C.

Klobuchar used personal and professional stories like these not to say exactly what *policy* she would champion in Washington, but what *kind* of senator she would be. When sharing this sort of information with voters, Klobuchar used a "show, don't tell" style of communicating. After all, would you trust a candidate just because she says, "You can trust me"? Of course not. But by *showing* people who she was and what she had learned in her life and career, Klobuchar did develop a deep trust with the people of the state.

Now let's look at a few television ads that Klobuchar used to introduce herself to voters. As with the examples from the speech, the ads used personal stories to establish a connection with people and show what she was made of.

My job is to hold people accountable when they break the law. [*Narrator*: Amy Klobuchar. For eight years, she's run a prosecutor's office.] We've gone after scam artists, child abusers, murderers. We even put a judge in prison. This is a judge who stole money from the bank account of a mentally disabled woman who he was supposed to protect. He was a Democrat and so am I. But that didn't matter, because this guy had to go to jail. I believe in standing up for people without fear or favor. Isn't that what they should be doing in Washington?

Here's another one:

When our daughter was born, she was very sick. She couldn't swallow, she was hooked up to machines, and yet our HMO had a rule that new mothers were kicked out in twenty-four hours. [*Narrator*: Amy Klobuchar took on the insurance industry.] We got one of the first laws in the country passed guaranteeing new moms and their babies a forty-eight-hour hospital stay. I believe in standing up for people without fear or favor. Isn't that what they should be doing in Washington?

Now ask yourself a few questions. What would tell you more about a candidate: that she has a thoughtful five-point plan on insurance industry reform, or that she took on and beat the insurance industry on behalf of mothers and families after being kicked out of the hospital with a sick newborn? Which of those would stick with you? Do you want a candidate who *tells* you they will be tough in office, or one that *shows* you they're tough by having thrown a judge in jail when he did something wrong? Do these stories give you the confidence that Klobuchar has what it takes to do what's right in Washington, even when facing tough special interests? Would she really be on your side? The answer to these last two questions for many Minnesotans was a resounding "yes." Part of the reason these stories were so effective is that Klobuchar engaged people in a conversation about the kind of representation they wanted.

None of this is to say that policy isn't important in a campaign. Voters need to know what kind of person a candidate is, but they do also need to know what it is they plan to do in office. As we discussed earlier, the "sweet spot" is where who a candidate is and what she plans to do come together. Here's another example of how Klobuchar connected her work as a prosecutor to her plans for tax fairness and reining in the control of big oil and drug companies in Washington (not necessarily an easy task):

In my job, I know, if you want to find the bad guys, you've got to follow the money. [*Narrator:* Amy Klobuchar. Her office prosecuted corrupt CEOs, scam artists, and tax cheats. In Washington, she'll stop the $70-billion-a-year offshore tax scam for billionaires, end the giveaways to the big oil and drug companies.]

As we discussed earlier, it's important to connect policy to personal narrative, but it's also important to connect policy to a set of shared values and contrast it with your opponent's record or policy proposals. Here's how Klobuchar did that:

In Minnesota, we've always believed in opportunity through hard work. But these days, no matter how hard you work, the price of gas, college, and health care is getting out of reach. Washington's been tilting the playing field against the middle class for the past six years. I think it's got to stop. But that's never going to happen with this crowd in charge. It's time to end the giveaways to the big oil and drug companies and bring a dose of Minnesota fairness to Washington.

It's also not easy to make policy proposals engaging. Policy is complicated, perceived as the work of bureaucrats holed off in secret office buildings and often disconnected from people's lives and values. Here's one example where Klobuchar succeeded in making a specific policy proposal very engaging as well as contrasting it with what her opponent had to offer:

So here's a good idea: the government negotiates big discounts for the prices of drugs for our veterans. That's *right*. What's *wrong* is that Medicare pays the drug companies 40 percent more for the exact same drugs for our seniors. The drug companies actually got Congress to make it *illegal* to negotiate for lower prices. We could save $90 billion a year if we changed that. The drug companies don't want to do it, but I do.

There is no question that this conversational tone is more engaging than a politician lecturing voters on the things they plan to do in office. It's also connected to something that people understand: the idea of right and wrong. Most people would agree that it's wrong (or just plain stupid!) that Congress forbade itself from negotiating lower drug prices for seniors because the pharmaceutical industry wanted to make more money and had enough power to make it happen. It would be hard to disagree that negotiating for lower prices is the right thing to do, and Klobuchar lays out that argument very clearly.

Remember, however, a question in most voters' minds when they hear any promise from a candidate: "Even if she wanted to, could she really get that done?" It's critically important to establish credibility that you can and will do what you say when talking to a rightfully skeptical public. But when you think back to Klobuchar's story of taking on and beating the insurance industry before—a story that is hard to forget—it's a lot easier to believe that she would be able to follow through on this idea. Not every candidate will have such a crystal clear example with which to build their credibility, but it's important to look hard for something from your life experience that will preempt doubts that are naturally in voters' minds.

Amy Klobuchar wasn't elected senator solely on the strength of her message or communication skills. But there is a lot to be learned from the way she used her personal narrative, focused on a set of shared values with voters, established credibility and trust, and talked about policy in a manner that was easy to understand and agree with. When it comes to communication that's clear, concise, credible, contrasting, conversational, and compelling, Klobuchar got the job done and is now serving the people of Minnesota in the U.S. Senate.

CHAPTER 4

Identifying Your Base, Swing Voters, and Opponents through Voter Targeting

A SUCCESSFUL CAMPAIGN PLAN hinges on knowing which voters you must target to win: who they are, where they live, what motivates them, and how you can reach them. Campaign targeting uses information from past elections, voter rolls, past identifications and voter surveys, demographic information from the census, consumer data, and other sources to identify how many votes are needed to win, where those likely votes are within a district, who the base voters are, whom you will need to persuade, and who will never vote for your candidate. Targeting identifies where potentially supportive nonvoters and sporadic voters live so you can focus your voter registration and get-out-the-vote efforts. Targeting helps break the universe of all voters into smaller subgroups of particular types of voters. It is about playing the percentages: targeting cannot tell you precisely how a voter will vote (people simply are not that predictable, and the data are never that complete). What it can tell you is where you will be more likely to find the voters you will need to win. It will be up to your field operation to actually contact, identify, persuade, and turn out voters.

The first step is collecting the data about your race. There are three categories of information: past election results down to the precinct level, the voter file (data on registered voters), and demographic information about the electorate and the larger population.

Before we go into the details of each of these categories, a note for those who are running in small races, like a city council race in a small community or rural districts: even if you do not need a lot of sophisticated charts and analyses, you can still target. Small-scale targeting relies on having individual campaign supporters target their own networks of voters from the voter file. The advantage to doing it this way rather than simply asking folks to contact their friends is that it allows the campaign to track contacts and organize a get-out-the-vote effort. While the following discussion might not apply to all races, the principles of targeting and the tools used to target voters are relevant to any campaign worker or candidate planning a campaign.

Past Election Results

The first category of targeting data—past election results—helps you predict voter turnout, calculate your win number, and quantify your base vote. It can help you geographically locate precincts where high numbers of support- ers, opponents, and persuadable voters live, as well as high and low turnout areas. Always use election results that are similar to your race: if you are run- ning in a down ballot race (a race for a relatively lower office) in a presidential year, use results from your race in other presidential years. If you are running in an odd-year election or if there are multiple candidates on the ballot, look for past elections that mimic the essential conditions you are running under.

The first thing you will be able to take from this data is your win number. Your win number is the number of votes that you predict it will actually take to win a race. Getting "lots of votes" is not a number, and while getting one more vote than the other candidate is technically the way you win, it is hardly a strategy. Without knowing your win number, you have no way of making rational decisions for spending your resources or even knowing whether the race is winnable at all. You get your win number by looking at total turnout for the past three similar elections and making the best estimate of the num- ber of votes required to win your election. For example, let's say you are run- ning for state representative in 2008 in a district that has 45,000 registered voters. Based on past election results you find the following voter turnout for your district:

- ▶ 2006: 68.1 percent
- ▶ 2004: 69.4 percent
- ▶ 2000: 65.2 percent
- ▶ 1996: 65.5 percent

Calculating an expected vote from this data is half math and half educated guess. In 2004 we saw one of the highest voter turnouts in many decades, and in 2006 we saw one of the highest voter turnouts in a nonpresidential year for many years. We can expect, given what we know now, that in 2008 there will also be a high voter turnout. We might want to predict at least as high as 2004, a reasonable assumption, or we may want to simply take a straight average of these four numbers, which is 67.1 percent. Since this represents a number higher than the traditional turnout, which seems to be around 65 percent, but not quite the record turnout of 2004, we choose making this straight average. If turnout numbers are relatively stable, as they are in this example, simply averaging the past three elections will get you pretty close. In our fictitious race we would multiply 67.1 percent (expected voter turnout) by 45,000 (registered voters) to predict that roughly 30,000 (the actual number is 30,195) people will vote on Election Day.

In a two-person race, the win number is a simple majority—50 percent of the expected turnout, plus one vote, or 15,001 votes in our case. No one, of course, wants to target to win a race by only one vote, so most campaigns add a buffer of 2 to 10 percent depending on the size and expected volatility of the race. Let us assume we are targeting to win this race by four points, 52 percent to 48 percent. That means we think our working win number is 15,600 votes. It can be more difficult to estimate a win number in multicandidate races. Targeting such races depends on trying to estimate relative candidate strength. Do not simply divide the expected voter turnout by the number of candidates. Seldom do multicandidate races break that evenly, but it will also likely be a plurality, not a majority. Similar past multicandidate races, if you are so lucky to have them, can help guide this estimation.

The next step in determining how many votes you need to secure is to determine your base vote, or the floor beneath which you are highly unlikely to sink if you run as a particular type of candidate. Quantifying your base will help you determine what we call the vote deficit, or the number of votes that you think you will need to find to achieve your win number. To determine your base vote, you will need to look at the past several races (at least three and preferably five or more cycles). If you are running in a partisan race, you will want to look at the years and races in which your party did the worst. These do not have to be races for the same office you are running for. You are looking for a pattern that indicates the relatively few highly partisan voters who will vote for you regardless of who you are as long as you represent the party label.

For example, in our fictitious race we discover that

- ▶ in 2006, the state senate candidate received 36 percent of the vote;
- ▶ in 2004, the secretary of state got 35 percent and the governor got 28 percent (in a three-way race);
- ▶ in 2000, the state legislative candidate got 33 percent.

Since we are dealing with a two-way race, we will want to throw out the outlier, the three-way race. These data indicate that you should be able to expect somewhere between 33 to 36 percent of the vote simply by virtue of being your party's candidate. An average of these numbers shows 35 percent, or 10,500 votes, and is a fairly good indicator of the base on which you can expect to start. Your vote deficit is 5,100 votes, which means that you need to find, persuade, or register and turn out this many votes.

Figuring out your base vote in a partisan race is fairly easy, assuming you have access to the data. It becomes more difficult, although not impossible, in nonpartisan or partisan primary races. Determining a base vote in these races depends on a discernable voting pattern. For example, in one city the nonpartisan mayoral race usually comes down to a probusiness candidate and a prolabor candidate, or a candidate from the western side of the city against a candidate from the eastern side. For both of these types of races a base vote can be roughly determined depending on what profile your candidate fits. Other factors to look at might be how past races break down according to race or gender or whether you have the party endorsement (in those states that have party endorsement prior to the primary).

The next step is to use past election data, down to the precinct level, to determine where you are most likely to find swing voters (those voters who swing between parties and are more likely to be persuadable), base voters (whom you will want to turn out to vote), and your opponent's base voters (on whom you will try to not spend any resources). If we diagram our hypothetical district, we could expect our base to be 35 percent of the voters and our opponent's base to be 40 percent of the voters. The middle 25 percent are swing voters. Most swing voters trend toward one political party, even if they consider themselves truly independent (relatively few voters are true swing, undecided voters without a tendency to vote one way or another). The task of your campaign, then, is to mobilize your base vote, solidify your soft supporters, and win over enough of the persuadable voters to achieve your win number.

Analyzing past election results can help locate where relatively higher concentrations of each of these types of voters live, and it begins the process of breaking the entire electorate into the key smaller universes where you will focus resources. For example, precincts that routinely support your party's candidates at levels of 65 percent or greater are your base precincts. Likewise, the precincts in which the opposing party receives 65 percent or more of the vote are their base precincts. These will likely be precincts your campaign spends little time or resources in. Swing voters are more likely to be found in greater numbers in those precincts that are roughly equal in voting behavior between the two parties. An even better gauge is to look at precincts that have a history of "ticket splitting," or supporting candidates from both parties, particularly in the same election year. These precincts will become a priority for your voter identification and voter persuasion program. You can identify these precincts by looking at the gap between your party's candidates with the best performance in the district and the worst performance in any given election. Those districts with the largest difference have more ticket splitters and become an identification and persuasion priority. Precinct-level targeting is very valuable but is one of the crudest targeting tools available. It works best for targeting the candidate's schedule, media buys, events, and get-out-the-vote efforts.

In the hypothetical example above we used nice round numbers. Now let's look at another targeting document from an actual campaign. The following chart was created by a targeting professional who looked at the past three similar elections and added data about voting age population to come up with key data points for each precinct in a district.

Your campaign team could determine all of the statistics on this chart simply by looking at the basic secretary of state data and census data. To find voting age population data, you can look at voting age naturalized citizen data from the U.S. census or contact either party officials or a professional targeting firm. Below are definitions of key targeting terms.

- ▶ *Registered voters:* the total number of registered voters in the district.

- ▶ *Voting age population (VAP):* number of "potential" voters (at least eighteen years old and U.S. citizens).

- ▶ *Percentage registered:* this is derived by dividing the registered voters by the voting age population.

PRECINCT	REGISTERED VOTERS	VOTING AGE POPULATION	REGISTERED (IN PERCENT)	TURNOUT (IN PERCENT)	PROGRESSIVE PERFORMANCE (IN PERCENT)	EXPECTED PROGRESSIVE VOTE	PERSUASION (IN PERCENT)	PERSUASION INDEX	MINORITY (IN PERCENT)
P-1	1,867	4,068	46	26	52.7	256	20.1	97	18.9
P-2	1,854	3,225	57	34	65.3	410	19	119	44.6
P-3	1,189	1,637	73	42	59.7	298	17.9	89	32.7
P-4	957	1,143	84	61	49	284	22.3	130	11.7
P-5	1,234	1,438	86	64	55.4	434	15.3	120	28.3
P-6	692	822	84	61	52.1	221	18.6	79	17.5
P-7	1,119	1,332	84	61	52.6	358	17	116	17.9
P-8	1,573	1,921	82	58	49.9	454	20.1	183	10.9
P-9	583	739	79	57	51.2	171	17.3	58	17.2
P-10	1,189	1,282	93	72	39.6	340	13.1	112	4.7
P-11	218	421	52	51	61.3	69	20.8	23	29.1
P-12	1,973	2,325	85	68	38.8	521	17.1	230	7.9

This targeting spreadsheet for a legislative campaign tells you a lot about each precinct in your district—everything from the number of voters to the typical performance of progressive candidates. While the spreadsheet contains a lot of numbers and might look confusing at first glance, walking through each item gives you a straightforward picture of how your campaign will likely perform in each precinct and where to allocate your campaign resources.

▶ *Turnout percentage:* expected voter turnout, based on the average of the past three similar elections.

▶ *Progressive performance:* the expected percentage of votes a progressive can expect given a typical campaign, based on the performance of progressive candidates in the past. Often this information is part of data provided by the party or by organizations such as the National Coalition for an Effective Congress.

▶ *Expected progressive vote:* the expected number of progressive voters given a typical campaign. This results from multiplying the expected number of voters (registered voters multiplied by turnout percentage) by the progressive performance percentage.

▶ *Persuasion percentage:* the estimated percentage of swing voters based on past voting history. This can be calculated by looking at the difference between high and low percentages for your party in a given precinct or district. For example, if your best-performing candidate received 58 percent and the worst received 44 percent, you can expect that about 14 percent of voters are swing voters and good persuadable voters.

▸ *Persuasion index:* the estimated "number" of swing voters. This is arrived at by multiplying the persuasion percentage by the number of expected voters.

Assume you are the manager of this campaign and you are responsible for devising the targeting strategy. Almost all key decisions—how to schedule the candidate's time, where to invest field resources, whether there are precincts the campaign should ignore—depend on getting this targeting data right. The district has twelve precincts. The total population of eligible voters in the district is 20,353. The total number of registered voters is 14,448. According to this chart, the likely turnout will be 8,015 voters, or 56 percent of registered voters.

Take a moment to study the table. Each precinct is not created equal. You will note that in Precinct 1, for example, there are more than 4,000 eligible voters, but only 1,867, or 46 percent, are registered, a low number compared with other precincts. On top of that, the expected turnout of those who are registered is quite low—26 percent of registered voters, or 485 people. Just by looking at the first five columns of numbers, you know a lot about this precinct. It is easily the most populated precinct, with at least twice as many eligible voters as other precincts. Yet in terms of actual votes, P-1 produces fewer than most precincts. You can infer some characteristics of the precinct without ever stepping foot in it. It could be heavily populated with students, which might explain the gap between eligible voters and likely voters, since many students are either not registered to vote or are registered in their hometowns. Another possibility is that this precinct is made up of low-income households, with a sizable population of disenfranchised residents who see little reason to bother registering and showing up at the polls. All of this data can be readily verified through census data or spot-checking the precinct.

What about the other information? The progressive performance for this precinct is 52.7 percent. That means your campaign can expect 256 votes going into the race (you reach that number by multiplying the progressive performance by the expected turnout, in this case: .527 x 485 = 256). The persuasion percentage is 20.1 percent: 20.1 percent of the voters in this precinct are "persuadable." That translates to 98 votes. Finally, you know that 18.9 percent of this precinct are minority residents. This information will be useful as you put together your field and political outreach program.

From this table, a targeting plan will begin to emerge. To start, you can tell just by looking at "progressive performance" that P-2 is a base precinct, because your campaign starts out with 65 percent of the vote there. P-2 also has a lot of voters—the second highest population and the third highest number of registered voters—although the expected turnout, 34 percent, is significantly lower than other precincts. Already you can start thinking about a strategy for P-2: this is a strong progressive precinct, but a majority of voters never bother to show up at the polls. This precinct should be a focus of major voter turnout efforts, including voter registration, ongoing base-building work, and intense get-out-the-vote efforts. You know from this data that if you randomly pull a voter off the street, you have a 65 percent likelihood of getting his or her vote. Those are good odds. This is a precinct that deserves attention.

Where are your other base precincts? P-11 also has a high progressive performance index, but look at the expected turnout: 113 voters (51 percent of registered voters). This is a very small precinct that, while important not to ignore, is not a top base area for the campaign. P-5, on the other hand, has a progressive performance index (55.4 percent) that is substantially higher than the overall district performance and has some other notable characteristics. It has a very high number of registered voters. Of the eligible voters in this precinct, 86 percent are registered. Of those, 64 percent actually turn out at the polls. So you have a high turnout rate relative to other precincts and a reasonably high progressive performance index. In terms of raw numbers, this precinct will likely turn out the third highest number of progressive votes. If your campaign focuses on base building and voter mobilization in this precinct, you have an opportunity to turn out even more votes. P-5 is definitely a base precinct, but because the density of supportive voters is significantly less than P-2 (55.4 percent compared with 65.3 percent), your base work in this district needs to be more targeted than turning out every voter as discussed earlier. Similarly, P-3 has a relatively higher concentration of base voters (59.7 percent performance) and a substantial number of likely base supporters (298). Like P-2, it has low voter turnout. This is also likely a base precinct. If resources allow, you would spend considerable time in each of these districts. If tough choices need to be made about where to focus your resources, and they usually do, the precincts that make the most sense for you depend in large part on your overall strategy to win and your candidate's connection with any given precinct or constituency in that precinct (e.g., with youth voters or disenfranchised voters).

Now let's look at your opponent's base precincts. If you just look at the "expected progressive vote" column, P-12 looks pretty good for your campaign; it is a heavily populated precinct that will likely turn out the highest number of progressive votes. But don't let that number confuse you. The progressive performance for this precinct is 38.8 percent; in other words, slightly above one in three voters will likely be supportive. It also has a relatively low persuasion percentage of 17.1 percent, which means that there is a lower density of swing or persuadable voters. P-12 is a base precinct for your opponent. Finding your voters in a precinct like P-12 using past election results is very difficult, yet there are many of your supporters who live there. Targeting these voters will need to rely on other tools like the voter file and microtargeting, which we cover later in the chapter. Your opponent's other obvious base precinct is P-10. This precinct has the highest percentage of registered voters in the district and the highest expected turnout. These are reliable voters who can be counted on to vote, and unfortunately fewer than 40 percent of them start out in your camp. Worse, there aren't many persuadable voters in this precinct, only 13.1 percent.

Which precincts deserve particular attention from your campaign's persuasion efforts? Take a look at the persuasion percentage in each precinct. You can see that four precincts—P-1, P-4, P-8, and P-11—have persuasion percentages above 20 percent. Yet if you look at the persuasion index, or the actual number of voters those percentages represent, precincts 4 and 8 stand out. P-8 is clearly your top persuasion precinct, as it has a lot of registered voters, a relatively high turnout rate, and a high number of persuadable voters. P-4 also has both a high percentage and high number of persuadable voters. However, there is one other factor to take into account: performance. Performance data gives you some indication of which direction those swing voters are likely to swing. Both P-1 and P-11 have higher performance percentages, indicating a likelihood that swing voters will disproportionately swing progressive. As discussed earlier, P-11 is very small and will not likely become a major target, although it should also not be ignored. P-1 also has low registration rates and low turnout. It could be viewed as a precinct to selectively target for voter registration and turnout and one in which to identify swing voters, as well. Depending on your campaign resources, all three would be good persuasion targets.

Finally, the campaign's top precincts for voter registration are P-1 and P-2. Both of these precincts have very low percentages of registered voters (46 and 57 percent, respectively) and abysmal turnout percentages. That represents both an opportunity and a challenge. A sustained voter registration effort will likely yield a large number of new registered voters, but registering a voter and turning him or her out to vote are two different things. If past experience in these precincts is any guide, registered voters may simply stay home. The campaign might also focus resources in P-11, despite the low population. With only 52 percent of eligible voters registered, the campaign may be able to add several dozen voters to the voting rolls in that precinct.

The Voter File

The voter file is an essential targeting data source and can be found in its most basic form at the secretary of state's office. At a minimum, a voter file will have name and address of the voter, the election district, and precinct. Most also include the person's phone number, date of birth, past elections the person voted in, gender, party registration (if in a state that requires party registration), registration date, and absentee voting status. Voter files vary greatly from state to state, and the cost can range from as little as twenty-five dollars for a CD with all the voters in the state and their voting history to several hundred and even thousands of dollars. If possible, you will want to get an enhanced voter file for your district, one that has the information from the secretary of state's office plus additional material that helps you know a voter better. These enhanced voter files are usually maintained by political parties or are available for sale by private vendors, often at a substantial cost. Some campaigns create a targeting analysis themselves, others get help interpreting the data from their political party, and still others may hire a targeting planner. Larger campaigns may get assistance from organizations like the National Committee for an Effective Congress, which provide highly detailed and sophisticated targeting data for progressive campaigns. For most small and medium-sized campaigns, you and your team can do the targeting you need.

The voter file provides invaluable information for targeting. From our geographic targeting, we have a better idea of where our voters live and we know where to look for persuadable voters. Let's say you are an organizer on the campaign responsible for Precinct 1. You know that 52.7 percent of the voters will likely vote for you, and that 20.1 percent are persuadable voters. That's useful, but it doesn't tell you who these voters actually are.

That's where the voter file comes in. A good voter file will be able to tell you the preferences of voters in previous elections, which helps you determine where to start identifying voters for the current election. For example, if you know that Jane Doe is a reliable conservative voter who identified herself in previous elections as a supporter of the most conservative candidates, it doesn't make sense for you to target her in this cycle. If, on the other hand, you know from the voter file that Jane Doe is a consistent swing voter, she is someone you want to prioritize when you start doing your voter identification phoning and canvassing (a topic we cover in detail in chapter 5). You can therefore use the voter file to run lists of voters who are traditional swing voters, or you can use it to run a list of people who consistently support progressive candidates; these are great prospects to call to find volunteers.

Since it is impossible in most races to speak to every voter, campaigns have to prioritize their contacts with voters. The figure below demonstrates the importance of strategically targeting voters. On the left is the voting history of voters: those who always vote, sporadically vote, or rarely vote. The top row is the voting pattern of these voters: whether they always vote for progressives, are swing voters, or always vote for conservatives.

	Very Strongly Vote Progressive	Persuadable/ Swing Voters	Very Strongly Vote Conservative
Always Vote	ID supporters (Recruit volunteers)	Persuasion priority 1	
Sometimes Vote	GOTV	Persuasion priority 2	
Seldom or Never Vote	Base building priority 1	Base building priority 2	

When you have limited resources, your campaign must prioritize your contacts. Your first target for persuasion should be swing voters who consistently show up at the polls. As a voter's likelihood of voting decreases, you will need to spend more time doing both persuasion and base-building work. Likely progressive voters who consistently vote will make up your base of volunteers, and you will want to focus particular attention on progressives who only sporadically or rarely vote. Reliable conservative voters should be ignored, as the blank boxes indicate; they will draw precious resources from the campaign.

Let's use another example to illustrate how to use this diagram. Say you have identified from the voter file Alex Martinez, who you know has voted in every election for the past twenty years. You also know, either because you have an enhanced voter file that contains this information from previous campaigns or because you called Alex Martinez on the phone or knocked on his door, that he always votes for the conservative candidate. What should you do with Martinez? Ignore him! Do not waste your time, money, or staff resources trying to persuade someone like Mr. Martinez; it's a lost cause. That's why the right-hand columns are blank in this diagram. If we know for sure (in chapter 5 we'll discuss how you can know for sure) that someone will never vote for your candidate, don't spend any time trying to persuade that person.

Now let's say you have a group of voters whom your campaign has identified as swing voters. These voters are your persuasion audience. The top targets among these voters are the ones who always vote. You know they are going to vote, and you know they are persuadable. They are number one on your persuasion list. In your field program, these voters will receive the most mail, the most phone calls, and the most knocks on the door from the campaign. They are highly valuable voters because you know they are going to turn out at the polls and could determine the election. The next most important group is the group of sporadic swing voters. The task here is not only to persuade these voters to support your campaign, but then to turn them out to vote. Finally, you will want to target the swing voters who rarely vote as voters who need to be brought along with a solid base-building and grassroots organizing strategy.

But what about the voters who will always vote for a progressive regardless of the election? You have three goals with these voters: first, you want to turn the progressive voters who rarely show up at the polls into active supporters. This will require a lot of base-building activities, which we describe in chapter 5. Second, the sporadic voters need to be turned into likely voters. This will require ongoing field organizing during the campaign and an intensive get-out-the-vote (GOTV) effort in the weeks leading up to the election. And those progressive voters who always show up at the polls? Don't ignore them! This is the heart of your campaign; these are voters whom you need to turn into volunteers and activists for the campaign who in turn will go out and recruit other volunteers and persuade voters.

In addition to helping you prioritize your work, the voter file can also provide data about what types of races turn out voters. Some voters only vote in presidential years. These voters are often referred to as presidential drop-off voters. They are good targets for get-out-the-vote efforts in nonpresidential general elections. Some voters vote in primary elections while others only vote in general elections. Some vote in local races or municipal races. If these races are done at a time different from other larger races, you can target specific voters who often vote in these races, usually a much smaller number than those who vote in a presidential or other even-year election. The term used for a voter who votes periodically is *sporadic voter*. The rule of thumb for identifying sporadic voters is to determine those who have voted in one or two of the past four elections. By contrast, a consistent voter is someone who has voted in three or four out of the past four elections. These voters are a top priority, since you already know they are highly likely to vote. The voter file will provide you all of this data.

For example, let's say you are running for school board in a nonpartisan primary election. Your targeting data tell you that women with children in the schools are highly persuadable and likely to vote. How do you find these voters? First, the voter file will tell you which voters are likely primary voters. Next, you want to focus on women. Some voter files have gender, but if not, it is easy enough to assign a gender marker based on first name (some first names are less indicative of gender, but usually you can create a highly accurate list). Finally, you are targeting women with children. Few voter files have this information (and what is available is incomplete), but you can still concentrate your probable voter universe by looking at women in the age group who are more likely to have children, say ages twenty-eight to fifty. Pulling out likely primary voters who are women ages twenty-eight to fifty will not give you complete coverage, but it will be much more efficient than contacting all voters and will cover a large number of your targeted voters: women with children.

Demographic Targeting

Demographic targeting is a strategy of predicting voting behavior based on characteristics we know about a person (race and ethnicity, membership in organizations or groups, gender and income, etc.). At the most basic level, certain demographic groups tend to support progressives and certain groups tend to support conservatives. For example, a progressive candidate will likely want to target the African American, Latino, and Native American communities, environmentalists, and pro-choice women. This targeting is also done by identifying personal networks, a tactic that has been used effectively by Republicans, and is often the most effective way to target a nonpartisan race or a partisan primary, especially in rural districts. This is based on doing a power analysis of the district (or relying on local knowledge) to determine which networks of organized people often put together (or could put together) a winning coalition. The targeting strategy is to identify these networks and its leaders, then target those leaders to win their support and provide access to their networks. Anyone who has run a rural township race or rural county commissioner race knows this intuitively based on who belongs to what church and who has connections with the local volunteer fire department.

Another demographic targeting concept that has become increasingly important in campaigning is microtargeting. Microtargeting is a way to predict voters' preferences through such things as their consumer preferences (if you drive a Volvo, you are significantly more likely to be a Democrat than a Republican, for example). Microtargeting is a concept we don't spend a lot of time on here because it gets highly complex, and for most campaigns it's not something that you will realistically master during the course of the race. You should know, however, that the party's voter file will likely have microtargeting information, and you should find out what that information looks like and how you can use it on your specific race. It is highly unlikely, unless you are working on a large statewide race, that you will conduct your own microtargeting work.

As we move into a discussion about base building and field organizing, remember that targeting data will inform most of the strategic decisions you make in your organizing efforts. Targeting also tells the campaign where it should schedule the candidate's time and where to focus paid media and earned media work. The scheduling work is particularly important, as a campaign will get dozens of requests for the candidate to appear. Choose those events wisely, and use targeting to inform those decisions. Schedule according to where the votes are. Like most things in campaigns, these are rules of thumb that often answer any direct question with "It depends." The key to targeting is to use it to maximize the time, money, and volunteer resources you spend on direct voter contact.

CHAPTER 5

How to Build Your Base and Use It for Direct Voter Contact

To UNDERSTAND THE IMPORTANCE of grassroots organizing in winning an election, consider Ralph Remington's race for Minneapolis City Council. When Remington announced his candidacy for Minneapolis City Council in early 2005, he knew he was up against long odds. He faced several well-known opponents for his party's endorsement for the open council seat, and a victory would make him the first African American ever to represent the 80 percent white Tenth Ward. Despite being active in community issues for several years, Remington was a newcomer to electoral politics and was not a party insider. While he had a compelling message—"There are two types of politicians. Those that want to be something and those that want to do something. I'm running because I want to get in there and do something"—he had never run for office before and lacked the experience of his opponents.

But Remington knew he could win with good organizing. Like most wards in Minneapolis, the Tenth is overwhelmingly progressive. Remington started by focusing on the endorsement of the Democratic-Farmer-Labor Party (Minnesota's equivalent of the Democratic Party), a process that begins with precinct caucuses (small local precinct meetings of party activists) in the winter. In a local race and in the heavily Democratic city of Minneapolis, receiving the party's endorsement gives a candidate a tremendous advantage over the opposition. Since it takes 60 percent support to win the party endorsement, conventions often end deadlocked, with no candidate receiving enough support. Remington knew the he was a long shot to win 60 percent support at a party convention and that he would be an even longer shot to win a primary or general election if another candidate had the party endorsement.

He focused on two goals: bringing new people to the precinct caucuses and having multiple, direct individual conversations with likely precinct caucus attendees based on lists of previous attendees. Getting new people to turn out to precinct caucuses is a common way of involving new people, yet one of the most difficult organizing tasks possible. It requires not only winning the support of voters, but also motivating them to come out for a couple of hours on a Tuesday evening in the dead of winter. It was a strategy that other candidates embraced as well, but Remington built on his long-standing relationships in the arts community (he is an actor and director) and with union members and community activists to create a campaign that brought new people into the process with a compelling message and per-suaded party regulars that he was someone they could trust.

In both cases—with new caucus attendees and party regulars—Remington built relationships by knocking on doors and meeting people face-to-face. Over the course of two months, he knocked on every door where a likely caucus attendee lived. When he wasn't out door-knocking, he was on the phone with delegates asking for their support. His campaign kept good records and entered identified caucus attendees into the database. The more people saw of Remington, the more they liked him. He was authentic, trust-worthy, and hard-working, as evidenced by his presence on people's front doors in subzero temperatures. By the time of the city conventions that year, Remington had spoken at least once to nearly every person in the room. His campaign utilized direct mail, literature drops, and phone banks to identify and turn out supporters, and when it came time for the convention, they created a specific strategy for the endorsing process. In the end, Remington defied all expectations and garnered the most support of any candidate in the endorsement contest—just shy of the 60 percent he needed to win official party backing. The other candidates were stunned, and his showing led an-other leading contender to drop out of the race. The momentum from this surprising success catapulted Remington into the summer and fall, when he expanded his grassroots organization and went on to win the primary and general elections. In early 2006 he was sworn in as the member of the Minneapolis City Council from Ward 10.

Ralph Remington's experience shows that while field organizing requires smart strategy and hard work, the mechanics are rather straightforward: if you have a good candidate and message, you can win by directly engaging as many voters as possible in a conversation about the campaign. A field op-eration creates opportunities for those conversations to happen on a scale necessary to win. Base building and field organizing are the foundations of Wellstone Action's training philosophy. Good organizing was the reason Paul Wellstone went from being a little-known community organizer to a U.S. senator in less than two years, and why candidates like Ralph Remington are now holding elected office.

Establishing a good voter contact program consists of five major components: base building, volunteer recruitment, direct voter contact, getting out the vote, and visibility. It is a process of expanding your base by connecting politics (and the campaign) with the lives of people who may not see any connection with politics. Then it is about consolidating your base, moving your supporters into active volunteers, and harnessing their energy and training them to contact and win over undecided voters. Finally, it is about mobilizing your supporters to turn out to vote. Throughout this process the field provides a face, or visibility, to the campaign. This can be signs, bumper stickers, and buttons, but may also include rallies, parades, and presence at community events. More will be said about each of these components in the rest of the chapter.

Base Building

The best candidates start their campaigns with a base of supporters. These supporters might come from the candidate's work in the community, through personal or work connections, or from the candidate's leadership on issues. There are two ways of thinking of a candidate's base: her personal base and her base vote. The personal base is the circle of the candidate's friends, family, and colleagues who are involved in the campaign from the start. If you are a candidate, these are the folks that you can absolutely count on; you raise money from them in your first letter, and they will be the first to step up to help. You don't have to explain to the person why she should support you; you need only let her know what you want her to do to help. A candidate's personal base cannot be claimed; the base claims you and is built upon a relationship of trust. Questions to ask about a person's personal base might include: Whom do you spend your time with? Where are you most comfortable? Where do you hang out?

Another way to understand your base is as a base vote. As we discussed in the targeting chapter, this is determined by predicting voter affinity using past performance, shared issue commitments, demographic and geographic proximity, and targeting. Putting together your base vote depends on contacting, stitching together, and mobilizing different groups of people who are likely to vote for you. The demographic component to your base vote is made up of people who fit the same demographic profile of the candidate. Students, for example, were a big part of Andrew Gillum's campaign for Tallahassee City Commission because Gillum himself had just graduated from college. Issue-based constituencies represent another part of your base vote. These are members of organizations allied with the candidate's agenda, like organized labor, environmental groups, and pro-choice advocacy groups. Another key base component exists within the candidate's political party and among party activists. While they make up a small minority of voters, these party activists can play a key role in establishing the legitimacy of a candidate. Finally, the candidate has a geographic base vote, which may include the neighborhood or district you live in as well as the areas where progressive candidates traditionally perform well. To say that these groups are part of your base vote does not mean that you can automatically assume that you can count on their vote. How many times have we seen candidates lose because they assumed that because they were young they would get the youth vote, or that as women they would get the majority of women, or Latino candidates the Latino vote? Determining your base vote is an important component for prioritizing your field program and candidate's time but it is still a vote that will need to be won.

Identifying and nurturing your base is important in both the short and long term. In the short term, the larger your base, the easier it is to get to your win number, generate active volunteers, raise money, and persuade undecided voters. Campaigns often give lip service to base building, but then revert back to conventional wisdom that focuses almost exclusively on winning undecided voters. Many campaigns devote the vast bulk of resources on the existing electorate and the 20 percent of the voters who are typically swing voters in any given race. Few if any resources are used to expand the electorate. The result is that the progressive base vote has dwindled over the years. This is not just about good civic stewardship. Expanding our base is the way we will ultimately win power and move our agenda in a sustained way. For example, one organizer in a very "red" district once asked us how to win in a state legislative district where she could expect only 18 to 20 percent of the voters ever to vote for the progressive candidate. The answer is pretty simple: you don't win in the short term unless you are very lucky. But what if we think of this district in terms of building the base, and think of elections (even losing elections) as part of building that base? If, a couple years later, that base goes from 18 percent to 26 percent and four years later to 31 percent, we may still lose that individual district (although it will be far easier to win), but this base building may provide the margin of victory for a statewide or Congressional race. Eventually the district may even flip and become a swing or even progressive district. The problem is that seldom do individual campaigns think beyond Election Day, nor do they often have that luxury. Long-term base building (party and movement building) operates on different timelines than an electoral campaign does. In most electoral campaigns a base vote is built from the candidate's personal base outward. As the election develops, you reach out to

▸ Key leaders of base or supporting groups and party activists (leaders, officers, caucus attendees)

▸ Party members and members of endorsing organizations, like labor unions or other advocacy groups

▸ Partisan primary voters (as opposed to swing voters)

▸ General election voters whose level of support is measured by voter identification work

▸ Nonvoters who are not yet in the electorate—the target of voter registration and the least likely to vote (unless specifically targeted with a message that motivates them and connects to their interest)

Identifying and consolidating your personal base is a process of reaching out to the people you know (even if they have never been involved in politics before) and enlisting their help in expanding the base. For example, even though Gillum had no electoral experience, he brought a significant base of supporters to his campaign because he had spent the previous four years as a student organizer. Not only was he a constant presence in student affairs, he understood the issues affecting students better than anyone. He also had a lot of friends. So when Gillum needed volunteers to knock on doors, make phone calls, or provide strategic help to the campaign, he didn't have to look far. "My volunteers were people I went to school with and weren't political at all up to the point of my running," he told us. "We went through a process of reaching back and thinking very thoughtfully about who I had known over the years and who I could engage. We were paying attention to people who had never even been asked to get involved in politics."

Once you mobilize that core base group, the next step is to start expanding it. Cory Booker's 2006 campaign for mayor of Newark, New Jersey, is a good example of a campaign that made a strategic effort to expand its base. After losing the 2002 election to the incumbent mayor, Booker maintained a strong presence in neighborhoods throughout the city. One of his former volunteers describes how this helped mobilize Booker's base:

> While maintaining a low profile, Cory expanded his base, building and strengthening relationships throughout the city. So when it was time to launch the 2006 campaign, and we canvassed neighborhoods, few people did not claim to know Cory "personally." In addition to his wide name recognition, the campaign was organized extremely well. Over a year prior to the election, headquarters were up and running in every ward of the city. Full-time staff at each office ensured anyone wishing to volunteer could do so immediately, whether this involved phone banking, door-to-door canvassing, or other administrative tasks. To top it off, the campaign was for a candidate who was extremely passionate and constantly inspired his volunteers.

The Booker campaign's aggressive base expansion work paid off, earning him a comfortable victory and creating a strong grassroots network to support his work as mayor.

As Booker demonstrated, expanding your base relies on deepening and strengthening your relationships with people who might not usually participate in the political process. That expansion work includes organizing disenfranchised communities and issue-based constituencies and registering new voters.

Organizing Disenfranchised Communities

If a progressive candidate hopes to represent communities of color and others that have been marginalized in the political process, the campaign must invest time and resources in working closely with these groups. Ideally, a campaign should assign a campaign staff person or volunteer who is from these communities to work as an organizer and campaign representative. The most important work this organizer will do is to establish ties to community leaders and key contacts who support the campaign's goals. This relationship between the organizer and the community leaders is fundamental, as it leads to trust, cooperation, and shared goals. It starts by scheduling meetings with community leaders to discuss issues important to the community, upcoming events, potential problems, and other key information that will help the campaign succeed. From those meetings, the campaign should build a list of key people who agree to work in a sustained and deliberate way, mobilizing their networks and bringing them into the campaign.

Another key to organizing in underrepresented communities is producing campaign literature specifically targeted to your audience. At least one, and preferably two or three, pieces of literature should be developed. These would include an introductory piece about what is at stake in an election or issues campaign, why it is important to be involved, and how to participate in the process. A second piece should focus on persuading a specifically targeted group within a community, and it should contain issue-specific information. A third piece of literature should be sent as part of the campaign's get-out-the-vote (GOTV) efforts, and it should focus on how to vote on Election Day, the choices people have when they go to vote, and directions to polling stations. Whenever possible, these literature pieces should be translated into appropriate languages if the campaign is working with immigrant populations.

Campaign workers should also identify key media outlets that serve each community. The organizer works with the communications director to publicize the campaign's connection to the community and the work it is doing. This can be done by holding press events, working to get articles and letters to the editor published in community newspapers, and (depending on the size of the campaign) running newspaper or radio ads targeted to the community. The campaign should produce lists of newspapers, radio shows, cable television programs, local Web sites and blogs, and other media outlets and coordinate a modest, focused strategy for each community. In addition, the campaign should develop a group of surrogate speakers who can speak for the campaign and are particularly qualified to communicate with the targeted communities.

Organizing disenfranchised communities, particularly immigrants and people living in poverty, presents unique challenges to a campaign. For many immigrants, even citizens who are eligible to vote, politics is an unfamiliar and intimidating process. Their experiences with politics in their home countries have often been negative, and they may be wary of getting involved in the U.S. system. Low-income communities often feel very much disconnected from politics and skeptical of politicians, and it is difficult to convince people that their participation will make a difference. Language can also be a barrier to immigrant communities, which is why it is imperative for the campaign to produce materials in multiple languages if there is a large immigrant population. Successfully organizing disenfranchised communities can only be done if there is a relationship of trust and confidence between the campaign and the communities. The campaign must connect with people and speak to the circumstances of their lives and make them feel that their interests are linked to the campaign's success.

It is important, too, for progressive campaigns to acknowledge their tradition of "electoral strip-mining" of communities of color and other base constituencies. In many places, base communities are all too familiar with the parade of candidates and campaigns that show up in the weeks leading up to Election Day. A year or even a month before an election there is no sign of interest or campaign presence in these communities, but then all of a sudden people are bombarded, told how important they are and how politicians are going to look out for them if they vote a certain way. Then, the day after the election, the tumbleweeds blow in and people know they won't see their elected officials until the waning days of the next election. Many of these communities rightfully feel as though they are taken for granted by campaigns and political parties and are simply helping fulfill someone else's political ambition.

No single campaign is going to change this decades-old problem, but it is possible for campaigns to organize more deeply, to build real relationships, to be present, to listen, and to be responsive to the concerns that people have. To begin with, campaigns should act with intention, begin much earlier, block out legitimate time in a candidate's schedule, and make a real commitment to spending resources on staff and communication in certain communities.

Organizing Issue-Based Constituencies

Field organizing is traditionally done geographically—by precinct, legislative district, or other geographical boundary. Constituency organizing cuts across these boundaries because it focuses on issues and organizations, not geography. It involves organizing groups like teachers, veterans, health care workers, union members, or advocates for reproductive rights. This work is often referred to as the "political" program, and the person in charge is often the political director. Constituency organizers motivate, mobilize, and empower individuals to actively support the campaign based on specific issues. Successful campaigns persuade these constituencies that their agenda will move forward if the campaign wins.

For example, some colleagues of ours were part of a campaign that brought in many different constituency groups fifteen months before Election Day. They held meetings, usually attended by the candidate, with leaders and activists. No one had to support the candidate as a precondition for attending the meetings. The purpose of the meetings was to understand the group's issues, so very little time was spent by the campaign talking; most time was spent listening. Ultimately, the goal of the campaign was to harness the energies and research of the different issue groups to help draft issue papers and to establish issue-based organizing committees to garner support within specific constituencies: workers, environmentalists, people of color, people with disabilities, and even Lutherans! Altogether, the campaign had eleven different constituency groups organizing on behalf of the campaign. Some of these groups grew to several hundred active members, and a few of them (Lutherans, labor, and peacemakers) were very adept at raising money and votes for the campaign. They were also involved in helping provide detailed information, research, and speakers for specific issue positions and events.

As with this example, constituency organizing efforts should be deliberate and strategic, with clear goals and a comprehensive plan. Here are four steps to setting up a successful constituency organizing plan:

1. *Create a steering committee with honorary co-chairs.* A campaign should establish a steering committee for each issue area it is organizing. The committee guides the organizing efforts and helps the campaign clarify its strategic decisions. It should not be a ceremonial committee, but rather an engaged and active group of people who can speak authoritatively about an issue and have credibility within a constituency group. Steering committee members should expect to commit significant amounts of time to this work, helping develop and implement a plan, working to expand the campaign's base, and helping solve any problems that arise. The steering committee should be chaired by prominent community leaders who are closely identified with the issues the campaign wants to highlight. Since many such leaders are often too busy to play an active role on the steering committee, creating an honorary position provides a realistic way for the campaign to engage these people.

2. *Use the campaign's database.* Keep track of the issues people care about and the work they are willing to do. Your database should include information about people's issue preferences and their interest in volunteering around specific issues.

3. *Create an action plan.* As with every other aspect of a campaign, it is essential to create a plan that guides the issue-based organizing efforts. The steering committee should help create and develop the plan, and it should include components like goals, timetable, surrogate speakers, media events, fundraising efforts, and the announcement of the steering committee. The campaign should also produce campaign literature and other material that summarizes its position on the specific issue.

4. *Implement the plan.* Once the campaign creates a plan that has been approved by the steering committee, then the staff, volunteers, and committee members should implement it.

On larger campaigns, at least one and usually several full-time staff members constitute the political operation. For small campaigns, a volunteer can coordinate the constituency organizing efforts, particularly someone with expertise in the issue area. Regardless of the size and scope of the campaign, its organizing efforts should focus not only on building a geographic base of supporters but also on building its base and adding to its credibility by galvanizing supporters who care deeply about particular issues.

Organizing Young People

If you listen to the rhetoric of most political candidates, you would think that issues concerning young people would be at the forefront of the national policy agenda. Young people have been hearing since middle school graduation that they're the future of our nation, yet rarely do they see political leaders speak to their interests, let alone make policy that is positive for them. They are strapped with school debt and largely uninsured, the majority of them are deeply concerned about U.S. foreign policy, they are worried about climate change, and many of them feel that our elected officials and candidates have no idea what is going on in their lives.

It's easy and logical for young people to be cynical about politics, and that's a problem for anyone who wants to change the face of power in our

country. But this disengagement is also an opportunity: done right, organizing young people expands the electorate, adds new voices to the political
process, and creates a powerful political constituency that can help change
our country.

So what are the keys for campaigns to engage and mobilize young people?
Here are some ideas:

▶ *Go to where they are and use peer-to-peer methods.* Empirical research
 has shown that the most successful field campaigns targeted at
 young people are those in which someone their own age and from
 their own community talked to other young voters at their doors
 and where they hang out. Young people turn off political ads and
 rhetoric, but turn on when another young person talks with them
 about matters that affect their lives. Find out where young people
 gather. Use teams of young people for "bar and café storming"
 and "vote mobbing" efforts. Send them to the places where they
 themselves hang out to register their peers.

▶ *Get good contact information.* Physical address and landline telephone number are not reliable sources of contact information for
 young people. When collecting information from young people,
 focus on obtaining their cell phone numbers, e-mail addresses,
 and social networking pages. These are the best ways of reaching
 your people. Plus, when young people move, you will still be able
 to reach them and turn them out to vote because you will have
 obtained contact information that moves with them.

▶ *Connect with them.* Make a conscious effort to reach out to the
 young volunteers and supporters who come to the office and
 want to help. Organize brown bag lunches or informal gatherings
 of your young supporters, and tell them about the inside work-
 ings of the campaign. They are well informed on the issues and
 have good ideas. They are willing to do grunt work on campaigns,
 but put their brains and skills to work as well. Use these regular
 gatherings with young people to ask their advice about what the
 campaign is doing well and where it needs improvement.

▶ *Give them responsibility.* One of the first things you can do with
 young supporters who offer to volunteer on the campaign is to enlist them as organizers of their peers. Challenge a young volunteer

to recruit five of her friends as volunteers for the campaign. Do the same with each of these five volunteers. You'll quickly identify the "super volunteers" to whom you will gradually give more responsibilities, like being a lead organizer on a campus.

▶ *Make them leaders.* Young people can become outstanding leaders on campaigns when empowered to do so. At the beginning of the campaign, identify different roles that you would like to see young people fill as the campaign evolves—volunteer coordinator, field organizers, press aides—and make a conscious effort to recruit your young "super volunteers" to fill these roles.

▶ *Use music and culture as organizing tools.* Local bands, particularly campus bands, frequently perform for your target audience of young people. Be sure to post your volunteers at the entrances to these shows, or better yet, use the contacts your young volunteers have with musicians to ask them to make a pitch for your campaign during their performances. You can also ask these groups to play at campaign-sponsored rallies or meet-ups.

Organizing this way only works when your campaign is compelling and your message resonates with young people. Some ideas for making a compelling case in your conversations with young people include the following:

▶ *Talk about power.* Young people don't want to hear about their "civic obligation" to the political process—particularly when so many of them feel that those in power have reneged on their civic obligation to look out for them. Instead, young people respond to the idea that powerful interests *benefit* from their disengagement, that they don't want them to participate: "The politicians that watched our tuition skyrocket, made our health care unaffordable, and sent our peers off to an endless war directly benefit from your staying quiet. They won't listen until you speak out and force them to."

▶ *Don't solely focus on the candidate.* Rather than talking about the qualifications of your candidate, talk about the policy choices of your candidate that will affect young people, for example, that the state legislature is scheduled to vote on educational appropriations, which will directly impact how much tuition goes up next year. You want to emphasize that your candidate has promised to vote in support of increased higher education funding.

▸ *Make your message urgent.* For example, "Your vote, your voice, is crucial. Student participation in recent elections has forced our issues to the forefront nationally. Issues like tuition and student loans are now high on the national agenda because of a rise in young people's participation in politics. Register to vote by October 13!"

▸ Because young people do not access media in the same way as their parents do, campaigns need to *focus on nontraditional marketing,* such as search engine ads, social networking sites, text messaging, and targeted cable advertising.

There is growing evidence that efforts like these to incorporate young people into campaigns are paying off. Voter turnout among young people in recent elections is up by record numbers, and they are being noticed as a voting bloc. This work is already paying off: student loan interests rates were cut in one of the first bills passed by the new majority in Congress.

Voter Registration

One of the most important ways of expanding a campaign's base beyond the existing electorate is to register new voters. A strong voter registration operation, combined with aggressive organizing, can dramatically increase the number of voters supporting progressive candidates. Like everything else in a campaign, the voter registration program should be carefully planned, based on a set of specific goals. These goals include the number of people the campaign hopes to register and the number of precincts and communities to target. The campaign should carefully consider how to spend its limited resources and invest in strategies that have the most potential for registering likely supporters in targeted areas. The plan should also include a specific description of how volunteer and staff time will be used to register voters and how the voter registration process should be coordinated. It should specify a timeline for the voter registration efforts, a location where voter registration will take place (e.g., specific precincts for door-knocking or targeted high traffic areas), and major events (parades, festivals, etc.) at which the campaign will have a voter registration presence. Of course, the plan should also include a budget for voter registration efforts, with specific information about where the money is coming from. You also need to know the laws around voter registration, felony voting, residency requirements, who can register voters, what forms of ID are necessary, deadlines for registering voters, and when cards need to be turned in once the card is signed. Unfortunately, in several past elections, thousands of voter registration cards were rejected for such issues as illegible signatures, too long a delay in turning in signed cards, photocopied forms, and even that the cardstock the card was printed on was too thin.

The most effective way to register voters is through direct personal contact, preferably by going door-to-door in targeted neighborhoods. These door-to-door efforts require time and volunteers, but they are worth the effort. If the campaign is already conducting a canvassing field operation (which it should), voter registration should simply be included in this effort. For example, if the campaign is conducting voter identification canvassing (which we discuss later in this chapter), the canvasser should ask whether a person is registered to vote. Canvassing is a particularly effective method of voter registration because it is conducted in a well-defined area that the campaign has specifically targeted. It initiates contact with unregistered voters and provides key information on every newly registered voter in each household, which is useful for later GOTV efforts.

When implementing a voter registration canvass, a campaign needs to assess the amount of work it intends to do in each targeted area. With targeting data in hand, prioritize specific neighborhoods for canvassing, estimate the number of people and hours you need to knock on doors in the targeted areas, and make clear "walk maps" that highlight the areas (and in some cases, individual houses) to canvass. Canvassers should carry materials that will help answer questions and make door-knocking efficient and easier. These materials include the walk map with highlighted areas, talking points, campaign literature, a contact sheet to be filled in at the end of canvassing, clipboards, campaign stationery for leaving notes with people who are not home, and, of course, voter registration cards.

In addition to canvassing, other methods of registering voters include setting up voter registration sites and having a presence at community events. Depending on the laws in different states and municipalities, some campaigns can establish registration tables at public locations like shopping malls, libraries, and community or campus centers. As with targeting of voters, the campaign should carefully assess in which neighborhoods to hold voter registration canvasses and at which events to set up voter registration tables. The key here is that it has to be targeted to events or areas that fit in with your plan to build a base and secure your win number. Focus on registering likely supporters; a shopping mall may have a lot of traffic but may not be a good place to register voters unless most of them will actually support your campaign and can vote in your race. Also plan to register voters at all campaign events (this is easy to forget!) and at community gatherings like local union meetings, block parties in progressive areas, rallies and events sponsored by other progressive groups, activities at religious institutions, concerts, sporting events (many ethnic communities have soccer games or other sports events), festivals, and town hall meetings. You should get permission from the proper authorities or contact the organizers of an event for their approval.

When registering voters, campaign staff and volunteers should be prepared to deliver a voter registration "rap" that anticipates people's questions and makes clear why it is important to register. The first step in that process is for the canvasser to get a person's attention with a friendly, enthusiastic introduction, followed by a statement about the purpose of the conversation. For example, a canvasser might start a conversation with a quick introduction followed by a statement like, "I am out here registering voters because I feel strongly that our environment needs protection, and Candidate X has made environmental issues a top priority of her campaign."

The next step is to ask the person if he or she is registered to vote. If she is already registered, it is important to ask if she has moved or has recently voted. It is always better to reregister voters than to leave it to chance. If a person is not registered, she may need help filling out the voter registration form and should be reminded to sign the form and provide the campaign with a phone number. Of course, if she is a supporter of the campaign, she should be asked to volunteer. Some people may have questions about whether they are qualified to vote, which is why the campaign should have a solid understanding of the laws surrounding voter registration efforts. Some states allow same-day registration, which means that people can register at the polls when they go to vote.

It is critically important (assuming it is acceptable under state law in your state) that you not only assist in completing a registration card, but also then file it with the appropriate office (secretary of state, county elections office, or other). *Simply handing out voter registration cards to people, whether at events or on their doorstep, is not voter registration!* Someone who has not voted before is unlikely to take the time to fill out the card, and even less so to turn it in. Moreover, campaigns should keep a record of every voter they register by entering the person's information into the overall voter file with a field that shows they are newly registered. These newly registered voters will merit extra attention during get-out-the-vote activities, so you need to know who they are and how to contact them. You can do this by photocopying the card before filing it or just entering the data from the card directly into the campaign voter file.

Your conversation with these new voters cannot end there, however. Since these voters were not engaged in the process in the first place, the campaign must continue to educate, nurture, and mobilize them throughout the process—and must not always assume they are with the candidate. It's not enough to get a voter to register. You must identify how to merge their interests with the campaign. It is not a guaranteed vote for your candidate until that voter actually goes to the polls and makes that choice. Voter registration is the beginning of a long conversation with this new voter. Voter registration is not the end, it is the means.

Volunteers

Base building is a process of growing the base of supporters and then activating those supporters by turning them into volunteers and leaders. Volunteers are the lifeblood of all grassroots organizing. The vast majority of electoral campaigns are managed and run entirely by volunteers, and you will probably not win your race unless you effectively harness the energy of a volunteer base. For example, in 2004, in Duluth, Minnesota, progressive campaign organizers had 850 people take the day off to knock on doors. That's 1 percent of the population knocking on the doors of the other 99 percent. The result was that Duluth had the highest voter turnout in the country that year. You can't pay for this kind of organizing, even if you had the money. The most effective persuasive contact is from a motivated, passionate, trained volunteer talking with an undecided voter. Yet many campaigns don't know how to recruit, use, and retain volunteers. Have you ever called a campaign and offered to volunteer and not received a call back? Or had an experience of volunteering for a campaign when no one really knew how to use your help? Have you showed up once to volunteer for a campaign and vowed never to return? So have we, and it is exasperating.

When you consider the attitude that many campaign professionals have toward volunteers, it's not surprising that many volunteers have a negative experience on campaigns. Here's what one political consultant recently wrote about volunteers in a guidebook for campaign workers: "A volunteer is a creature who tends to come late and longs to leave early, who telephones to say, 'I'm on my way,' then never shows up. Ask a volunteer to take a vital mailing to the post office, but don't be surprised to learn, a few days later, that the mailing is still in the trunk of his car. Place a group of volunteers in the same room to work, and each will be convinced that the others have been given sharper pencils, more comfortable chairs and better light. Volunteers are a pain in the neck." Such an attitude isn't just insulting, it's also strategically foolish. Treated well and used correctly, volunteers can dramatically increase a campaign's capacity to engage in highly effective direct voter contact.

In fact, the problem for most campaigns isn't that volunteers are a pain in the neck; it's that there aren't enough of them. We recently asked participants in one of Wellstone Action's Campaign Management Schools to analyze the strengths and weaknesses of campaigns they had worked on in the past, and a common response was that they wished they had more volunteers to help with the work. Here are some of the things we heard:

▸ "I should have recruited a few more serious volunteers."

▸ "The key to our victory was that we had a solid core of consistent volunteers who would canvass, phone bank, put together mailings, and do anything else that was necessary to win."

▸ "Unfortunately, we were not able to get enough volunteers to cover all of our targeted precincts."

▸ "In retrospect I have come to realize how expanding the group of volunteers could have had exponential effects on the success of our phone program."

▸ "Finding enough volunteers to accomplish the campaign plan was a big challenge."

Lack of clarity is one of the reasons that campaigns run short on volunteers and that volunteers have a bad experience on a campaign. Volunteers are motivated by their own interests, not by a sense of charity or an overabundance of time on their hands. They will have something they want to get out of the experience. Campaigns sometimes see volunteers solely as envelope stuffers or lawn sign deliverers, only capable of doing the grudge work that no one else wants to do. But it is a myth that campaigns have an ever-present number of envelopes to stuff or lawn signs to pound. Recruiting and retaining volunteers is a balancing act between satisfying a volunteer's interest and the campaign's needs. For example, some volunteers say, "Anything but phone calling and knocking on doors." This can be frustrating from the campaign's perspective, since most of the work is focused on direct voter contact. Volunteers need to know how critically important these activities are. Direct voter contact is the primary objective of the campaign, and it should be the primary objective of your volunteers. It's all about direct voter contact. Next to the candidate, volunteers are the best people to carry the candidate's message to voters. Focus their work on talking to their neighbors, identifying voters, and having one-on-one conversations with undecided voters.

Still, there are some volunteers who cannot do these activities (or aren't very good at them). For these folks, there are always tasks to do, including data entry, answering the office phones, or being a greeter at campaign headquarters. Cooking for and feeding the other volunteers (so the campaign doesn't have to spend precious money on food) is another way to utilize volunteers. It is much easier to move a volunteer who opens the mail to the phones or doors than to ask someone with little commitment to the campaign to take on direct voter contact. In smaller campaigns volunteers do most, if not all, of the campaign functions. Be clear about upcoming opportunities and maintain an ongoing list of needed volunteer tasks so that there is never a time when a willing volunteer doesn't know what to do.

A focused, well-organized volunteer operation will keep volunteers coming back because they will feel that they have an important role in bringing the campaign to voters. Over time, "super volunteers" will emerge—committed volunteers who can take responsibility for key aspects of the campaign, particularly when the campaign doesn't have a paid staff. You should give these super volunteers a job description, which is a way of giving them clarity about their roles and also holding them accountable for the responsibilities you give them. In return, they get more access to the inside of a campaign and gain experience that could help them get a job on a future campaign.

Recruiting Volunteers

Recruit volunteers from your base, starting with your identified supporters or constituencies. The most likely kinds of volunteers from within your base will be students, seniors, regular campaign volunteers, party activists, and constituency groups. The best place to begin to find volunteers is a list of identified supporters and databases from other campaigns or like-minded organizations. Other sources include donor lists, college campuses, senior centers, retiree groups, constituency organizations, and the Internet (be sure that your Web site has a place for volunteer sign-up). Once you convert someone as a supporter, you ask him or her to be active in your campaign by giving time and giving money. For example, when Paul Wellstone ran for reelection in 1996 and 2002, his campaign employed a house party strategy as a way of reconnecting with its base voters. With supporters from previous elections, the campaign held a series of house parties that raised money, but they were designed primarily to reactivate Wellstone's base. At every event, Wellstone asked people to do three things: volunteer for the campaign, donate money, and take Election Day off to help with getting out the vote. If they signed up, they were asked to recruit a friend to do the same thing (also called "friend-raising"). This is the essence of grassroots campaigning, which is called force multiplying: volunteers recruiting other volunteers, who will in turn recruit others.

Volunteers will keep coming back if they have an enjoyable experience. Many campaigns understand the importance of treating volunteers well, but they view volunteers as a separate entity from the campaign itself. On good campaigns, the line between the organizers and volunteers is broken down. Volunteers are not just an important part of the campaign, nor are they viewed simply as people who could help out with the work. On the contrary, volunteers define the campaign's identity. Once someone agrees to volunteer, his or her experience—particularly the first one—should be positive. Recognize volunteers' contributions and include them in briefings about what's new on the campaign, including "inside" information they would not get from the media. The campaign should also take time to listen to your volunteers and ask them about their experiences and how these could be improved. Volunteers are on the front lines, directly communicating with the public, and they may have a good sense of how the campaign looks to the outside world. Finally, volunteers will not come back if they are not asked, and campaigns often lose track of volunteers because they do not track them in their database. You should have a well-managed and frequently updated list of all the campaign's volunteers—their interests, strengths, preferred working hours, and other relevant information.

Although every campaign should have a commitment to volunteers, it is the job of a field organizer to recruit, train, and manage volunteers. The typical field campaign often has paid organizers making the calls to undecided voters. While it is important to have field staff calling voters to hear what is being said and understand how undecided voters are reacting to the campaign, it is equally important that they recruit and train volunteers. Often in well-run grassroots campaigns, the largest bulk of a field organizer's time is spent recruiting, training, and managing volunteers. Field organizers are responsible for ensuring that a volunteer is made to feel welcome as soon as he or she walks in the door. Some campaigns have a full-time volunteer coordinator to manage volunteer activities, track their progress, answer questions, and maintain a positive working environment. If your campaign has paid staff, they should participate in the volunteer activities themselves when possible, which demonstrates to the volunteers how much the campaign values their work. Don't ask someone to do work that you wouldn't do yourself.

The volunteer operation must provide thorough training before activities begin, support while they're happening, and a quick but thorough debrief afterward to make sure that the experience was positive and that volunteers understand how the work they did got the campaign closer to victory. The training should also include a campaign update and some information that makes volunteers know that they're on the inside, that they have access to information that the general public doesn't have. After the debrief and a hearty thanks, the campaign should ask the volunteer to commit to coming back for another activity. With the difficulty in reaching people by phone and e-mail, it is very important that people don't leave a volunteer experience without committing to coming back. Moreover, this face-to-face commitment is likely to mean more to the volunteer than one made by e-mail or over the phone.

In thinking about volunteer recruitment and retention, it's important to understand why people do and don't decide to volunteer. Following are some of the reasons people are often hesitant to volunteer:

▸ The activity will be too hard or they aren't "good at it."

▸ It will take too much time.

▸ They won't be supported or given enough information to succeed.

▸ It won't matter to the outcome of the election.

▸ It doesn't matter *now*.

On the positive side, there are lots of reasons people decide to volunteer, including these:

- ▸ It's a social activity, a chance to be with other like-minded people.
- ▸ It provides a sense of accomplishment, a sense that what they're doing matters.
- ▸ It is an opportunity to be part of something bigger than themselves.
- ▸ They believe in the cause or candidate.

Successful field organizers or volunteer coordinators think critically about creating an environment that generates regular volunteers while preempting any pitfalls that would keep someone from returning.

Direct Voter Contact

The objective of your direct voter contact program is simple: identify, persuade, and turn out voters. Your targeting information tells you where your base and swing voters generally live. Your voter file gives you the names of actual voters, their addresses, and often their phone numbers. But even with an enhanced voter file that contains information about a person's past candidate preferences, you still need to find out whom they support in your race. The first stage of direct voter contact is about finding out exactly who is supporting you, who is undecided, and who is supporting your opponent. In other words, targeting tells you where to find voters; field organizing tells you who they are and what they are thinking.

This process is called voter identification (voter ID), and it starts with taking a look at your voter file. Depending on how good your voter file is, it should contain information on voter preferences, either because you are in a state with "party registration" (voters have to register as a member of a party, as an independent, or as "declined to state" or "DTS" voters) or because the voter file has been "enhanced" with ID information from past campaigns. Campaigns that have voter preference information from the start are at an advantage; they have a general idea of who their base voters are and who the conservative voters are. But of course, the best way to identify voters in a district is simply to ask them.

A voter ID is like a survey. Voters are asked a simple question or series of two or three questions about their election preferences, starting with: "If the election were held today, which candidate are you likely to support?" There are two types of ID calls: identified IDs and blind IDs. Identified IDs are calls that inform the voter who is calling ("This is John, and I'm a volunteer from the Blue for Senate campaign. I'm calling to ask if the election were held today, would you vote for Patricia Blue or Terry Green?"). Since revealing to the voter the identity of the campaign making the call can bias the response (some voters will be more inclined to say they support the candidate if they are speaking to a representative of that campaign), the campaign can also use what's called a "blind ID," which is asking the question without revealing to the voter where the call is coming from. Blind IDs are the best way to get an unbiased response from voters, but they have a drawback: if a voter really wants to know who is calling, the caller either has to reveal the campaign's identity or lie (which you obviously shouldn't do).

One way for the campaign to manage the large number of ID calls is to hire a paid phone vendor to make the calls. Paid phones can be a great way of making a large number of phone calls in a short period of time. There are many phone vendors available for campaigns to hire, and chances are good that if you are running for or managing a race for statewide office or Congress, you will receive multiple solicitations from phone vendors looking for business. Before you think about hiring someone on your own, find out if your political party is conducting any paid IDs. In most states, party-coordinated campaigns hire phone vendors to do voter ID calls, and then share that information with individual candidates. If you find out the party is not doing paid IDs and you're still interested in hiring someone, don't hire the first person you talk to. Phone vendors have very different styles, experiences, and approaches to voter ID. Good phone vendors will work with you to come up with a voter ID program that is both comprehensive and cost-effective. But don't assume you can do paid phones for cheap: phone vendors can charge up to a dollar per completed phone call (the average is about sixty-five to seventy cents per ID call), which can add up to hundreds of thousands of dollars very quickly in a large race.

Whether you are using volunteers or paid phones, the timing of voter ID calls is an important factor to consider. The earlier you do your voter IDs, the faster you can start to focus on persuadable voters. On the other hand, if you make your voter ID calls too early, most people won't have made up their minds or even know who the candidates are. The timing of these calls ulti-mately comes down to the campaign's budget, its overall direct voter contact program, and the primary election schedule. If ID calls are being done chiefly by volunteers, the timeline usually has to be longer. One of the advantages of using a paid vendor is the ability to do a large number of ID calls in a very tight window of time.

Voter ID calls often include a separate question or two about which issues matter most to voters. This is called an "issue ID," and it is particularly useful for targeting voters who say they are undecided. Since you don't know candi-date preferences of undecided voters, one way to focus your persuasion work is to talk to these voters about the candidate's positions on the issues they care about. If the campaign knows which undecided voters care a lot about education, for example, you can tailor your message to them. Let's imagine that you are working on a U.S. Senate race for candidate Augusta Gray. She is running against May Brown, a formidable conservative candidate who is running on a strong family values theme. Here is an example of an issue ID script:

"Hello, my name is *[give first name]* and we're calling today to talk about the upcoming election for U.S. Senate. May I ask you three quick questions?"

If no: "OK, thank you."
If yes: "Which of the following is the most important issue in this election: jobs, security, environment, education, health care, the war in Iraq, or other?

"If the election were held today, which candidate would you vote for: May Brown or Augusta Gray?"
[Let them volunteer undecided or supporting another candidate.]

If supporting Augusta Gray: "Great! Are you a registered voter?"
If no: "I'd be happy to help you register to vote. Does that interest you?" *[If the person is interested in registering, follow the voter registration process described below.]*
If yes: Thank them and ask if they would be interested in volunteering.
"Thank you for your time."

When the call is complete, enter a record of it into a computer or make note of it, including the issue identified by the voter as well as the voter's support level. Voters called can be categorized according to a five-point system:

▶ 1 = strong supporter. This is someone who essentially says, "You had me at hello. I totally support the campaign and I'm telling my friends to vote for you." Support is support only when you hear the magic words "I will be voting for the candidate," not merely "I like the candidate." Otherwise the person is a 2 or 3.

▶ 2 = soft supporter. A soft supporter is inclined to vote for you but could be convinced otherwise. This may be the person who supports all the issues, is intrigued, but isn't yet ready to utter the magic words.

▶ 3 = undecided. Undecided voters often don't make up their minds until the very end of the campaign. An undecided voter usually specifically identifies herself as such.

▶ 4 = soft opponent. The campaign will have a hard time changing the minds of 4s, but their support for your opponent is soft enough that they are open to persuasion, especially if they belong to a demographic or constituency group that is more likely to vote your way. Many 4s are actually 5s who are too polite to tell you that they don't support your candidate.

▶ 5 = strong opponent. This is the person who chases you off his property. Don't bother.

The 1s are your core base voters. They should be recruited to volunteer and play an active role on the campaign. The 2s, 3s, and some 4s are considered the persuadable universe. They are going to decide the election, and they will be subject to an aggressive voter persuasion program. Those who are 5s and many of the 4s are people the campaign should waste no time or resources on. At the end of the campaign, 1s and 2s are the universe used for the get-out-the-vote program.

Once the persuadable universe is identified, the core work of the voter contact program begins. The campaign can contact voters in a variety of ways—face-to-face, on the phone, in the mail, through e-mail, with literature drops. The rule is the more personal, the better, starting with face-to-face conversations. Because canvassing and phone contact rates have become somewhat lower in recent years, many campaigns now employ a hybrid identification-persuasion script when first contacting voters. In this type of contact, you would immediately deliver a persuasion message to a person who self-identifies as undecided or is just leaning one way or another. The rationale for this is that while gaining information from an ID is very important, you may have a hard time reaching that same voter again. While you have them on the phone or at their door, it's smart to deliver a message to a voter you could win over or firm up right then and there.

Face-to-Face Communication: Door-Knocking

By far the most effective way to directly engage voters is one-on-one, face-to-face. While this has been common knowledge among community organizers for years, academic research now backs it up as a campaign best practice. A recent book, *Get Out the Vote,* by Donald Green and Alan Gerber of Yale University, uses empirical data to demonstrate that door-to-door canvassing is the most cost-effective way to reach voters as part of a get-out-the-vote campaign. It makes sense that this applies equally to direct voter contact and persuasion. Canvassing allows a campaign to personally have genuine conversations with voters on their turf and deliver a message that connects the voters to the candidate or campaign. For smaller campaigns, like local and legislative races, door-knocking by the candidate is the primary direct contact method for the campaign. A common characteristic among most winning legislative candidates we talked to was an intensive and systematic focus on candidate knocking on the doors of the entire universe of voters multiple times.

One state legislator, who described himself as "a door-knocking freak," said that in his experience, door-knocking was both more effective and more efficient than other ways of contacting voters. "If you show up to a generic ceremony in your district, let's say there are a hundred people there," he said. "Many of the people aren't from your district. Some of the people who are from your district might know who you are, but of those people, you won't be able to interact with all of them. On the other hand, if you door-knock for a couple days, you could meet a hundred people right at their doors. All of them are your constituents, all of them will know who you are, and all of them will remember their interaction with you." Another candidate told us that she liked to door-knock both on weekends and on weekdays. "You get different people"; she told us, "during the weekday you get to talk to a lot of stay-at-home parents. On the weekends you often talked to their spouses. You'd be surprised by how many people are home during the day. Those people usually have more time to chat than when you knock on their door at six o'clock at night." In a rural district, a candidate told us that she would door-knock on Sunday afternoons, the traditional time when people in her district visited their friends and neighbors at their homes. This meant the candidate was invited to more "coffee and donuts" than most campaigns would usually encourage, but it was part of making powerful connections with voters in her rural district and would have a "network" effect far beyond the individual voter. The key here is to understand the patterns of the people who live in the district. In some areas, door-knocking during the weekday makes no sense because people aren't home, while other candidates have found it to be a great time. You need a strategy not only for when you go, but where. If there are locked apartment buildings or condos in your district, you might need to enlist supporters who live in those buildings to let you in for door-knocking.

Door-knocking can be difficult, especially at the start, but most candidates find it becomes easier with practice. Here's how one successful state legislative candidate goes about door-knocking in his district:

> I was very nervous about going door-knocking for the first time, but once I got past that first door, it came pretty naturally. Since I live in a rural area, I have to drive to most houses in my district. With so much ground to cover, I try to go from door to door as efficiently as possible. I quickly discovered that I needed a driver, so I enlisted some of my friends. Each of them took a day, and we would spend the evenings canvassing. I came to really look forward to the time in the car—to talk about the campaign and catch up with friends. We would pull up to a house, I'd hop out and go knock on the door, and my driver would turn the car around and be ready to go when I was done. I had all my canvassing materials—a clipboard, list of voters from the voter file, water, dog snacks, and my brochures—in a bag. When no one was home, I would scribble a note—"Sorry I missed you"—on a brochure and leave it at the door (if I heard a dog barking behind the door, I'd leave a snack). When people were home, I would try to keep the conversation brief and to the point, leave a brochure with my home phone number, and head on to the next house. When I got home at night, I made a commitment to write a follow-up note,

before I went to bed, to everyone I had spoken to that evening. Once I got into this routine, I came to actually enjoy it!

Of course, candidates on larger campaigns cannot make a big dent with door-knocking, which is why your field and volunteer organization should be focused on conducting a regular and large door-knocking operation. This large door-knocking effort deploys campaign workers and volunteers into given areas to speak to targeted voters. Canvassing works best in areas with high population density. Some rural and suburban areas are very spread out and may be difficult for volunteers to reach, and the campaign may instead want to emphasize phoning as a primary contact.

Details matter when it comes to setting up a canvass. When possible, your canvassers should be from the areas in which they are working (don't send a team of people who speak only English to a predominantly Latino community, for example). Take time to train your volunteers and prepare them for what they will experience in the field: Always plan on fifteen to thirty minutes to brief folks before the canvass begins. A typical precanvass briefing includes a campaign update (which helps build ownership and gives volunteers a sense of the campaign's momentum), a description of the campaign's goals, a review of the script and the walk packet (make sure all volunteers are familiar with the materials), and a mock door-knock that helps volunteers practice before they go out.

If a canvasser is new, the team leader will need to spend extra time helping him get comfortable with the task. This should include providing additional background on the candidate and issues, giving helpful hints, such as why you can't leave literature in the mailbox (it's a federal offense), how to handle stressful situations, and what to do when you don't know an answer to a question. Take extra time to explain the maps, script/rap, and lists and tally sheets, then pair the person with another canvasser and work with that canvasser to practice the script until the volunteer feels comfortable.

Once out on a route, canvassers should keep in mind a few guidelines. First, if a person expresses support for the campaign, be sure to ask that person to volunteer. Conversely, if the person is hostile, thank him or her politely and be on your way. In general, do not enter the home of either a supporter or an opponent; speed and efficiency (to say nothing of safety) is critical. There are exceptions to that rule; in certain communities, it would be culturally inappropriate not to step in and chat in more depth, especially if you are from that community. Be considerate and do not walk on people's yards or linger at a door if someone obviously does not have time or interest in talking. Be mindful of the safety of your canvassers and travel in pairs when necessary. Often one person can knock one side of the street while the other does the opposite side. Keep each other in view and check in with one another.

When you speak with voters, be sure to ask them (unless they are obviously hostile) for their vote. If you don't ask for a vote, don't expect to get one. And finally, get as much information as you can from the short time you are at the door. One technique that worked well for Andrew Gillum in his race for city commission in Tallahassee was to include "commitment cards" in his walk kit. When Gillum or a volunteer found a supporter at the door, they would ask the supporter to sign a commitment card that simply said, in writing, that the person supported the campaign and would go out and vote on Election Day. The campaign then collected the names of these supporters and followed up with them to see if they would volunteer and to remind them when and where to vote. Some campaigns actually mail these commitment cards back to the supporter as part of the campaign's GOTV effort. These commitment cards were useful not just during the campaign but also after Gillum won. "To this day," Gillum told us, "everyone who signed a commitment card is on my mailing list and my personal Christmas card list. It's not just out of political strategy; it's my responsibility to my constituents. We have to keep these people engaged in politics."

It is important to do a postcanvass debriefing with your volunteers. Spend five to ten minutes asking volunteers how it went. This helps establish trust between the campaign and volunteers, and it gives the campaign an opportunity to track which volunteers are particularly good and might be ready to assume more leadership roles. The campaign can get feedback from volunteers about what they are hearing at the doors about the campaign and the candidates. Of course you also need to get all the information gathered on the canvass from volunteers—without that information, the canvass can't be considered a success! The postcanvass briefing also gives you an opportunity to thank your volunteers again and to sign them up for future canvasses.

Phoning

Phoning is a very efficient way of reaching large numbers of voters, but it is becoming more and more difficult, given the backlash against telemarketing phone calls and the increased use of caller ID, message machines, cell phones, and call blocking. It is not uncommon for callers to talk with a live person (the "connect rate") less than half the time. While this is an increasingly important problem that limits a campaign's ability to connect with voters on the phone, there is a reason why telemarketers are so prevalent: phoning still works. It is an inexpensive, fast, and convenient way to have a personal conversation with voters in a highly targeted way. A volunteer phoner doing persuasion calls can make twenty-two to thirty calls an hour and talk to twelve to fourteen people. They will be able to make significantly more with predictive dialer technology, which is increasingly more accessible. They may be able to make even more calls if the script is a simple voter ID or GOTV call.

Phoning is a particularly effective way to reach voters who are otherwise very difficult to reach: in locked buildings, college campuses, and rural districts that are very difficult to door-knock efficiently. Many campaigns will use the voter file to look up addresses with multiple voters living at that address (more than eight, say) to identify likely locked apartment buildings, then build a phone contact program focused on reaching into those specific buildings in an otherwise walkable district. Phoning into these buildings is another way of identifying a supporter who can let volunteers into the building to go door to door.

Volunteer phoning usually takes place in the evening (the best calling hours are between 5:00 and 9:00 p.m., Sunday through Thursday nights), and volunteers make the calls at a phone bank, a location with multiple telephones and lines that is typically donated or leased back to the campaign by a supporter. Like candidate door-knocking, though, certain calling is done best during the day. Calls to seniors, for example, are more successful during the day than during the evening. Phone bank locations could include law firms, real estate agencies, unions, and the campaign office itself. With cell phones, any large space can be a phone bank location. A campaign that we know of had a youth outreach program that brought in pizza for students on the weekends. Typically forty or fifty students would show up with their cell phones, and chargers, and would use their free weekend minutes to call fellow students about the election. At break everyone ate pizza and shared stories. In another example, one union created a "phone bank in a box"; it had a complete phone bank kit, including a cell phone, that could be delivered to any part of the state to create an instant phone bank and was reused in subsequent elections. Depending on the size of the campaign, the phone bank should be managed by a field organizer, volunteer coordinator, or "super volunteer" who has been given the responsibility of managing others. These organizers are responsible for recruiting, training, and supervising volunteers. Here are some things to keep in mind when running a phone bank:

▸ *Overrecruit:* live by the "Law of Halves." If the campaign has six phone lines available, recruit twelve volunteers. Inevitably, some of the volunteers will cancel when you make confirmation calls, and a few more will not show up or will find that they would prefer to do other work. If the phoning takes place at a location outside the campaign (which is recommended, as the campaign office should be busy with other activities in the evenings), be sure to have some nonphoning work as a backup.

▸ *Make confirmation phone calls the night before.* If a volunteer does not receive a reminder phone call the night before, he or she is much more likely to forget or to assume that the campaign no longer needs the help. These calls should be brief, but should include a reminder about the urgency of the activity to be done and how it is critical to winning. Confirmation calls are mandatory!

▸ *Write scripts in plain language* that volunteers use as a guide rather than a recitation. This should be a short, succinct script that the volunteers should feel comfortable with. Once phoners learn the script and are comfortable, encourage them to just use the script as a guide and add their own words (although be sure they always stay on message). The types of scripts will vary depending on the nature of the calls.

▸ *Take time to train people.* As we discussed in the chapter on volunteer recruitment, new volunteer phoners need time to ease into this work. Explain the reason for the phoning and why it is important to the campaign. Ask the volunteer to read through the script aloud for practice, and be prepared to give feedback. Have the new phoners listen to others before starting themselves, and train people in how to record data on the call sheets.

▸ *Be available to answer questions and respond to comments.* Phone bank managers should practice MBWA: management by walking around. Phoners will often have questions once they begin to make calls. If you are the supervisor, you must be accessible and approachable to all volunteers and must answer their questions.

Check in with volunteers regularly, and ask them how the calls are going. If they are getting frustrated, tell them to take a short break and return to the calls when they are refreshed. It is equally important for the phone bank manager to be on the phone. There are few things more demoralizing than seeing your boss not working. Managers can call voters so they have an idea of what their volunteers are hearing on the phone, and can call no-show volunteers to say they are missed, find out if everything is OK, and recruit them for another night.

▶ At the end of the night, *debrief the volunteers* to address any problems that occurred, look at the numbers of calls made or supporters identified, and reinforce how important their work was for the campaign.

▶ *Finally, be sure to ask the volunteer to sign up to come back again!*

For many campaigns, phoning, particularly to persuadable targets, is conducted by volunteers. Paid persuasion phoning is generally less effective than volunteer calls, because paid phoners rarely have the personal connection to the area, the campaign, or the issues, and it is very expensive.

Persuasion phoning is a longer and more in-depth call than ID phoning, and it usually takes more time to train volunteers for that task. Whereas ID phoning consists of simply asking people about their views of the different campaigns and the issues they care about, persuasion phoning is more substantive. In a persuasion call, the caller focuses on engaging a voter in a short conversation to find common ground on issues. Ideally, the campaign will know which issues the voter cares about most and can tailor a message to that voter. For example, if a voter identifies the environment as the top issue, the persuasion caller can probe to see if the voter agrees that the previous four years have seen an erosion of environmental protections. If agreement can be found on an issue, the caller then highlights the candidate's position on environmental issues and points out how he or she will address the voter's concerns. The call ends with a specific request for the voter's support. The key to effective persuasion calling is connecting with a voter on an issue that is important to that voter and having a conversation. Remember the key rule of voter contact: the more personal, the more effective. Too often campaigns do what we call "verbal direct mail," in which they read a message statement to a voter just as if they were reading a piece of mail.

Scripts are an important part of your phoning program. Ideally, volunteers will familiarize themselves with the script and then adapt it in their own language so they don't come across as automatons on the call. There are three basic types of phone bank scripts:

▶ **Voter ID script.** A voter ID script is very brief and is used early in a campaign to identify who the person is supporting (a candidate ID) and/or what issues are most important to him or her (an issue ID). See the example of a typical voter ID script in this chapter's account of the fictional Augusta Gray campaign.

▶ **Persuasion script.** A persuasion script is usually used after the voter ID and stops within a week before the election. For example, you may be calling a voter who was previously identified as undecided on the race and who has health care as the number one issue. A persuasion script is usually a bit longer and attempts to engage the voter in a brief conversation about an issue—in this case health care—that is important to him or her. Here's an example of a short persuasion script:

> "Hi, my name is *[give first name],* and I'm calling on behalf of the Paul Orange for City Council campaign.
>
> "Paul is the progressive candidate for city council in Ward 6. His lifetime of experience has readied him to serve the ward. He will respond promptly to your concerns and work to create affordable housing and private development that improves the city. He wants fair community-based policing and a greener city with better city services and transit. He'll work to improve relations between the university and surrounding neighborhoods and to give our kids early assistance to succeed.
>
> "If the election were held today, would you vote for Paul Orange, Olive October, or are you still undecided?
>
> "Thank you very much for your time."

▶ **Get-out-the-vote script.** A GOTV script is a brief script that is directed to a voter who we already know is supporting the campaign. The purpose is to urge the voter to get to the polls and vote. The script should also provide polling locations and should ask if a ride is needed to the polls. For a GOTV call, unlike ID and persuasion calls, a message left on a machine is usually as good as actually talking to a voter. The key to a good GOTV call is to remind people of the stakes in this election: "Your vote will help make the difference between moving toward affordable health care in our country or watching our health care costs continue to skyrocket." You are not reminding people to vote; our supporters know when Election Day is. You are reminding them of how important their vote is to our shared values.

Visibility

Visibility is an additional component to the field plan. While it does not constitute direct, personal voter contact, it does play an important role in campaigns: a campaign's visibility activities are one way many voters encounter a campaign. Visibility—which includes signs, bumper stickers, people standing on street corners waving, parades, rallies, literature drops, sound trucks, and T-shirts—increases name identification and can energize the base. Since most visibility activities are fun and relatively easy, they are also an effective way to motivate supporters to volunteer and express their support in some concrete action. Successful field operations use visibility actions like parades, rallies, and dropping literature to recruit new volunteers and help move those volunteers into more difficult activities like canvassing or doing persuasion phone calling.

While visibility activities play an important role in campaigns, they can also be a distraction and a drain on resources. Visibility activities move relatively few undecided voters. Seasoned field organizers often say, "Signs don't vote." This is certainly true. In addition, signs are expensive and serve mainly to motivate the candidate and people who already support the candidate. They are extremely poor choices for persuasion or convincing undecided voters. A formula that is worth considering is this: the one sign that will likely be stolen on Halloween night equals about five direct mail pieces to targeted undecided voters. A button is about the same as a direct mail piece, and how many of us have walls of candidate buttons? You choose which is the best way to spend limited campaign resources. Signs and buttons and bumper stickers have a role to play in campaigns, but obsessing about who has more of them (or worse yet, having the candidate obsess about it) is a common waste of campaign time and money. Every visibility action taken by the campaign needs to be for a strategic reason; must be weighed against other more effective, direct, and personal ways of contacting voters; and should be integrated with other more direct methods. If you have volunteers putting up lawn signs, ideally they are putting them up as they knock on doors and identify campaign supporters. To help cover the costs of the lawn signs, have your volunteers ask for a five-dollar donation (or better yet, even more!). Ultimately, if lawn signs become a central focus of your campaign, they are not advancing the goal of winning the election. Use lawn signs in the context of a direct voter contact program: the first thing volunteers should do is contact voters, and their visibility work should complement, not supplant, their contact with voters.

Despite the limitations of visibility, there are times when it plays other useful functions. Take an example from the town of South Prairie, Washington. A progressive community activist named Peggy Levesque decided to run for mayor, and recruited a group of friends and neighbors to help her campaign. "I had about twenty people who were helping me out," Levesque told us. "I don't think any of them had ever been involved in campaigns before. They really wanted lawn signs that we would put on lawns but also hold on a street corner for visibility. I knew that signs had only a limited impact, and I resisted. But they wanted signs! So I figured, 'If they want signs, we'll get them signs.' They were so excited about them, and they wanted to stand on the main corner in town and wave the signs. That was something that had never been done before, and even though I had doubts about how effective it would be, I figured that if these supporters were willing to stand on the corner and wave signs for me, then I was too." The volunteers turned out to be right; their sign waving drew all kinds of attention from the town's residents, who had never seen such a thing. Mayor Levesque's story illustrates a point about base building we made earlier in this chapter: good grassroots campaigns stay connected to their supporters. Levesque puts it simply: "Listen to your supporters. Thank them. Know that they have their eye on the community and take what they say seriously."

E-mail and Text Messaging

Despite, or perhaps because of, the wide use of e-mail among voters, e-mail is generally not an effective persuasion tool. People's in-boxes are filled with spam and mass e-mails, and they rarely take the time to read a persuasion message. And a campaign wouldn't want to send an unsolicited persuasion e-mail to an undecided voter; that has the potential to turn a voter off. (What undecided voter will proactively give an e-mail address to a campaign?) But, following the rule of "the more personal, the more effective," targeted e-mail by means of an individual supporter contacting his or her e-mail list can be effective, especially for volunteer recruitment. E-mail is very effective as an organizing and grassroots fundraising tool and can make your work much easier. While an average voter might ignore a persuasion e-mail from the campaign, your supporters actually want to hear from the campaign, as long as you don't bombard them with e-mails every day but instead communicate with them on important and timely issues with a specific call to action. Capture as many e-mail addresses as possible—through your Web site, at events, and when you are knocking on doors—and use your growing e-mail list to send out action alerts, organizing requests, notices of upcoming campaign events, and fundraising appeals. You need the technology to send out bulk e-mails (using Microsoft Outlook won't work for hundreds or thousands of addresses), which might require the campaign to purchase bulk e-mail software or to use an e-mail program connected to your database. It is vital that campaigns only e-mail individuals who have asked to be on the campaign e-mail list!

Text messaging can also be a good organizing tool when you're targeting young people, particularly those you have a hard time reaching through traditional methods. Like e-mail, text messaging has its limits as a persuasion tool, but if your campaign is organizing a rally, building a crowd for an event, or implementing a GOTV plan, text messages are useful to send to certain audiences. A wide variety of companies offer text messaging services that allow you to send a message from a computer to your list of cell phone numbers. Be sure your list contains cell phone numbers, not home numbers, or the campaign will be spending money on wasted calls. Again, be sure that every person you have on the campaign's text messaging list has agreed to receive the text messages.

Other Forms of Contacting Voters through the Field

▸ **House parties.** A house party strategy based on personal networks is an excellent way both to build the base and to target individual undecided voters. Undecided voters can be personally invited to a house party by a neighbor who is supporting the campaign, with the invitation followed up by a phone call. Even if the voter does not come, he or she has been given two contacts and connected to a neighbor who supports the campaign. The house party can be one of the few ways to contact voters on a wide scale in apartment buildings, senior high-rises, and other difficult-to-reach geographies.

▸ **Literature drops.** Lit drops—or leaving a piece of literature at a person's door—is less personal and hence less effective. It is best combined with door-knocking as a "knock and drop"—knock and give the lit to the person who answers (even if the conversation is not of any depth, the person is still more likely to pay attention to the piece of literature) and drop the lit at those doors where no one is home. Lit drops can be targeted by precinct and by neighborhood. Although less effective than a more personal contact, in low-visibility races it is a cheap and effective way of contacting voters. In a county commissioner race run a few years ago in a rural district, the campaign had only a $4,500 budget for a race in which they expected 25,000 people to vote. Without the resources to mount a mail program, the campaign decided to lit drop the entire district five times (using the newspaper boxes, not the mailboxes!) with five different pieces, each building off each other (just like a direct mail campaign) five weekends in a row. The candidate won, unseating a long-term incumbent, and was the first woman to win in the district. Along with a highly targeted volunteer phone program, the lit drops were the principal way the campaign contacted voters.

▸ **Automated calls, or "robo-calls."** Computerized calls—those calls from the president or a star celebrity—are increasingly used. They are effective to augment other forms of voter contact, or provide basic information, but they are not effective for persuasion. A high percentage of people hang up in the first ten to fifteen seconds, so if used, be sure the message is delivered very quickly and succinctly.

Putting It All Together

There's a lot to do when it comes to direct voter contact—voter ID, persuasion, and getting out the vote (a component that we'll discuss in far more detail in chapter 14)—and not much time to do it. Putting your activities into a timeline, with clear goals and repeated voter contacts, will help you manage all the work and ensure that you're contacting the right voters at the right time. The reason you need to create a voter contact program and write it down, with a clear timeline and description of activities, is that voters need to be contacted repeatedly (five to nine times or more) in a variety of different ways over the course of the campaign. That requires good planning; calling an undecided voter five to nine times in the last week is not only counterproductive, it is irritating. A more effective voter contact program is to have the candidate door-knocking in the spring or summer. Several months out from Election Day, a volunteer phone bank would start identifying supporters, opponents, and the critical undecided voters and their issues. This ID call could then be followed up a couple of weeks later with a piece of direct mail specific to the voter's issues. The initial mail piece would then be followed by a volunteer door-knock, another piece of mail, a phone call, a call or door-knock from the candidate, another piece of mail, and finally another phone call, with each contact spread out a week or so apart. Spreading out both the type and timing of the persuasion contacts minimizes voter fatigue while allowing the campaign to continually have its message before the undecided voter.

The sample voter contact plan on the next page shows how a city council race in a medium-sized city contacted voters. This was an actual campaign, although we're using rounded numbers here for simplicity. There were 18,000 registered voters, which equals 86 percent of the voting age population. Based on past elections, the campaign calculated an expected voter turnout of 75 percent. There were 12,000 voting households, of which 6,000 households constituted the persuadable universe (those identified as undecided voters, or 3s, as well as the traditional swing voters in the voter file). A runoff primary was September 8, with the top two vote-getters moving on to the general election on November 3. The campaign's total budget was $6,500. Let's walk through this program step by step.

1. From the beginning of May through the summer and into September, the candidate was out door-knocking the entire district, all 12,000 households. This was the first contact voters received. More important, it was a crucial way for the candidate and the campaign to learn the issues of the district. While campaign leaders thought the race would be about economic development, it

Sample Voter Contact Plan (approximately $6,500 budget)

City Council District 2
- Registered voters: 18,000 (85.7%); estimated voter turnout: 75%
- Households (HH): 12,000
- Persuadable universe: 6,000 HH (from voter file: registered swing voters)
- Primary day: September 8; general election: November 3

TIME FRAME	ACTIVITY	UNIVERSE	BRIEF DESCRIPTION
May–September 1999	Candidate door-knocks entire district	12,000 HH	Introduce self, secure sign locations, identify supporters
August 28	Mailing to likely primary voters	3,200 HH	From voter file: direct mail piece to 3,200 likely primary voter HH
September 12–October 1	Phone ID likely swing voters: support and key issues	6,000 HH	From voter file: two-question script (preference and top two issues)
September 12–November 2	Candidate persuasion calls to ID'ed undecideds with follow-up note to contacted voters	~2,400 HH (target to complete = 1,200 calls)	Candidate makes calls to ID'ed undecided voters
September 15–October 4	Mail introductory letter and first issue piece to ID'ed undecideds	~1,200 HH	Targeting ID'ed undecideds from an ID field program: issue pieces specific to ID'ed issues
October 1–October 16	Mail second issue piece to ID'ed undecideds	~2,400 HH	Second piece, and send general issues piece to uncontacted voters
October 4–October 31	Volunteer persuasion calls to ID'ed undecideds	~2,400 calls	Calls made by volunteers to ID'ed undecided voters
October 15–October 31	Mail third issue piece to ID'ed undecideds

Volunteer persuasion door-knocks to ID'ed undecideds | ~1,200 HH | Volunteers will door-knock ID'ed undecided voters |
October 31–November 1	Lit drop district	12,000 HH	General campaign doorhanger
October 31–November 3	Visibilities (a.m. and p.m. rush)	Key district intersections	Supporters with signs waving
November 1–November 3	GOTV calls and GOTV mailer	~4,500 calls and mailers	Supporter target

This example of a voter contact program for a campaign for city council shows how a campaign layers various types of contact on top of one another. Direct mail and phone calls work to complement one another, as does the campaign's door-knocking strategy. Every campaign should lay out a similar timeline for the final weeks of the campaign, making sure that the message delivered in the mail, on the phone, and at the door is consistent.

was really about the quality of life issues in the neighborhood—everything from parks to the pesky problem of insufficiently prompt garbage pickup, resulting in neighborhood dogs knocking over trash cans. This information became invaluable later in the campaign when one of the major issues became whether snowmobiles would be allowed on a city walkway within the district.

2. On August 28, the campaign sent out a single mailing to the 3,200 households of likely primary voters. Since it was a primary, the piece reminded people of the importance of voting and reinforced the message the candidate had been delivering to voters over the summer. These 3,200 households were taken from the voter file and represented highly likely primary voters, those voters who have voted in the past three off-year primary elections. This was a minimal preprimary voter contact program, and the result was a distant second-place finish in a multicandidate field. Conventional wisdom would say that this race is lost. Even an optimistic reading of the results made it an extremely uphill fight.

3. Immediately after the election, the campaign started a focused visibility campaign to get lawn signs for the candidate in the yards that already had signs for two very popular elected officials. The idea was to tie the candidate with these more popular and better-known candidates, even when one of those candidates was supporting our opponent.

4. The campaign then started the postprimary voter contact program, which included volunteer phone ID calls to 6,000 likely swing voter households. These households were identified as likely swing voters in the voter file based on past voting history and performance for the precincts they live in, but the campaign didn't have specific information about supporters. The purpose of the calls was to winnow down likely general election voters to actual swing voters for an intensive voter contact program. The call was a simple two-question script: a question about preference in the race and a question about the top two issues on the voters' minds.

5. The results of these calls were then put into two categories for action: persuasion and getting out the vote. As the volunteer phone ID program produced identified undecided voters, those calls

then went to the candidate, who made persuasion calls to actual identified undecided voters whose major issues were known. These were extremely effective calls for the candidate and the best use of his time. He committed to forty-two straight days of calling, four hours a day, to make about 1,200 contacts. Many of these calls resulted in a persuasion, for the single most effective contact is from the candidate himself. This became the candidate's most important activity (he was still working full-time), and despite protestations from the candidate, he was pulled off door-knocking, for it was a far less efficient use of his time at this point. Every voter who was contacted received a handwritten follow-up note from the candidate. Every answering machine after the second try had a message left from the candidate inviting a call back. Surprisingly, many actually did call back.

6. Now the campaign started layering its volunteer and candidate phone calls with direct mail. They did three pieces of direct mail to undecided voters specific to the issues that they had indicated were important to them and a separate piece of mail, a general issues piece, to voters not yet contacted by phone. The first piece went out to roughly 1,200 households and was targeted according to the issue IDs. For example, of those 1,200 households, about 400 received a piece on development issues (since they identified it as their top issue), another 400 received a piece on the living wage policy, and another 400 a piece on parks and local issues. Everyone received information on the candidate's proposal to prohibit snowmobiles on the district walkway, a very quiet plan being explored by the city and supported by business that was surfaced by the campaign through research. This issue was thrust into the campaign by the candidate and likely became the decisive issue. His opponent knew nothing about the issue and was caught flat-footed and in an awkward position of having to repudiate her backers in order to take a position in line with the district.

7. The second piece in the direct mail program went to the same audience of identified undecided voters, with the addition of voters who had not yet been contacted, making an estimated universe of 2,400 households. The uncontacted voters received a general issues piece, while the identified undecideds received another specific issue piece.

8. During the month of October, volunteer persuasion calls, which complemented (and took place at the same time as) the candidate's persuasion calls, went to approximately 2,400 undecided households. All of these calls were taken from the results of the voter ID program.

9. The third and final persuasion mail piece went to undecided voters.

10. In the final two weeks of October, volunteers door-knocked approximately 1,200 identified undecided households, adding a personal, face-to-face contact to the phone calls and mail they were already receiving. This was made even more personal by sending volunteers who were well versed in the various issues—housing, environment, development, and so on—to talk with voters who indicated those as their top issues.

11. GOTV activities kicked in during the final five days of the campaign, starting with a citywide literature drop over the course of two days.

12. In addition to the citywide lit drop, the GOTV operation also sent volunteers to key intersections and high-visibility areas to hold signs and wave at cars during the morning and evening rush hours.

13. In the final three days, the campaign's identified supporters received at least one get-out-the-vote phone call and a piece of GOTV mail, which included information about polling location and hours. Volunteers conducted the GOTV calls.

The net result of this campaign was a narrow but important victory in a very tough district.

You can see from this example that voter contact methods have to be layered. Door-knocking is great, particularly if the candidate can door-knock an entire district, as in this example. But it's not enough; voters need frequent contacts. Phoning, both by the candidate and by volunteers, complements the more personal contacts obtained from door-knocking, and allows the campaign to get IDs more efficiently. And mail gives people a graphic, tangible piece of literature with the campaign's message. One piece of mail isn't enough; you need at least three pieces. Regardless of the size and scale of your campaign—you might send more mail, use paid phones, or have a paid canvassing operation, for example—your voter contact program should paint a comprehensive picture of who the campaign is contacting, when, and by whom.

Another example of layering contacts that has proved very effective is what many in the labor movement have called the sandwich technique. A robo-call goes out to targeted voters telling them they will be receiving an important message from the campaign (or their union) about an issue. The next day the mail piece arrives. Because of the call, the likelihood is greater that the person will read the mail. Then a week later this contact is followed up with a phone call or a door-knock, asking if the person received the mail piece and has questions. This type of focused, highly targeted, and layered voter contact makes each of the contacts in the "sandwich" more effective than it would be on its own.

CHAPTER 6

Using Direct Mail to Reinforce Your Message and Target Specific Voters

Dᴏɴᴇ ʀɪɢʜᴛ, direct mail is one of the most effective and efficient methods of direct voter contact with your target audience. For many small races, direct mail will be the only form of paid communication that you do, since it is a highly targeted and relatively inexpensive way to combine field strategy with your communications and paid media plan. Direct mail is designed to get people's attention and to provoke an emotional response from voters. Voters need to care about an issue or a candidate before you can persuade them to support your campaign. As one direct mail professional put it, "You can't make voters think until you get them to feel." Good direct mail uses photographic imagery, evocative language, and clear and concise messages to make a connection with voters.

While television and radio advertising can reach more people, direct mail has several advantages over other paid media methods:

▸ **Targeting.** TV and radio will often be seen and heard by people not in your target audience more than by those who *are* in that audience. You are therefore spending a lot of money on delivering a message to people who don't live in your district, don't vote at all, or won't be voting for you. Direct mail, on the other hand, is sent to the individual voter you are targeting and can be customized to specific content or issues that are important to that voter. One voter might get a direct mail piece on the environment and global climate change while her neighbor might get one on fair trade and

the need to stop outsourcing jobs. Using precinct-level information from past elections, your voter file, and the information you
have gathered from your voter ID work, you can target your mail
specifically to voters you know are undecided. To that end, direct
mail is far more efficient than other paid media tactics.

▸ **Repetition.** Direct mail is a great way to deliver multiple contacts
to your audience, and it relies on repetition. In fact, a mail piece
is only really effective if part of a series. Adnaan Muslim, a direct
mail professional and veteran of many campaigns, describes the
importance of repeated contacts bluntly: "If you're doing just one
piece, you might as well just take the money you're spending and
burn it." A rule of thumb to follow is that you should do a minimum of three pieces, and potentially several more, for direct mail
to have an impact. One advantage of direct mail is that you have
more control over how many times your audience is contacted.
With TV and radio advertising, you never really know how many
times your intended audience is seeing or hearing your message.
You can make accurate guesses (through sophisticated ad buys
that a media consultant will help you make), but there's no way
to guarantee that a person who needs to see your ad will see it
once, much less multiple times. With direct mail, you control the
frequency of message delivery and the sequence of that contact.
(This can be done with other paid media as well, but high production costs make great flexibility impractical for most campaigns.)

▸ **Use of contrast.** Direct mail is a very effective means of contrasting your position with your opponent's. For some campaigns,
that means direct mail is a way of delivering hard-hitting messages against an opponent without broadcasting that to a wide
audience. While we don't believe in over-the-top personal attacks
(which you often see in direct mail, particularly at the end of a
campaign), campaigns are ultimately about choices, and mail is
well suited for hard contrasts on issues.

While direct mail has many benefits, you should also understand its limitations. The biggest problem, of course, is that many voters treat direct mail
as junk mail. It's easy to ignore direct mail when it lands in the mailbox amid
the bills and credit card offers received every day. In addition, despite your
ability to target direct mail to individual voters, direct mail remains a rela-

tively impersonal mode of communicating. As we know, the best way to reach voters is with personal, one-on-one conversations, preferably at their doors.

These limitations are why it's important to do direct mail the right way. The biggest challenge with direct mail is making a connection with voters as quickly as possible. Keep in mind, for example, that there are three types of people who will be reading your direct mail.

In the first group are the people who read the mail piece between picking it up in the mailbox and throwing it in the recycling bin. These people essentially treat the mail as junk mail, but in the seven seconds they spend glancing at it, they notice the photo, a headline, and maybe a campaign slogan. That's about all they see. It's not much, but it is a contact. This is the group newspapers target with large headlines and front-page photos above the fold. The second group consists of people who actually stop and look at a mail piece, read the headlines, and scan the text to see if they are interested. They take about ten to twenty seconds to look at the piece, and then throw it away. Using the newspaper analogy, these people are readers newspapers try to capture with the increasingly popular longer subheadline, cutout quotes, cutlines under photos, etc. Most Web sites are created for this type of a glancing/scanning audience. In the third group are the readers. They read every word of the mail piece, are probably well informed about the issues, and have been following the campaign. These are the folks who buy the Sunday paper and try to read it all. This audience will always want to know more, so mail pieces with their limited size need to point the reader to a Web site where they can find more information.

To the extent possible, you want your mail to connect with each of these groups. Here are some ways to make that happen:

▶ *Use good photos.* Bad photos equal bad mail. Period. Photos capture people's attention and draw them into the mail piece. Avoid using bland headshots of the candidate—use action photos of the candidate interacting with people, preferably not those horrible posed shots of candidate with worker and hard hat, candidate with senior and prescription drug bottle, candidate with student and knapsack or student loan application, or candidate with farmer in bibs. These are not only boring and predictable: they waste precious space without communicating any message besides the fact that you have some friends who are willing to pose for you. Make sure the photos are big enough for the seven-second voters to see and remember.

▸ *Keep it simple but make an impact.* This is not the time to show off how many different fonts you can use and all the different colors you can cram into a mail piece. The rule generally is that less is more. Headline fonts should be crisp and large enough to read. Text fonts should be easily readable and should not go below 11 points. Font sizes less than that are not readable for a broad audience. Tightly packed or dense pieces will be tossed or set aside more easily. The layout should direct the eye to read the piece according to the sequence you intend. The rules on good messaging apply to direct mail: simple, straightforward messages connect with voters.

▸ *Generally, do not put direct mail in an envelope.* Persuasion mail should be in the form of a self-mailer—front and back—that can easily touch the three audiences described above. Of course, there are exceptions to this. If you want to guarantee that your voters open your piece and look at it, send them your message in a first-class, stamped, hand-addressed envelope that looks like a person sent it, not a campaign stationery envelope. They will open it, and what they see once they open it needs to follow the rules we've just described. The more overtly political a piece looks, the less likely that it will connect with most voters.

▸ *Make the mail noticeable.* Big is one way to send mail, but big is often terribly overused. Full-page flats (8½ x 11) tend to get folded over by many letter carriers and the beautiful layout seen in the mock-ups is not at all what the voters see in their mailbox. Odd-sized mail stands out when you pull it out of the mailbox. Square mail, elongated, and oval mail are all unusual and stick out from the pile. You can also use oversized postcards or single- and double-fold mail pieces.

▸ *Other considerations:* Make sure that the candidate's vital information is on the piece: Candidate name, office, election, the "ask" (vote, contribute, register). Each mail piece needs a disclaimer. A disclaimer can be in a smaller font. Know the rules as to what needs to be in the disclaimer. Most progressive campaigns use union printers and will want to use the "union bug," which is a small symbol that indicates that the piece was printed by union printers and which union firm printed it. In regions of the country where union printers are few and far between, or nonexistent, you may face the trade-off between using local printers and out-of-town union printers. Learn the political culture of your region and ask around to see what is available. Homemade postcards or mailers printed in house should state, "Printed in House." Finally, be sure to include basic contact information—Web site, phone, or e-mail address—some way to contact the campaign to volunteer, contribute, or find out more.

There are endless examples and varieties of mail pieces. Here are a few that illustrate the points we've made above. The first is a mail piece that is simple and clear. The candidate was Harry Kennedy, who was running for reelection to the Missouri State Senate. This is a pretty catchy mail piece; the penny with the candidate's head superimposed on it catches your attention, and the message makes you want to read more. Some might say that calling him "cheap" (even with tax dollars) is a negative, and that might be true, but it's catchy enough that it's a risk worth taking. This entire mail piece consists of sixteen words, yet anyone reading this gets the message. It's clear, simple, and conveys the point that Harry Kennedy is on your side if you think that government needs to be more frugal and that he backs up his words with actions (by not taking a pay increase).

A good example of a mail piece that really fits a candidate is one from Elsie Mosqueda, a candidate for House delegate in Virginia. This is a great direct mail piece: simple, attractive, inviting, and clear. It portrays Elsie Mosqueda as likable, and the words used to describe her fit with the photo and represent what voters want to see in their elected officials: authentic leaders they can relate to.

For a great example of using repetition to reinforce message in direct mail, look at the series from Marty Markowitz's successful run for Brooklyn borough president. It's not hard to see the consistent theme in these mail pieces, which were timed to hit mailboxes over the course of several weeks. In the first example, the photo of the couple is almost all you need to know about Markowitz's character: no one can fake that look. This is another direct mail piece that really conveys a message with few words. The focus is less on Markowitz and more on Brooklyn; you get the sense that this guy really loves Brooklyn (and his wife). And of course, the photo is great—note the Brooklyn Bridge in the background. The theme continues in the next two pieces. Each piece in this series builds on the last one. After seeing these three pieces, it's hard to argue with the slogan: "As Brooklyn as they come!"

This is a good example of a direct mail piece that conveys a clear message with very few words. While other mail pieces or direct voter contact methods can fill in more details about Harry Kennedy's positions, this mail piece leaves voters with a clear impression that Kennedy is fiscally responsible and committed to representing them.

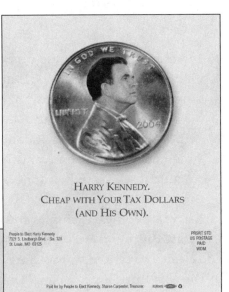

HARRY KENNEDY.
CHEAP WITH YOUR TAX DOLLARS
(AND HIS OWN).

People to Elect Harry Kennedy
7321 S. Lindbergh Blvd. - Ste. 320
St. Louis, MO 63125

PRSRT STD
US POSTAGE
PAID
WDM

Paid for by People to Elect Kennedy, Sharon Carpenter, Treasurer.

He voted down his own pay.

People to Elect Harry Kennedy
7321 S. Lindbergh Blvd. - Ste. 320
St. Louis, MO 63125

PRSRT STD
US POSTAGE
PAID
WDM

Paid for by People to Elect Kennedy, Sharon Carpenter, Treasurer.
KEN0404

Good direct mail can focus on issues or on the personal qualities of the candidate. This piece doesn't mention the issues (something other pieces can focus on), but instead concentrates on the person. The photo in this mail piece nicely complements the list of Mosqueda's personal attributes, which depict her as someone you would be glad to have as your neighbor.

Elsie Mosqueda
Daughter
Wife
Mother
Grandmother
Neighbor
Activist
Leader

1522 King Street
Alexandria, VA 22314

Prsrt Std
US Postage
PAID
CSI

Paid for and authorized by Elsie Mosqueda
MO50501

After 54 years in Brooklyn, 21 as our State Senator, thousands of breakfasts at Junior's, and hundreds of walks through Prospect Park, he could've gone absolutely anywhere to begin his honeymoon.

Where did he choose to take his bride?

Brooklyn.

Marty Markowitz *As Brooklyn as they come!*

While in Albany for the January 2001 legislative session, Marty broke his ankle in three places. The E.R. physician recommended surgery and gave him two choices of where to have it done: Albany or Manhattan.

Marty picked

Brooklyn.

Marty Markowitz *As Brooklyn as they come!*

Most learn the tradition of public service from a statesman or politician. Marty learned the finer points of service from his father, who happened to be neither.

Robert Markowitz was a waiter at a kosher deli.

In Brooklyn.

Marty Markowitz *As Brooklyn as they come!*

This series of mail pieces for Marty Markowitz in Brooklyn illustrates the importance of message repetition. The goal of this multipart mail campaign was to reinforce the idea that the people of Brooklyn will have no greater advocate than Markowitz. The stories are personal and reflect his enthusiasm for the borough, and each piece builds on the last.

The direct mail pieces we've shown here have several characteristics in common. First and most important, they capture your attention and make you want to read more. That's most of the battle when it comes to direct mail—making sure people actually read it. Second, they don't use too many photos, and the photos they use are good. They are not "busy" pieces that overload the eye with information. Third, they are simple and use words sparingly. And finally, they reflect the personality and message of the candidate. Voters can sense fake politicians, even in a direct mail piece. Although not all of these candidates won, they were all good examples of the kinds of candidates progressives need to run for office.

If your campaign is planning to use a large volume of mail, you should hire a direct mail professional with experience in political mail. There is a difference in how people read and see mail that is about candidates compared with how they read and see mail about an issue or about a product. There are countless firms around the country that specialize in creating direct mail for progressive electoral campaigns. Find out from other campaigns or previous candidates whom they used for direct mail and have conversations with various vendors. If you are managing a campaign, particularly a large one, you will likely receive a lot of phone calls and packages in the mail from direct mail firms hoping to enlist you as a client. Take your time in making this decision, and ask questions:

▶ What do they charge per piece? Usually the answer will depend on things like the size of the mailing, the colors you want to use, and the quality of the paper, but every firm should be able to give you a price breakdown. Don't hesitate to bargain with them. If they give you a quote at a certain rate, try to talk them down a few cents per piece. If they really want your business, they should be willing to negotiate on price.

▶ What is the turnaround time? Clarify with the mail firm how long it will take for the mail to hit mailboxes from the time you give final approval for a piece. This is really important, particularly at the end of the campaign. These firms will likely have dozens of other clients, and you need to be sure you are a priority. It doesn't do you any good to have your mail hit mailboxes the day after Election Day.

▶ Who will the campaign be working with? The person who sells you on the firm isn't always the person you work with on a day-to-day basis. Often the president or head of the company will make the sales pitch, but once your campaign signs up with the company, you end up working only with associates. While that's not always a problem, you do want to have assurances that the top people in the firm will be available to you and have direct input into the creation of the mail pieces.

▶ Can the campaign see samples of the firm's work? Any good direct mail firm will be eager to share examples of previous work. Be sure the examples you see are from recent campaigns.

▶ Ask for references and call those campaigns; ask for winners and losers and check the references!

Once you hire a firm, your work is not over. Stay closely involved in the conception and development of the mail. Remember that this is your campaign, not theirs. You know the issues better than anyone and understand what works in your district and what doesn't.

Many small campaigns cannot afford to use direct mail consultants. You can still produce effective mailings if you follow the same rules. There are many good desktop publishing programs available, and with luck you can find a volunteer who is skilled in graphic design and layout. Home-designed direct mail can be sent using a mail house (a business that specializes in preparing and sending bulk mailings) or by using a bulk mail permit secured by the campaign from the post office. Mail houses can often package your mailings in the most cost-efficient way and even recoup any additional cost of sending mail by the campaign itself. Doing direct mail in-house can be considerably cheaper, but also risks being less effective if not done right.

CHAPTER 7

Reaching Voters through Paid Advertising

W HETHER AND HOW your campaign uses paid advertising—television (both cable and network), radio, Internet, and print—depends on the size and geography of the race. National, Congressional, and statewide campaigns usually rely heavily on television to communicate to their targeted voters, and they supplement this primary media with Internet, newspaper, and other forms of paid advertising. Anyone brave enough to turn on the television or listen to the radio in October of an election year knows that the advertising levels can reach a deafening pitch, with back-to-back campaign ads from one side or the other. It seems to get worse each season. In fact, the trend in major races has been toward starting earlier and spending more on television advertising to counteract the problem of reduced viewership of traditional television, the growth of the Internet, and innovations like TiVo and digital video recording (DVR) that eliminate advertising from the viewing experience. Because television plays a major role in large races and is still effective at moving voters, large campaigns will usually spend millions of dollars on television and radio advertising. But relying solely on television is by and large a losing strategy. A much better approach is to combine and integrate broadcast media with robust direct voter contact in the field. This means that during the planning process, the broadcast media budget needs to be weighed alongside your budget decisions about direct mail and other direct voter contact methods.

Medium-sized campaigns may use television in a targeted or limited way, especially by running advertising on cable channels. Cable channel advertising does not give you the reach that broadcast television does, but it is much more affordable, gives you the ability to target specific kinds of voters watching certain cable channels, and allows you to geographically target your advertising in a way you cannot with broadcast. (Satellite cable presents a unique problem in that most satellite cable won't let you pick stations, removing the targeting ability that traditional cable buys used to provide.) Radio will often be a major part of medium-sized races, and 95 percent of Americans listen to the radio at least once a week. It's also sometimes the only options for Congressional races in the biggest media markets, like seats in New Jersey, where TV covers either New York City or Philadelphia and is unaffordable. Radio can be targeted generally by demographic group and geography, but like television it is a "broadcast" medium, so your ads will reach many people who are not in your target audiences (or even in your district). Radio can be an important tool for base organizing and getting out the vote as well, because it can be the best way to reach your base voters through a broadcast medium. Print advertising is often used for base organizing as well, such as when placing advertising in ethnic or constituency-based press. As in the major races, decisions on the use of paid advertising need to be made in the context of the whole question of how the campaign reaches enough voters enough times to win.

Smaller races may do no paid advertising at all, instead relying exclusively on direct voter contact—direct mail, door-knocking, telephoning, and other tactics. But small campaigns rely on targeting and identifying sufficiently large pools of specific base and persuadable voters, and then keep their communication program directed to them. Sometimes radio and print advertising makes sense in these races, but those are planning choices that must be weighed against whether there are adequate resources to do the direct voter contact you need.

For both large and small races, paid media is always a balancing act between which of the effective means for reaching voters the campaign would ideally like to use and what the campaign budget will allow. As we discussed in chapter 5, on direct voter contact, there are rules of thumb but seldom ironclad dictates, for the effective use of paid media. Each is a tool and each has its uses and its limitations.

Television

Television is still the most dominant form of media and is one of the most effective because it appeals to eye and ear, emotions and mind. TV reaches a broad audience with relative efficiency and cost-effectiveness on a per contact basis. Still, it is still extremely expensive because it reaches so many people. You are somewhat able to target (e.g., cable by geography, demographics based on shows, etc.), but since it is broadcast, you may be talking to the wrong people or to people who can't vote for you.

Radio

Radio can be broadly targeted and can reach people in places TV cannot—cars, for example, during drive time, and at work on the office radio. Radio is not as dynamic as TV because it appeals to one sense, hearing. Although on a per spot basis it is much cheaper than TV, radio can be almost as expensive as TV, in many media markets, to cover the same number of target listeners. Radio is effective for reinforcing other paid media more than serving as the backbone of a paid media program.

Newspapers

Newspapers are a relatively static medium and appeal only to readers—and an increasingly fewer number of them, as newspaper readership declines. On the plus side, newspaper ads can convey more substantive information, and the newspaper readership overwhelmingly consists of voters. In dailies, you can target specific types of voters (like readers of the sports section as opposed to the front page), but targeting is very imprecise. Other advantages include the general legitimacy that is still given to newsprint over other forms of paid mass media. However, most ads are placed amid the clutter of other ads. If you place an ad, it needs to be placed multiple times and be large enough to stand out (one-quarter to full page). You will often get better results by utilizing specific constituency or ethnic press (like women's newspapers, labor papers, and minority press). In addition, in rural districts, community weeklies (not the shoppers; they are a waste of money) are well-read media for a campaign message. Community weeklies can be highly targeted by geography and are read differently, for local information.

Internet Banner Ads

The Internet is an emerging medium, and more people are getting information from the Web as newspaper readership declines. Banner ads are relatively inexpensive and can be targeted to pop up when certain pages are accessed (like local newspaper front pages or issue-related blogs) or tagged so they emerge when a specific word is searched for or pop up in articles. This allows for extraordinary flexibility in targeting ads. The downside is that banner ads are often the junk mail of the electronic world, annoyances that are clicked through to get to what you really want to see. One of the effective uses of banner ads is to drive base voters to take an action or steer potential voters to another site that provides more information or action. Banner ads themselves are not the most effective conveyers of a campaign's message.

Consider package deals. If you are buying print ads in local papers, ask them to throw in some banner advertising as well, and make sure the links go to a page on your Web site that is not the home page, but one that has a quick, concise message and a request for action—either fundraising, volunteering, or attending an event. Don't get sold a bill of goods on Internet advertising. Ask about click-through rates, how many folks visit the Web sites you are considering, and how many are from your district. Also, some campaigns produce ads that would traditionally have gone on TV, but now they put them on the campaign's Web site, as an Internet ad. This is a creative idea, but the campaign should decide if the production time and money is worth it for the audience the ad will reach. Generally, persuadable voters are not your Web site's audience. Unless the ad is so creative and so provocative that it increases interest in the campaign through more sign-ups and fundraising, it may not be a good use of campaign money and resources.

Billboards

Billboards usually don't work as a persuasion tool. They are mostly like supersized lawn signs and have about as much impact as lawn signs in moving undecided voters: very little. They don't contain much information, are not particularly effective at delivering a message, and cost a lot of money. There are times when billboards can be used to draw attention to the campaign, but rarely is that more effective than using those resources on going door to door and having direct conversations with voters. Sometimes, however, billboards can be used to get free media for the campaign. For example, when Paul Wellstone ran for reelection in 1996, the National Republican Senatorial Campaign identified him as their number one target for defeat. The Wellstone campaign used this to rally our supporters and motivate our base. As it turned out, there was a billboard immediately above the Wellstone campaign headquarters, so the campaign leased it for the duration of the campaign and replaced it with a sign that featured a large target with an arrow beneath the words "Millions of Republican dollars aimed here." The campaign then held a press event with a crowd of cheering supporters, unveiling the ad to the press. The cost of the billboard in this case was worth it, given the exposure it received in the press and the effect it had on motivating our supporters.

Another example of leveraging outdoor advertising beyond its normal impact took place overseas, in the Irish parliamentary elections in 2002. At the time, the Progressive Democrat Party was the junior member in a coalition government with Fianna Fáil, a much bigger party. Fianna Fáil was cruising toward a huge election victory, so much so that it appeared they might have enough seats in Parliament to form a majority government all by themselves. In a desperate but strategic move, a senior member of the Progressive Democrats held a press event where he personally scaled a lamppost to put up a giant poster that said, "One party government? No thanks!" The party accompanied the stunt with a very limited purchase of billboards, essentially so they could say they had done so. The event garnered a huge amount of media coverage, dominating the print, radio, and television news for many days. It began a protracted debate about whether single-party government without anyone to hold the dominant party in check was good. In the end, it became the defining moment of the campaign, with voters moving to the Progressive Democrats to make sure that no one party exerted too much power. Without a strategic delivery of the advertising, it would have had a limited effect. But done right, it transformed a national election and returned a party to power that appeared to be on its way out.

Use Professionals When Possible

Paid media usually requires the involvement of professionals to produce your advertising and in larger races, to buy your advertising time. Candidates sometimes attempt to do their own television advertising, almost always with bad results. There are times when radio ads can be done effectively in-house, but with television, well-written scripts, professional voices, and good production values make all the difference in grabbing and keeping voters' attention.

Frequency and Repetition

One of the rules of effective campaign messaging is to deliver it with frequency and repetition. When we discussed direct voter contact, we talked about the importance of repeated voter contacts—primarily at the door, on the phone, and in the mail. Ideally, by the end of the campaign, a persuasion target voter should have received six to nine direct contacts from the campaign. The same goes for paid media. The goal is to maximize the number of times the right voters hear the message. Because of this, it is important when planning your paid media strategy to dominate one medium and not spread yourself too thin. If, for instance, a campaign has $100,000 to spend on its paid media, doing some radio and some cable television and a couple of direct mail pieces may not get you to the levels you need to have an impact. Instead, the campaign may decide to dominate radio with all of the paid media budget, assuming that sufficient numbers of targeted voters are included in the radio audience in a cost-effective manner. The dominating strategy applies when you are deciding on direct mail versus paid advertising as well. Deciding to put some money into mail and some into radio or cable television can lead to too little for any one of the approaches to be effective. One or two scattered direct mail pieces will have almost no impact at all.

There are rules of thumb for effective frequency and repetition of a single ad. For television, an ad should run a minimum of "1200 points" or "600 points" per week. Paid media is calculated based on what percent of a target audience can be reached through a particular medium. This is done through a measure called gross rating points (GRP). Gross rating points measure the total volume of delivery of your message to your target audience (that is, the percent of your target audience exposed to the message times the frequency of exposure). A rating point defines the audience size as a percentage of the universe (the "universe" is the single market or geographic region you are targeting). One rating point is equivalent to covering 1 percent of your target universe or market. Although confusing (this is why professionals should buy media time), the most important number to remember for most campaign media buying is that for one ad to cover 100 percent of its target universe requires purchasing 100 GRP in that medium. A hundred rating points means that an average person in the market universe will likely see an ad once.

For our example above, 1200 GRP means virtually everyone in our target viewing universe will see the ad: about 80 percent of average viewers will see the TV ad twelve times. About 10 percent won't see it at all (because they are sporadic viewers), and another 10 percent will see it more than twelve times because they watch more television. One radio ad should run a minimum of thirty times per week on the same station to break through and be heard in sufficient repetition to make a difference. Timing is important with paid media. The reason airwaves are filled with political ads in the last two to three weeks of an election is that this is the time when many undecided swing voters make up their minds. Block out your media buys from Election Day backward. If you are going to put up media early, there is a general rule of thumb that reads, "Once up on the air, stay up on the air." Early exposure followed by silence means the early media money ends up being wasted because people forget the message. When buying broadcast media, you want to target to your audiences as best you can. For instance, if women are an important persuasion and base target, then you'll want to buy radio and television that attracts that group (e.g., Lifetime and the Oxygen network) and avoid media that attracts a more male audience (such as the Spike network).

Layering Paid Advertising with Your Campaign Plan

Given the gloomy trends for traditional broadcast media, more and more campaigns are working to fit radio and television advertising into a holistic approach to direct voter contact by integrating and then layering paid contact with your mail and volunteer contact program. When advertising, you should always integrate what you are doing on the ground with your paid media. For instance, if you just put a new ad on the air, your volunteers can carry PDAs ("PalmPilots") when they are door-knocking that play the same ad at the door, giving voters an opportunity both to have a personal contact from a campaign volunteer and to see the TV ad. Creatively combining paid media and volunteer contacts can lead to breakthroughs with voters. For instance, if you are running a race in a suburban community with lots of commuters, you may be buying drive-time radio advertising to reach people, and you may want to reinforce the ad with a billboard on the main commuting route that ties into the radio ad (one of the only times buying billboards may make sense). An effective use of this technique in Minnesota was to put billboards at key areas where traffic backups occurred during rush hour that read, "This traffic jam brought to you by [the opponent's party]." Or you could buy a print ad and then do a robo-call to your target audience encouraging them to look at your ad in that day's paper.

Let's turn to some examples to illustrate the process of deciding whether and how to invest in broadcast advertising.

The first example is from Tony Lourey's successful run for an open seat in the Minnesota state Senate that was being vacated by his mother, Becky

Lourey. Let's imagine you are the manager of Tony's campaign. The Eighth Senate District sits between Minneapolis–Saint Paul to the south and Duluth to the north. It is a geographically large rural district, running about one hundred miles long and fifty miles wide. There are 79,384 eligible voters, but your targeting estimates that 50,000 voters will turn out on Election Day. You have also identified a target persuadable universe of about 10,000 voters scattered throughout the district. Your total budget for the campaign is $65,000.

Here are the available media sources:

▸ There are two network television markets: Duluth and the Twin Cities. Three local cable networks are located in the district.

▸ There are many radio stations in Duluth and the Twin Cities, and six local radio stations throughout the district.

▸ There are three daily newspapers—two in the Twin Cities and one in Duluth—with coverage in the district. In addition there are eight local weekly newspapers.

Although television is the way to connect with the largest number of target voters in the district, you quickly conclude that television advertising is too expensive. In addition to production costs, purchasing ad time is impossible. A minimum ad buy in Duluth costs $36,000, and a minimum buy in the Twin Cities is $330,000. Obviously this is not an option, unless you want to spend half your entire budget on a minimal purchase on Duluth TV, which only reaches half the residents of the district, but also reaches people in northern Wisconsin and the western edge of the Upper Peninsula of Michigan. Metro radio is also too expensive. A minimum buy in Duluth is $20,400, while a minimum buy in the Twin Cities is $228,000. Like television, this is one of the most powerful ways to reach broad numbers of voters in the district, but your ads will also be heard by hundreds of thousands of listeners who live outside the district as well. On the other hand, advertising on local radio stations is quite inexpensive. For a minimum buy on all six local stations combined, the cost is $990 per week, which is a fraction of the cost of metro radio. While there are obviously fewer listeners to these local stations and the coverage of the district is incomplete compared with metro radio and TV, the listeners all live in the district and can be targeted for specific messages.

What about newspapers? The dailies in the two metro areas are much too expensive: a minimum buy in Duluth is nearly $4,000, and the minimum buy in the Twin Cities is $31,500. Moreover, the metro dailies do not reach many of your targeted voters. Fewer than 2,000 of those voters live within the circulation area of the Duluth newspapers, and an even smaller number live within the Twin Cities circulation area. Weekly newspapers, however, reach a wide number of voters in the district. The eight weekly papers reach an estimated 20,000 voters, ten times the number of voters reached by the metro papers. And the cost, of course, is far less. A minimum buy—one fairly large ad (27 column inches) in each paper every week for five weeks—is a total of $4,410.

Look at these numbers and take a couple of minutes to figure out what you would do in this situation. Remember, the campaign's total budget is $65,000. In general, you should plan on spending about 65 to 75 percent of your budget on direct voter contact, which is roughly $50,000. How would you spend that money?

Here's what actually happened. The bulk of the money for voter contact went to direct mail to the identified 10,000 persuadable voters (based on previous IDs and the voter file). Eight mailings equal 80,000 pieces, or about $40,000 of the $65,000 budget. The campaign's paid media program then aimed to augment this targeted direct mail with local paid media. Three weeks of decent radio coverage on all six stations cost $5,000. This was further supplemented with the relatively inexpensive weekly newspapers ads, which accounted for another $5,000 for a five-week run (one ad per week) in all eight weekly newspapers. In total, $50,000 was spent on direct voter contact and paid media, or 76.9 percent of the overall budget, and the campaign won both a contested primary and general election.

In this example, it wasn't worth it to make a significant investment in broadcast advertising. It was too expensive and too inefficient relative to other methods of voter contact. Since you always want to dominate one medium first before moving on to others, in this case you want to dominate direct mail, and then complement those contacts with limited radio and newspaper ads.

CHAPTER 8

Working with Reporters and Communicating Your Message through Earned Media

THROUGHOUT THIS BOOK, we focus on ways to contact voters with a clear and compelling message that motivates and persuades target audiences. Unfortunately, the campaign doesn't always control the message that voters hear. While the direct voter contact and broadcast advertising methods we have discussed—paid media, door-to-door, and phones—are critical to the success of a campaign, voters are also getting information from a third party: the news media. Despite the decline of traditional news sources, the press can still play a defining role in political campaigns. Good press coverage can turn unknown candidates into viable contenders, reinforce the campaign's message delivery through the authority of an "objective" source, and help the campaign gain legitimacy with base supporters and donors. Bad press, on the other hand, can torpedo even the most well-organized and well-financed campaign.

There are several reasons to pursue an aggressive media strategy. First, it's a low-cost way to get into the broadcast media and reach a larger group of target voters. Unlike television or radio ads or direct mail, getting a good story written in the newspaper doesn't require an expenditure of money. That's why you often hear about a campaign getting "earned media." Earned media has also been called "free media," but the reality is that a campaign has to work too hard to call it "free." Second, earned media lends credibility to a campaign. While it's essential that voters hear directly from a campaign at their doors, in the mail, and (depending on scale) in television and radio ads, voters also need to know that a candidate is legitimate and has a reasonable shot at winning. Good press coverage allows a campaign to say to voters, "Don't just take our word for it, read what others are saying about us." Third, good press coverage is important for keeping your base informed. When your supporters see articles about the campaign in newspapers or see television or radio news coverage of the campaign, it gives them a sense of progress and forward momentum. Active, progressive voters disproportionately read the paper and follow current events compared with other voters, and the better the campaign is doing, the more you are likely to recruit and retain volunteers and base supporters.

To see how a campaign uses earned media to maximize its exposure to a broad audience, consider the example of Rebecca Otto in Minnesota. A former school board member and state legislator, Otto ran for state auditor in 2006 against a well-known conservative incumbent. It was a busy year in Minnesota politics, with contested races for U.S. Senate, governor, attorney general, state auditor, secretary of state, and several Congressional seats. With so many races dominating headlines, Otto faced a huge challenge: how to convince voters, who were already overwhelmed with news about other races, to pay attention to the state auditor campaign, a boring-sounding job that most Minnesotans don't even understand. She was running against an incumbent, an additional disadvantage for someone running for an office most people don't know about. Complicating matters further, she was limited by state election law to spending just over $200,000, a tiny sum for a statewide race in a state of more than five million residents.

Otto understood that she needed to implement a highly aggressive earned media strategy that would increase her exposure while saving precious campaign resources. Using targeting data, her campaign identified the regions of the state where she needed to spend as much time as possible and created a schedule made up primarily of media visits, based largely on those targets. The campaign built the list at no cost by using an Internet directory of news outlets and building a spreadsheet from that data, which allowed them to match circulation figures with their targeting data to maximize their bang for the buck. Then they made appointments with as many newspapers and television and radio stations as possible. The key to those conversations, Otto told us, was to explain how the job of state auditor affected people's lives in a given community. "I localized everything," she said. "I would talk about what the state auditor actually does and what it means to Tracy, Minnesota, for example. Reporters often didn't know what to ask of a candidate for state auditor, so I needed to explain why this office is so important. People knew who I was because I had received media attention when I was in the legislature, but even people who liked me still needed to understand what a state auditor does and why the race was important to their own lives."

Otto understood the importance of knowing her audience. "I always had briefings on everything about the community I was going to," she said. "My staff would put together press clippings and do research on the key issues that were going on in the community. It made me more comfortable when I could walk into a newspaper office in a small Minnesota town and have a good understanding of what was happening in that town. I was true to my own style and I was confident in who I am, but it was so important to know my audience and be able to connect with them."

To maintain that connection after the visit was over, Otto's campaign paid a clipping service, a company that scours media outlets across the state looking for mentions of the candidate's name and sending the news clips to the campaign on a regular basis, to track the articles that were written about her visits, as well as those of her opponent. The campaign would then ask supporters in those communities to send letters to the editor addressing issues raised in those clips, in an effort to keep her name in the news. "The clipping service tracked what was going on," she said. "We could count how many 'hits' we got versus my opponent. We were able to measure our success and make adjustments where we needed to." Otto credits her extensive earned media coverage for putting her campaign in the minds of voters across the state. By Election Day, their success was clear: Otto won by 11 percentage points.

Rebecca Otto's strategy embodied a half dozen key characteristics of effective earned media work. First, by using targeting data to inform her schedule and choice of media outlets, she integrated her field plan into her earned media strategy. Second, she said no to going just anywhere, instead focusing her time talking to media in her target areas. Third, she got to know the communities she was traveling to and came to her interviews prepared. By doing her homework and having good briefing materials, she got local reporters interested in the race by drawing local connections. Fourth, her campaign was constantly looking for opportunities to get Otto's name in the newspapers and other media outlets. Fifth, her campaign kept track of every news story in which she appeared, giving them opportunities to extend the life of good stories or respond to any criticism she received. Finally, because she had such a limited budget for paid media, she was able to broadcast her message to her targeted voters through this earned media. For a statewide candidate like Rebecca Otto to show up in small, rural communities across the state was news in its own right. Simply showing up, demonstrating to a town or community that a candidate takes their concerns seriously enough to visit, is worthy of a news story.

Despite her success with earned media, Rebecca Otto would be the first to tell you that getting reporters to cover your campaign can be difficult, and that controlling the quality of that coverage is even more challenging. With the exception of very small markets, the sheer volume of news and information coming into most media outlets is overwhelming, making it very difficult to generate attention for any candidate or issue. When reporters do cover a candidate or a campaign, it can be difficult to control the outcome, resulting in a diluted or distorted message. Getting good press coverage therefore requires a lot of time and effort, and it requires presenting a clear contrast and simple message that is delivered consistently, backed up with examples relevant to the lives of voters in any given community. Campaigns that receive frequent earned media are persistent and, like Otto's, opportunistic. They have staff or volunteers who think every day, "What can we do today to move members of the media and get our message out?" Reporters are often wary of being used or gamed, and successful campaigns realize this. They know the reporters covering the campaign, and they understand that the best way to get a reporter to write a story is to give him or her a unique and newsworthy subject to cover from an angle that has an impact on the lives of their readers.

Building Relationships with Reporters

Getting consistently good press coverage often comes down to relationships. The relationship a candidate and campaign manager (or press secretary) builds with reporters and other members of the media determines, more than any other variable, the quality of coverage you will receive. Just as strong relationships with a broad range of people are crucial in moving voters and raising money, they are also important in a campaign's ability to deliver its message effectively through the media.

You can't build relationships with reporters unless you know who they are, so the first step is getting a list of reporters who will be covering your race. This is not difficult to find. Many states have media associations that publish listings of all press outlets in the state; look on the Internet or ask your party how to find such a list. Another resource could be other campaigns or a campaign you've previously worked on. Good campaigns add details to their lists, including not only phone numbers and e-mail addresses, but also information on deadlines and any other information that makes your interaction with that outlet more efficient and mutually beneficial (for example, it might include something like, "This reporter prefers e-mail to phone calls and is known to write unfriendly articles about progressive candidates"). One successful candidate for state senator, early in her campaign, assigned a volunteer to be her media liaison. "At the beginning of the campaign, I had a volunteer with a lot of computer skills and some spare time because he was between jobs," she told us. "He did an inventory of all the local newspapers in my district, including a couple that I didn't even know about. We kept in constant touch with these newspapers, sending them press releases and notices about my campaign appearances. Then we kept track of whether stories about me appeared in these papers, and it turned out that they did!" If you are running a smaller campaign, for school board or city council, for example, you may have only one or two reporters covering the race; you can find out by identifying the media outlets in your district and asking them who is assigned to your race. When the campaign begins to build relationships with individual reporters, update your media list to include any relevant notes about the reporter. By the end of a campaign, the media list should be a dog-eared and frequently referenced source of information.

Once you get a list of reporters, get in touch with them. While interacting with reporters can seem intimidating at first, most reporters are eager to have contacts on campaigns and are amenable to engaging in conversations with you. You should designate one person, in addition to the candidate, to interact with reporters. At the beginning of the campaign, the candidate (or, if it's a large campaign, the campaign manager or press secretary) should schedule an introductory visit with reporters, either at their place of work or over lunch, bringing a simple media packet containing a bio of the candidate or background on the issues, a photo, and relevant press clippings. "Most of my communications with reporters is done over e-mail," a communications director for a Congressional race told us. "But it's so important to sit across a coffee table with a reporter. The relationship is ten times better, really. Just having had that face-to-face time makes it so much more personal, and I feel a stronger connection, and a stronger obligation to doing what I can to help reporters get information, which in turn benefits me and my candidate in the long run."

Relationships with reporters are unique. As Dane Smith, a veteran political reporter who recently stepped down from the Minneapolis *Star Tribune* after thirty years, told us, "You really need to learn as much as you can about the media players you're dealing with. Read everything you can about what they've written and be able to talk to them about it. Don't be fawning; they'll see right through it. Be perceptive and intelligent about the work they've done, but don't go over the top." Campaign workers and candidates should also be careful not to tell reporters that they are a "perfect person to cover this race" or that they wrote a "really great story." As Smith says, "Reporters never like to be told by a campaign staffer, 'Hey, that was a great story,' or 'thanks for being on our side.' It just makes reporters cringe, it makes them feel that they did something wrong. If you really like a story they wrote, tell them you thought it was a fair story." It's a reporter's job to be objective, and if they feel like their coverage is perceived as favoring one side, they will compensate for it. Likewise, if you think a story was negative to your candidate or campaign, do not call up the reporter screaming; remember the adage that you will always lose the argument with someone who buys ink by the barrel. Certainly, if a reporter missed a big piece of the story, it is appropriate to call to discuss it. Yelling rarely (if ever) gets you the result you want, and can often damage a relationship that has the potential to help get your campaign's message out. Finally, in an era of twenty-four-hour news and online newspapers that print stories throughout the day, quick responsiveness is more important than ever. Give reporters all your contact information, especially how to reach you after hours and on weekends.

Keep in mind that your relationship is not just a one-way process. You want to get good stories from reporters, but you also have something to offer them; you are in a position of having knowledge that reporters want. If you have tidbits of information that you think they would find useful and that will help your campaign, even indirectly, pass them on to reporters. Sometimes you will have story ideas that might not even mention your candidate, but that could set up future stories that will include the candidate. For example, one press secretary told us that because affordable housing was a central theme of his candidate's campaign, he frequently alerted reporters about information related to the housing crisis in his district that could be turned into stories. In one instance, he told a reporter about an affordable housing study that was being released, giving the reporter a head start on finding an advanced copy of the study. The candidate's name never made it in the story, but the following day the campaign held a press event in response to the story.

Creating Story Opportunities

Keep in mind that in your interactions with reporters, you have one goal: creating positive news coverage for your campaign. Reporters understand that that's your role, and they'll expect you to try to pitch them stories. That means reporters are used to people like you calling them and e-mailing them all the time with ideas for stories. The busier these reporters are, the less amenable they will be to hearing you pitch your story. So always remember: if you want a reporter to run a good story about you, give him or her a story to tell. This sounds simplistic, but too often campaigns forget that they need to create news, not just recycle the campaign's message, if reporters are going to cover them.

Here are some things that reporters are likely to write about:

▸ **Campaign announcement.** You might make your formal campaign announcement months after you start running. Sometimes you can get two stories—when you first start running and when you formally announce. A formal announcement is a big event that requires a lot of planning, a crowd of volunteers, and a speech from the candidate that lays out the campaign's message and prevailing themes. Take advantage of this opportunity: it's the one time in the campaign when you have a free shot at conveying your message and your candidacy.

▸ **Campaign filing,** when you formally file for office. Most papers (and sometimes TV) list who has filed for various offices. Think about what gives you the most exposure. Maybe you want to be the first person to file, so you let reporters know that you'll be arriving very early in the morning to stand outside the secretary of state's office until it opens. Another option is to demonstrate your grassroots support by bringing a group of enthusiastic volunteers with you to file.

▸ **Profile story.** In most higher-visibility races a profile story will be written about each candidate. This is often your classic "puff" piece. Think very carefully about what information you want to pull together for background. What stories do you want the candidate to tell? What events do you want the reporter to go to? If TV is the medium, what visual do you want? Profile stories can also be suggested to a reporter when there is an interesting angle. For example, Debra Shore ran in 2006 for the Chicago Water Reclamation Board, a low-visibility race for a job that manages a billion plus budget and all of the water issues for Illinois. She had a $300,000 budget to reach the entire city of Chicago. She ran an aggressive grassroots campaign, often standing outside El stops early in the morning and talking with every citizen group imaginable. She could not afford paid media, so her campaign aggressively pursued earned media. She was also running for one of the most environmentally sensitive jobs as an environmentalist, a first for the office. Altogether this made for an interesting "hook"—the quirkiness of the race (its invisibility and the very, very aggressive grassroots nature of Shore's effort), that she was the first environmentalist to run for the office, and the connection between her name, Shore, and the Water Reclamation Board. Her campaign was able to get a large profile story in the paper with a full-page photo of the candidate standing on the shore of Lake Michigan. This spread came out a couple of weeks before the election and graced news boxes on street corners all over Chicago, invaluable exposure for a low-visibility race. She ended up winning a big upset victory.

▶ **Weekend before election.** Most races, particularly big ones, have a last-weekend-before-election story. Think of what last impressions you want to leave voters before they go to the polls. Here's a good example from the Midwest: a state legislative candidate had planned a big door-knocking weekend, but a huge snow storm dumped thirty-eight inches on his district just four days before Election Day. Instead of canceling the door-knock, he sent out a press release saying he was going ahead with his plans, but that he would be going around on his snowshoes. A television crew filmed the candidate trudging through the snow, knocking on people's doors. The same crew then filmed the incumbent state legislator sitting snowbound in his comfortable house, sipping brandy (a case in which the TV news practice of always having to cover the other candidate for balance was used to great advantage). The resulting news story was devastating for the incumbent, and probably cost him the election.

▶ **Primary election night.** The press will often cover primary election results even in races where there is no contested primary. If you are a candidate in a contested primary, think carefully about what your victory speech will be. What will be your one victory quote? If you are running for a high-profile office, you may get television news to carry your acceptance speech live. In that case, remember that the cameras will stay with you for only a few minutes, so be sure you deliver the right message during this time. Several years ago, a candidate for governor in Minnesota won a huge upset victory for party endorsement. The campaign timed his acceptance speech to coincide with the ten o'clock news, and all three network stations covered the speech live. Everything worked out perfectly, except that the candidate spent five minutes thanking a long list of campaign supporters and volunteers. The cameras actually cut away before he started addressing the crowd, costing the candidate a full five minutes of invaluable media exposure.

▶ **General election night.** You are guaranteed to get coverage on election night, win or lose. If you win, think about the message you want to deliver about how you will do your job. If you lose, what do you want to leave in voters' minds in case you decide to run again? A word of advice: do *not* make the decision on election night not to run again. You never know if you will run again, and you need to avoid statements like the famous "You won't have Nixon to kick around anymore."

Of course, reporters will also cover the issues of the campaign if the campaign can turn them into stories. "In my experience, reporters are really hesitant about going to 'campaign-y' events," the communications director for a Congressional campaign told us. "They don't want to feel like they're being used for a cheap publicity stunt. They want to report news. To these reporters, the fact that we got an endorsement from a group of first responders (firefighters, paramedics) is not really news. We tried to do press conferences around endorsements in the past, and reporters started to lose interest. So instead of sending out a media advisory saying we were getting an endorsement from first responders, we focused instead on the issue and sent out an advisory saying we were announcing our first responder plan. Once reporters arrived, they saw that not only were we announcing our plan, we were also receiving the endorsement, and we had dozens of uniformed first responders there to participate."

Holding Press Events

Press events can be an excellent method of showcasing a campaign's message and level of grassroots support. Press conferences and other events are great ways to demonstrate momentum, broad support, and focus, and they give the campaign a forum for speaking directly about its message. Events are particularly important for grassroots campaigns; they are a great volunteer activity, and if an event is well attended, it gives the impression of strength, which reporters note. But there is a risk to holding events. Just as a successful event will highlight a campaign's strength, a poorly attended or weak event can make the campaign look disorganized and unfocused. Unless you know you can pull off a good event and that the press will cover it, you should not have it. Also, if your candidate has any doubts about the event, is too tired, or for whatever reason is not ready for the event, don't do it. The candidate has to be ready to deliver.

When planning an event, there are three things to consider: content, location, and timing. The content of the event will determine whether the campaign should hold a press conference, a campaign announcement, or a rally. Regardless of the type of event, it should always be driven by the campaign's message. Once the decision to hold the event is made, the next step is to find a location and set a time. An ideal location is one that reinforces the message (a press conference on environmental issues held in a park, for example), is free of distractions and noise, and is easily accessible. Careful consideration should be given to the backdrop of the event: what will a photo of the speaker look like? Also remember that reporters don't want to sit through endless press conferences. If you hold an event with "regular people" or people who are impacted by the issue the campaign is focusing on, limit the number to one or two people. "You don't want a parade of speakers," Dane Smith told us. "Your events should be crisp and short."

The best time to hold an event is between 10:00 a.m. and 2:30 p.m., Monday through Thursday. If the event is scheduled too late in the day, television reporters will not have time to file stories before the nightly news. Mondays are not ideal press days because reporters are often busy catching up from the weekend. A Friday event will be reported in Saturday's newspaper, which is the least read news day. Sometimes Sundays work well because it is a slow news day and the late news on Sunday night is the most watched news night. The campaign should also find out if other events are scheduled for that day.

Once the location and time are set, the campaign should alert the media two or three days in advance (longer if prepublicity is an objective) by sending a media advisory to the campaign's press list and following up with phone calls. A media advisory is a simple, single paragraph that describes the purpose of the event and then lists the who, what, where, and when.

While it's simple, the language of an advisory is very important. As one press secretary told us, "An advisory needs to sound 'sexy' in some way. It needs to be somewhat exciting and inviting, and even somewhat mysterious. You don't want to give away what you're doing, but you don't want to be overly general. Don't say you're going to make a 'major announcement' unless it really is major. The bottom line is that you have to have an advisory that makes it seem like there's going to be news coming out of this event."

The key to a good advisory is that to be covered as news it has to be actual news. It is important for campaigns to understand what that means for many reporters and editors. One of the biggest problems is that often campaigns want news media to be their public relations firm—that's not their job. The campaign's task is to make the issues of the campaign news worth covering. If an issue is not news, or very important news, perhaps a press release, phone call, or visit with reporters will be more effective than a press event. Create a "news hook." Can we hook into an already existing news event (like a proposal for fair taxes on April 15)? Is it new? Different? Exciting? Visually interesting? Does it have significant impact or affect many people? Will there be a prominent person endorsing (a key elected official endorsing your candidate)? Is there potential conflict? Reporters love to cover conflict; often that is all that can get coverage. But conflict can also be used to leverage your campaign into another person's story by presenting a contrasting opinion or alternative explanation. Finally, gimmicks can work, but they can also backfire. Your candidate bungee jumping off a local bridge may get coverage, but is that the image you want to show? (Yes, this actually happened.) Always ask why your story is of interest to the larger community; that's your hook. Your hook can be local, regional, national, even international.

Ultimately, whether it's a media advisory or making sure the sound system works, a successful event depends on the campaign's attention to detail. Every aspect of the event should be carefully planned in advance. Think about the ideal headline and ideal picture you want on the news or in the paper the next day and plan your content and location accordingly. Early on, make a list of the five questions you hope will be asked and the five questions you want to avoid. Develop answers to these and practice the answers, and always bring the interview back to what the campaign wants to talk about. If the event will feature speakers from outside the campaign, they should be given clear instructions on the content and length of their remarks. If a speaker is not familiar with the campaign message, he or she should receive a briefing and talking points from the campaign and should be aware of what your opponent might say in response to your event, because a good reporter will call your opponent. Having good self and opposition research is key to this process. Other details include setting up a good sound system, having contingency plans for outdoor events in case of rain, using well-placed visual aides like banners and signs, and preparing press packets to hand out at the event. In addition to containing background information, press clippings, and photos, these packets also include a press release that reporters can refer to when filing stories.

A press release is a short summary of the news that the campaign is trying to create. Ideally no more than a page in length, a press release can be handed out at an event or it can be sent out to reporters as a way to make news or comment on a story. To the extent possible, a release should read like a mini news story, as the campaign would want it to appear in the next morning's paper. It contains a headline that catches the eye, a lead paragraph that clearly summarizes the campaign message, quotes from the candidate or campaign spokesperson, and any relevant data or statistics that bolster the message. Utility is the key to a good press release: a reporter should be able to use the release as a quick and clear reference while writing a story. The release should be factually accurate (with citations for any data provided), grammatically correct, and free of typos. Keep press releases short and to the point. A press release from Rebecca Otto's campaign for state auditor, reproduced on the next page, is a good example of a release that gets to the point and draws a clear contrast with the opponent.

FOR IMMEDIATE RELEASE
July 12, 2006

Contact: Rebecca Otto   phone (111) 222-3333
name@email.com

Rebecca Otto files to run for State Auditor

REBECCA OTTO'S FIGHTING TO GET PROPERTY TAXES DOWN;
HER OPPONENT HAS DRIVEN PROPERTY TAXES UP
"THIS RACE IS ABOUT PROPERTY TAXES AND COMPETENCE," SAYS REBECCA OTTO

SAINT PAUL – The DFL Party-endorsed candidate for State Auditor spoke to supporters today after filing papers declaring her candidacy.

"This race is about property taxes and competence," said Rebecca Otto. "I'm fighting to get property taxes back down and strengthen your home town. My opponent has worked to drive them up and to weaken your community. That's the difference between us, and we've got the charts to prove it. If you want lower property taxes and a stronger community, vote for me. If you want more tax hikes and service cuts, vote for my opponent."

Otto said she also has "serious concerns" about the "series of major errors" coming out of the State Auditor's office lately. "She's been making dozens of accounting errors in her reports, and she's taken no responsibility for them," said Otto. "It's the State Auditor's job to *catch* errors. And then there's the stolen laptops."

PROPERTY TAX HIKES AND WEAKENED LOCAL COMMUNITY FINANCES

Otto says the current State Auditor was the first to propose the deep cuts to local communities that have driven property taxes up sharply. "There's simply no question about it – the cuts to local government correspond almost dollar for dollar to the $2.1 billion in new property taxes."

Otto says that by contrast she has proposed property tax reform that would bring property taxes down and strengthen local community finances by restoring property tax relief such as Local Government Aid, which was cut at the suggestion of the current State Auditor. "Our families cannot afford the ramp up that we are on with property taxes. As Auditor, I will fight for good policy at the state and federal level that moves us away from this direction."

ERRORS

The State Auditor's office has made several serious errors lately, ranging from accounting errors in major financial reports, to the theft of three laptops containing sensitive personal identity information from the State Auditor's office. "You could say that's just bad luck – if the same thing hadn't happened a month before," said Otto. "It's the pattern of not addressing these problems or taking responsibility that concerns me. It's not prudent management."

###

Rebecca Otto's press release announcing her campaign for state auditor in Minnesota is a good example of how to incorporate contrast into a positive message. Otto had to make the case that the current auditor needed to be fired, while at the same time establishing herself as the best person to take over the job. In just a page, she effectively summarizes the core message of her campaign.

Staying on Message

A highlight of our campaign trainings is a crisis simulation in which participants play the role of candidate or campaign spokesperson and the trainers
play the role of reporters. In addition to being a lot of fun (especially for
the trainers, who get to ask all the tough questions), the exercise provides a
lot of teaching moments. One of the first things our participants say after
the simulation is, "I didn't expect to be so nervous and put on the spot."
But that's the way interacting with the media can be, even for experienced
campaign spokespeople. It's normal to be a little nervous, but you want to
project confidence, speak fluently about the issues, and above all, stay on
message. In the following pages we describe some strategies for interacting
with reporters.

Pivot

Try to pivot back to your message whenever possible. This is probably the
hardest thing for a candidate or spokesperson to do. Ultimately, what you
are trying to do is answer the question that you want to be asked, not the
question that was actually asked, without being overly evasive. Remember,
you have precious few chances to deliver your message to a broad audience,
and you want them to hear your message on your terms, not the terms of a
reporter asking tough questions. This is best explained through examples.

The first is from the 2008 presidential election. When John Edwards of-
ficially announced his candidacy, he went to New Orleans to highlight the
major theme of his campaign, that he was committed to bridging the gap
between the "two Americas." The Edwards campaign timed the announcement between Christmas and New Year's Eve of 2006, a traditionally slow
news period. The announcement dominated the news for two days, in part
because Edwards deftly answered tough questions from reporters and kept
pivoting back to his central message. Here's an excerpt of an interview he
gave with CNN on the day of his announcement:

> CNN: You talk about two Americas, it's a populist message, but you're
> a real rich guy. We have some pictures of a house you're building near
> Chapel Hill, three-million-dollar mansion. That image, when it's jux-
> taposed with an effort to work with the poor . . . look at that, it's a big
> house. . . . Is that image a hard thing to get around for you as you try
> to make this appeal, that you're a man of the people, of poor people?

EDWARDS: Well first of all, I'm glad you like my house. You know, I've been very lucky in my life. I've always said that I've had everything that you can have in this country. It's not where I come from; it's not the place where my life started. I started in a very different place; actually I joke with everybody about being the son of a mill worker, because everybody's heard that so much they're sick of it now. The truth is there's a lot of good to be done about the two different Americas that exist in this country today, a vivid example of which you can see here in New Orleans. And instead of just talking about the problem and complaining about it, I want to see us actually do something about it. In the last couple years, we actually got the minimum wage raised in six states; we've made college available to kids who were willing to work for it. We've gotten workers organized around the country so they could earn a decent wage. All of these are efforts to try to bridge some of the divide that still exists in this country. I think there's a lot left to do.

Notice that Edwards brushes the question aside quickly by joking about it ("I'm glad you like my house") and then immediately returns to his message about the two Americas. He's not defensive about being wealthy, nor does he dwell on the central question, which is whether he's really qualified to talk about poverty. Instead, he demonstrates his commitment to ending the gap between the rich and poor by focusing on the actions that need to be taken.

Here's another example, this one from Paul Wellstone in his 2002 reelection campaign. This is also an interview with CNN, done just after Wellstone announced that he would vote against the resolution authorizing the war in Iraq. It was a huge political risk, with observers in Minnesota speculating that Wellstone's career was over. The message of Wellstone's campaign was "You can count on Paul to fight for you," a theme that is present in this exchange, even if he doesn't use those words. Notice how he turns a question about politics back to his fundamental message, which is that he would always do what he thought was right for Minnesota, even if it meant taking bold stands on issues.

CNN: Senator, you've come out and you said you will vote against this resolution authorizing the president's use of force in Iraq. How difficult a decision was that, and are you going to pay a political price back in Minnesota?

WELLSTONE: It's a difficult decision because it's a question of life and death. Minnesota's sons and daughters could be in harm's way. With that kind of decision you talk to a lot of people you respect, you think deeply about it, and then you make an intellectually honest and personally honest decision. So it was difficult for that reason. And on the political consequences? I don't honestly know. I think if I had come to the floor of the Senate and uttered words I didn't believe in or voted for something that I was really against, well I couldn't do that. So I think that it's always better to make the decision that you honestly believe in, and I'll leave it up to the people of Minnesota and what they think.

Here's the important thing to remember about pivoting: unless you have a strong message, you'll have nothing to pivot back to. These and other examples of effective pivoting have in common that they have an anchor—the message—to which they can always return. One candidate we spoke to described it this way: "Once you really have your message down by heart, you've practiced it, you believe in it, then it becomes like a magnet. Every time someone tries to throw you off balance, you just get pulled back to that magnet."

Finally, we're not suggesting that you ignore questions that are asked of you. Voters see through that, too. If you get a question about a controversial issue that you'd like to avoid, you need to be clear, but brief, about your position. For example, if you're running for state legislature in a conservative-leaning district and you get a question about whether gays and lesbians should have the right to marry, voters deserve to know your position on that issue. If you are in favor of marriage equality, here's one way to answer that question:

You know, we have a huge set of challenges facing our district, starting with the failure of our current state representative to create jobs with living wages and make health care more affordable. I don't believe the state should spend its time telling two people in a loving relationship that their love and commitment is inferior to anyone else's, so I have no problem with marriage equality. I suppose it's not surprising that Representative Smith would want to talk about this issue, since he sure doesn't want to talk about the things that matter most to the people of our district, like our rising cost of living and unaffordable health care, which keep going up despite Representative Smith's election-year promises.

With this answer, you are keeping the focus on your contrast with your opponent and on your message, but you're still answering the question. And you do want to answer the question. It's important that voters see a candidate taking a position and being clear about it. However, you should also be strategic about what you emphasize. We're not suggesting you run away from your positions on issues; in fact, we think voters reward candidates who take clear stands on issues even if they are unpopular. But remember that you have a message, and your number one priority is to deliver it to voters. You don't want to spend the majority of your time talking about something that isn't part of your message.

Note also the importance of language in this example. Instead of using the term "gay marriage," which is a conservative frame that makes homosexuality, not equal rights, the focus, it is referred to as marriage equality. "Marriage equality" is far different from "gay marriage" in the message it conveys. The equality argument—or a similar frame, "freedom to marry"— invokes principles that most Americans value. Equality and freedom are core American beliefs, and by rejecting the frame of "gay marriage" and evoking the rights of all citizens to pursue their freedom of equality, the message is more compelling.

Practice

Practice makes you better at every aspect of campaigning, but particularly at interacting with the press. The more you repeat your message and familiarize yourself with ways to answer tough or unexpected questions, the more likely you will be to remain calm and confident when you're talking to reporters. That's why we always tell candidates to role-play with a trusted member of their campaign team. Think of all the questions you might get, and start walking through your responses. Have the other person time your responses and give immediate and honest feedback. Talk through how you could have given a different answer, and then role-play it again. We can't emphasize this enough: keep at it. Ask the most difficult questions you can think of, and practice each one until you feel totally confident of your answers.

Be Careful about Going off the Record

As a general rule, every time you are talking to a reporter, he or she can quote you. That is always the assumption unless you and the reporter specifically and verbally confirm that your comments will not be used in a story.

The graveyard of political careers is full of candidates who made offhand or throwaway remarks that ended up appearing in the newspaper or on TV the next day. This often happens when candidates or campaign spokespeople assume they can trust reporters and let their guard down while talking to them. Whenever you talk to reporters or see them at events, you should always have in the back of your mind this thought: every word I say could appear on the front page of tomorrow's newspaper.

There are some instances when you have reason to give a reporter some information that you do not want to say publicly but that you think is important for the reporter to hear. In those instances—and if you don't have much experience working with the press, these should be rare instances—you want to clarify and have confirmed that you are speaking "off the record." For example, you say, "Let me tell you a couple things off the record, OK?" Before going ahead, make sure you get a verbal agreement from the reporter that it is off the record. Then continue: "Everything I'm about to say is off the record, and I will tell you when we're going back on the record, OK?" Again, get confirmation from the reporter. And continue, "OK, off the record, here's some background information that you might want to know about . . ." Notice that you have said three times that the statement is off the record, and you've received verbal confirmation twice. The reason that we sound so paranoid about going off the record is that you should be paranoid, too. We've seen too many people burned (and we've been burned ourselves) by sloppy interactions with the press that result in terrible stories. In general, always assume that you are on record.

Never Lie

This is a simple one. Don't ever lie. It will come back to haunt you later on, and once you lie to a reporter and people find out about it, your credibility is shot. In addition to being unethical, telling lies, even small ones that a reporter will not likely discover, puts your campaign at an unnecessary risk. If you have to lie to win an election, you shouldn't win.

Here's one good way to avoid lying: admit it when you don't know. Usually lies to reporters start innocently. You get a question that you don't know how to answer, but you're worried that if you say you don't know, you will lack credibility. Don't fall into that trap. You are not expected to have the answers to every question a reporter asks you. If you don't know, just say it: "Well, I actually don't know the answer to that. Let me find out and I'll call you back within the hour. Is that OK?" Reporters are pretty forgiving when you are up front with answers like that. Ultimately, what matters to them is getting the story, not whether you know every answer. Go find the answer and get back to the reporter in a timely way. One note of caution: if you are a candidate, reporters might be less forgiving, particularly when you are asked a values question such as your position on abortion.

Constantly Look for Opportunities

One of the biggest challenges of working with the media is finding opportunities to get stories written about the campaign. While the type of event that will work for your campaign depends on the dynamics of the campaign and the reporters in your district, one way to be proactive about press opportunities is to think early in the campaign about what issues you want to highlight. Reporters tend to cover substantive issues, particularly when they are accompanied by news hooks. We mentioned the example of the campaign that used the announcement of its plan for first responders as an opportunity to announce the endorsement by a first responders group. There are countless other examples of issues that can be used in similar ways, whether it's health care or foreign policy. When the campaign is against an incumbent, use the incumbent's record on the key issues to stage press events that both attack his or her record and announce what your candidate would do differently.

If possible, try to have a theme every week, with either a press event or a press release to reinforce that theme, but make sure that each week's theme connects with the campaign's overall message. Too often what results is a campaign that has a buffet of proposals and plans and themes, none of which adds up to a coherent whole or a crisp and clear message about the candidate. One gubernatorial candidate launched a multiweek thematic earned media program. One week was health care for seniors. Another was higher tuition costs. Another week was the growing crime problem. Still another was on the environment and renewable energy. What ended up was a laundry list of issue themes without any message. Like pivoting, each theme must always return to the core message of the campaign.

Use anniversaries, holidays, and significant events to tie in an announcement or event. For example, one week the theme might be prescription drugs. To figure out the timing of your announcement of a prescription drug plan, find out if there are any other upcoming events on which you could piggyback—Congressional hearings, the release of a report on prescription drugs, the anniversary of the day that the original Medicare bill was passed—

and schedule several activities during that week, whether it's a press event at a senior center, a send-off for a busload of seniors heading to Canada to get lower-priced drugs, or a radio ad on the issue. Then use this event to return to the campaign's overall message. Plan these press hits in advance, keeping in mind that the chaos of a campaign might force you to be flexible with your timing. Having a series of good press opportunities "in your pocket," ready to go when you need them, will save you hassle and time when the campaign heats up. It will also help you get ready for attacks from your opponent.

Be Ready to React

We spoke with several press secretaries and communications directors and asked what advice they would give about staying on message. A consistent response was the importance of being ready to respond quickly to your opponent's activities and attacks. "Fifty percent of the time, we're reacting to our opponent," one told us. "When we're ready with a response—we know what the opponent is saying, we have enough research to be able to pull together a response, and we move quickly—we are often able to turn his attacks into net positives for us. It drives the other campaign crazy when we get better press than they do even when they're attacking us."

Another press secretary told us about a time when the opposing candidate, who had struggled to gain any media traction during the summer months of the campaign, announced on a Tuesday afternoon that she was going to release her plan for reforming the Federal Emergency Management Agency (FEMA) the following morning. When the press secretary learned about this announcement, he pulled together the campaign's research on FEMA and called members of constituency groups who were advising the campaign on emergency management issues. They created their own plan for FEMA, which turned out to be far more comprehensive than the opposition's. The following morning, before the opponent's press conference, the campaign released its FEMA plan. The maneuver enraged the opponent and led her campaign to accuse the opposition of dirty tricks. That evening on the news and in the next day's newspaper, the press covered the story with such headlines as "Candidates announce plans for FEMA" and showed clips and quotes from the opponent complaining about the other side getting a head start. In the end, the story became a net loser for her campaign and reinforced a perception among reporters that the progressive campaign was better organized and more aggressive than its opposition.

One of the most common questions we get from our participants is how aggressively a campaign should respond to attacks. After all, if you respond to every attack, aren't you just giving credibility to the issue and drawing attention to it? Moreover, if you respond to an attack the media isn't interested in, you may turn a nonstory into a story about the back-and-forth. These are decisions that have to be made on a case-by-case basis. Some attacks are indeed not worth responding to, either because they have no credibility with the press or your constituents or because they don't reach many people. But in general, attacks that go unanswered can have a corrosive effect on the campaign and give the impression that the attacks are true. We all know about the Kerry campaign's failure to respond to the Swift Boat attacks, but similar examples abound in local and state races. One campaign manager of a race in California told us, "When the mudslinging began, other candidates began to circulate nasty pamphlets about our candidate. All this literature was full of half-truths, lies, and misrepresentations. Because my candidate viewed these slights to his character as unfair and petty, he saw little need to respond to them in kind. We, as a campaign, did not publicly point out the hypocrisies of the other candidates. Nor did we extend ourselves to respond to such ridiculous behavior in a supposedly friendly race. During this campaign, I learned that a good defense is the best offense, and that any candidate must anticipate the future actions of his or her opponents, no matter how lowly, and be prepared to respond."

Get Your Sleep

As hard as you will be working on the campaign, you have to remember to get plenty of rest, particularly when you are going to talk to reporters. The most common mistakes are made when a candidate or spokesperson is over-tired and gets careless. "When you go to an interview with the media and you're not 100 percent, don't walk in the door," Rebecca Otto told us. "If you walk in haggard and not making sense, you're not doing yourself a favor. I found that five interviews in one day was the absolute maximum I could do. Even when I had the opportunity to do more and thought that I could keep going, I always put a limit at five." Even if you're not doing that many media interviews in one day, put your own limits around how much and when you talk to reporters. If you have had a long day of door-knocking and you arrive home to a message from a reporter but are too tired to give the best answer possible, find out if you can wait until the next morning. If the reporter is on deadline, that might not be an option, but whenever possible, do the interviews in the right frame of mind.

Be Ready for a Crisis

Even the best campaign plans can't always anticipate a crisis, but usually the extent to which a crisis affects the campaign depends not on the crisis itself but the campaign's response to it. Crises are common—something from the candidate's past suddenly makes news, the candidate makes a stupid remark and needs to explain it, a campaign aide files a campaign finance report incorrectly. There is an endless number of ways that campaigns can screw up, and it's impossible to anticipate all of them. But you can be prepared with a few things in mind. First, if you made a mistake, take responsibility. The best way to kill a bad story about a mistake the campaign made is to own up to it forthrightly and move past it. You might have to endure a day or two of bad press, but ultimately you want the story to go away as quickly as possible. As you should know from following national politics, it's not the mistake that brings politicians down, it's the cover-up. Second, be careful not to affirm a statement by denying it. For example, if you get a question like, "Are you a slumlord?" (this is a real question we heard asked of a candidate), do not respond with "No, I am not a slumlord." Why? Because imagine the headline the next day: "Candidate Jones: 'I am not a slumlord!'" It's like Nixon saying "I'm not a crook." By repeating the negative statement, we affirm it. The better answer to the slumlord question is simply, "Absolutely not" and then pivot back to your message. Third, relax. Stay focused on what you need to say and remember to pivot back to your message. Flustered and nervous candidates send signals to the press that they should keep pursuing the story.

Finally, avoid distracting attacks, like calling your opponent a liar. Even if true, hot words can often come off as over the top and not credible. In a recent mayoral race the incumbent mayor, who had previously pledged not to run for reelection on multiple occasions, announced his run at the last minute and launched an attack on the public employees union as a key reason for deciding to run. In the announcement the mayor made numerous charges, most of which could not be substantiated, about ongoing tough negotiations. The local union responded with a press conference that opened by calling the mayor a liar. This was what led every story. What was lost was the long history of the mayor's inaction at resolving the issue, his history of rather bizarre and inappropriate behavior in the past, and his own credibility for reneging on his multiple promises not to run. The satisfaction of calling the person out got in the way of delivering a much more effective message.

The most important thing in responding to a crisis is quickly assessing your options and then getting all decision makers or people who might interact with the media on exactly the same page about what your response will be. Once you've decided on your response, with carefully chosen words and an idea of what questions you will or will not answer, you should hold the line, regardless of the pressure you feel. You will feel like you're under siege, and the bad headlines or news reports will make you think about doing or saying something different, hoping that if you changed your line you could shut the story down. In all but the very rare case, this instinct is exactly the wrong approach. First, the "crisis" is likely barely registering with voters, no matter how horrendous it seems to you. Second, campaigns turn little bad things into very big bad things when they drip out new pieces of information, new excuses for something they did wrong.

The best thing you can do to end a crisis is to deprive it of oxygen. After all, your opponent and the media don't usually have access to new information to keep a story going. Only you do. You can be your own best friend or own worst enemy at these points in a campaign. There are situations where you may need to change your strategy in the midst of a crisis, but it should be done with great care. Either way, it is critical that everyone, especially the candidate, has bought into the strategy and sticks to it when they're in public or talking to the media.

Delivering Your Message on the Opinion Page

Another great way for a campaign to deliver an unfiltered message is through "opinion media," including letters to the editor, commentary and editorials, talk radio appearances, and more. By enlisting grassroots supporters in the effort to gain earned media, the campaign expands the base of people active and engaged on an issue or with a candidate, expands its reach, and develops its capacity to respond to opponents with speed and accuracy. When recruiting volunteers and enlisting supporters, a campaign should always ask people to become a part of its rapid response network. Guided by the campaign's overall press strategy, a rapid response network is a structured way to target media outlets, place letters to the editor and guest columns in newspapers, monitor talk radio for mentions of the campaign or issue, and strike back when attacked.

Letters to the Editor

Although they have a short shelf life, letters to the editor can be an effective media tool. The best letters are short and pithy. Recruiting people throughout the state or district who are willing to write letters should be central to the campaign's media strategy. These guidelines can help ensure that the campaign gets the most out of its letter-writing strategy:

▸ Designate a letters-to-the-editor coordinator. It is a perfect job for a key volunteer. This person is responsible for tracking stories in all relevant newspapers, contacting letter writers in each area (these letter writers should already have been identified by the field staff), and sending them examples of letters.

▸ Distribute talking points and sample letters that people can use as a guide so letters stay on message.

▸ Identify volunteers who are willing to sign letters or write them on their own.

▸ Encourage local supporters, opinion leaders, and local elected officials to write letters on the campaign's behalf.

▸ Always include the letter writer's name, address, and signature (unless sending the letter via e-mail).

▸ Keep the letter short and to the point. The best letters to the editor are concise, written in the first person, and compelling. Of course, they also reinforce the campaign's message.

▸ Keep them coming. Papers will not always print every letter, but they will publish letters in proportion to those they receive. A steady flow is important.

Letters to the editor are a frequently read section of any newspaper, particularly those in smaller communities. A letter-writing effort that mobilizes a large number of people, comes across as authentic, and stays on message is an invaluable asset to any campaign.

Here is an example of a good letter to the editor, from a newspaper in Oregon:

Having been a World War II prisoner of war, I can say it was a frightening and bitterly humiliating experience. We did not know from day

to day what the Germans had in store for us. The torture of prisoners
is reprehensible and only sinks us to the level of the terrorists. Vice
President Cheney's reasoning puts our troops in danger.

This is short, personal, and directly to the point.

It's not only the quality, but also the quantity, of letters to the editor that
can make a difference. When possible, flood a newspaper with letters. Even
if they don't publish every one, the more they get, the more likely they will
be to publish at least one, if not several. You never know when you might
have the kind of success that a candidate for school board had in Billings,
Montana. In two successive days, Kathy Kelker's supporters dominated the
Billings *Gazette*'s letters pages, with headlines like, "School Board needs
members such as Kelker"; "Kelker shows passion for helping children"; "Vote
for Kelker to move School Board forward." You might not know anything
about the race for school board in Billings, but you do know just from reading the letters to the editor that Kathy Kelker has a lot of support in the
community and her campaign has momentum.

Op-Eds and Editorials

Op-eds are a great way for your campaign to deliver your message in a substantive way. Depending on the newspaper, campaigns can expect a paper
to run at least one, and sometimes several, op-eds during the course of the
campaign. The characteristics of a good op-ed are the same as a letter to the
editor, but op-eds are an opportunity to extend the argument. Use op-eds
as an opportunity to explain your position on an issue rather than give a
laundry list of reasons to support your candidacy. Just as you would piggyback a press event to other things that are in the news, use op-eds to seize
on a news story that fits into your overall campaign message. Keep it short
and succinct (usually not more than 650 words), and when you get the op-ed
published, keep it alive by reproducing it and sending it to your supporters
and ask them to write letters to the editor in support of the piece.

Editorials are the positions taken by a newspaper after deliberation by
their editorial board. Your candidate should meet at least once with the
editorial boards of newspapers in your district. Be prepared. Editorial writers ask tough, substantive questions and are often more likely to delve into
policy details than other reporters. Do your homework, and come prepared
not only with clear and concise messages, but with background material,
facts and figures, and the ability to respond to your opposition's arguments.

Think of this meeting as an informal press conference and apply the rules for interacting with reporters.

Talk Radio

Another way to get earned media is to call in to radio talk shows. Almost every community has at least one radio station with talk shows that incorporate listener call-ins. While these shows tend to be conservative, talk radio offers a way to deliver a campaign's message directly to listeners and voters. Just as the campaign recruits letter writers, so should it ask its rapid response members to listen to talk radio and call in with comments. A few things to keep in mind when thinking about how to utilize talk radio:

- ▸ Recruit volunteers to monitor (and call into) radio shows for discussions that mention the campaign or candidate. Use your constituent groups to your advantage, and enlist their help: when they hear something relevant, they should alert the campaign and call in and comment.

- ▸ Monitor when the campaign's opponent will be on a radio show and get the rapid response network to call in and ask him or her questions that you want asked.

- ▸ Record your opponents' appearances so you have them on record for later use.

- ▸ Make sure when the candidate or campaign spokesperson is on the radio that the campaign has lined up a large number of supporters to call in, thereby decreasing opportunities for the opponent's supporters to get through.

For many progressives, listening to conservative talk shows is about as enjoyable as listening to fingernails on a chalkboard. Yet we ignore talk radio at our own expense: studies show that many talk radio listeners are independents who are, in fact, open to hearing other views, and we miss an opportunity to deliver a message when we forgo calling in to talk radio shows.

Targeting Bilingual, Specialty, and Community Press

With all the attention paid to securing earned media in larger markets, campaigns sometimes overlook smaller media outlets. As Rebecca Otto's example illustrates, this is a missed opportunity. The smaller, weekly papers that became a focus of Otto's campaign ended up carrying her message to a large number of voters. Small papers are far more likely to run stories about your campaign (they are often actively searching for stories to cover) and frequently will publish a campaign's press release verbatim in the paper and treat it like a news story. This is a great opportunity to deliver an unfettered, unfiltered message to your voters. Take advantage of it! Having a presence in smaller media outlets is important not only for issue campaigns and local candidates, but also for those running in Congressional or statewide races. Smaller outlets include ethnic and bilingual media, as well as media serving specific constituencies such as labor, disability or faith communities, and neighborhoods. It includes newspapers, radio (AM and FM), cable TV, and some Internet formats.

In many larger cities there are independent newspapers that focus on certain ethnic communities, including African Americans, Asian Americans, Native Americans, or Latinos. These might also include newspapers for immigrant communities, some of which publish exclusively in English or in the native language of the reader. Other publications are bilingual. Bilingual publications are especially prevalent in the Latino and African immigrant communities. In the Minneapolis–Saint Paul metropolitan area, for example, there are three newspapers for the African immigrant community, three for the Spanish-speaking community, and one publication written exclusively in Russian.

These media outlets are eager to interact with political candidates and issue campaigns, especially if the candidate or campaign is relevant to them. They will publish photos, stories, interviews, notification of appearances, and paid political advertising. In addition to newspapers, there is a growing number of small commercial Spanish-language radio stations. One can also usually find community radio and cable TV stations with programs for almost any community in a given media market. Radio and cable TV may be a crucial way of communicating with new voters and new immigrants.

Other forms of specialty media include faith-based publications, newspapers for people with disabilities, neighborhood newspapers, and union newspapers. All of these reach a targeted audience, and many are eager to get the word out about progressive issues and candidates. As in so many other arenas, building relationships is the key to working with ethnic and specialty media. This can be very important in building name or issue recognition, mobilizing underrepresented constituencies, and creating a sense of excitement and enthusiasm. It also helps in negotiating favorable advertising rates.

As we discussed in chapter 5, on base building, the person responsible for organizing a certain community should get to know the publishers, producers, and writers for all the specialty and bilingual press outlets targeted at that community.

Blog Outreach

In the past few years, blogs (Web logs) have become a growing source of political information and are now objects of earned media outreach for a campaign. Just as with traditional media, identify the major political and progressive blogs in your district, city, and state and try to assess, with the help of your supporters, their impact on the race. Start with the major state-based blogs; don't focus on just getting a DailyKos front-page story (which is almost as difficult as getting the *New York Times* to cover you). Media tend to pick up stories from those before the smaller, more obscure ones, so find the more local blogs that reach your target audience faster, while researching which national blogs may be interested in your race, especially if it is a federal or gubernatorial campaign. That way, when you get good polling information or other notable news to share, you can get it to the right person. (Polling information can be fed to Political Wire, Politics1, and Pollster.com, and they write about it more than the daily papers do).

Also, find out if there are any major bloggers who live in your district (you can use LeftyBlogs and Technorati to figure this out). Give them the same access you give to the media (press release distribution list, invitations to interviews, etc.), and give them exclusives, too. Bloggers tend to be a cross between a supporter and a reporter. Treat them well, but don't ignore their reporter instincts and need for a good scoop. Campaigns should reach out to bloggers: don't just send them press releases; provide them with exclusive feeds or interviews with the candidate. Be professional and be truthful if you are blogging and working on a campaign. Always disclose your relationship to the campaign when you post on blogs, or someone will call you on it. Finally, don't bother reaching out to hostile bloggers; that will likely be used against you.

CHAPTER 9

Raising Money and Knowing How to Spend It

In talking to dozens of candidates and campaign managers about what they would say to people just starting their campaigns, there was one thing that nearly every one of them told us: don't underestimate the importance of raising money. Raising the resources you need to win is fundamental to your success. It allows you to implement the plan you so carefully crafted: base building, field organizing, direct mail, visibility, paid media, and your other voter contact tactics. Of course volunteers are also important to the success of a campaign, but even a volunteer organization costs something. Every campaign needs to raise money and should designate at least one person to be in charge of fundraising, a paid or volunteer finance director.

Kathy Hartman, who raised over one-third more money than her incumbent opponent in her successful bid for Jefferson county commissioner in Colorado, told us, "The sad reality is that money matters. Unless you get the money, you will not succeed." While recognizing that money plays far too great a role in campaigns, progressive candidates should look at fundraising as an extension of their organizing and direct voter contact work. Raising money the right way—with gifts from major donors and PACs, along with grassroots fundraising from low- and medium-dollar donors, while using fundraising to build the campaign's base—provides the campaign with necessary resources and allows your supporters at all income levels to have a part in the campaign's financial success. Whether it is for radio and TV ads, direct mail, or campaign literature for lit drops, more money means more direct voter contact.

Your fundraising goals flow from the campaign plan and budget. You first need to figure out what it takes to win, then figure out how much that strategy costs, and then develop the fundraising plan to raise the necessary funds for the budget.

The Importance of the Campaign Budget

The budget is a tool for managing the campaign, avoiding unnecessary expenditures, and keeping focused. It reflects the strategic and tactical choices you made in the plan and can be an effective fundraising tool: "We need to raise _____ dollars in order to do _____ activities. Can we count on you to help?" Remember when we talked about the importance of planning in chapter 2? The campaign plan is a "buy-in document," a written agreement on how the campaign will be implemented. The plan establishes a shared understanding of how the campaign will spend its scarce resources. The budget serves the same function. In effect, a budget is simply your campaign plan in the form of numbers. It is a blueprint for making the spending decisions that correspond with the strategic choices outlined in your plan.

Budgets help you to say no to unnecessary expenditures. Everyone, from your kitchen cabinet to your volunteers and especially your candidate, will have ideas for how to spend money, whether it's on more staff, brochures in multiple languages, or cell phones, new computers, bumper stickers, bobblehead dolls, or lawn signs. A budget, once agreed on, is a way to make strategic decisions about which of these expenses are most critical, what trade-offs are involved in making them, and how to control the impulse to make expenditures that do not contribute to achieving the win number. In that sense, it's a great management tool that allows a campaign manager to say to that vocal member of your kitchen cabinet who insists that you *have* to buy two thousand books of matches with the candidate's picture on them: "Here's the budget that we agreed to at the beginning of the campaign. This is consistent with our plan, and it maximizes the resources so we can talk to as many voters as possible. Tell me what you would cut from the budget so we can buy matches." If you are a campaign manager, you might be surprised by how often someone will come to you with a new idea that requires spending money. Since you don't want to discourage your staff and volunteers from being creative and coming up with new ideas, it's better to know whether the new idea is worth the extra expense (sometimes it is) or to explain why the idea doesn't fit into the plan than it is to simply say no to someone without a clear explanation of why.

Your budget is both an expense and income document broken down for the duration of the campaign. This is particularly important for managing cash flow. There are generally two times when you need as much money in the bank as possible: before a campaign finance report deadline and just before the election. The campaign finance report is a crucial indicator of a campaign's fundraising success. Some campaigns make headlines with how much money they raise, but the key number to look at is cash on hand. Campaigns that manage their budgets well have significant cash on hand to report. If possible, hold off on making big expenditures until after the reporting period is over, using your budget as a guide. You also want to make sure that while you have enough money at the end of the campaign to pay the bills, you don't want to have too much money left over. One campaign manager of a state Senate race told us that his biggest mistake was not writing a budget. "As a result," he told us, "we had $5,000 in the bank on Election Day. That's a huge amount of money for a state Senate candidate. Had a proper budget been planned in advance, we would have had a plan to spend the money, rather than placing last-minute advertisements in the local papers." Another candidate we spoke to who ran for city council ended up losing his race with $2,000 left in the bank, which he had intended to use to run for mayor two years later, if he had won the council seat. A general rule of thumb is that along with planning for payment of bills after Election Day, the budget should end with zero in the bank. In addition, campaigns must have the cash available to pay for direct mail, television, and radio at the time of purchase; these paid media options do not allow billing and often require wire transfers and can pile up at the end of the campaign.

Another campaign manager told us that writing a budget isn't enough; you have to constantly check actual income and expenditures and update the budget. "We had a budget, but basically ignored it until the end of the campaign," he told us. "By that time, we didn't have enough money to do the things we had originally planned, and it was demoralizing for the entire campaign. We made a lot of plans for a last-minute door-knock, but we couldn't afford enough literature. We also had hoped to send out a couple pieces of direct mail. Didn't happen. I learned you should pay attention to the budget, check in every week to see if you're on track, and make sure your candidate knows when you are not reaching your budget goals." If you have never run for office or run a campaign before, you might be surprised at how easy it is to forget this budgeting process, which seems so basic. But like a lot of things about campaigning, writing a good budget and sticking to it is harder than it looks, and it demands constant attention from the campaign manager and your finance director.

The campaign manager and finance director should lead the process of writing a budget, and while the candidate should sign off on the budget, he or she should leave it up to the campaign manager to implement it. While doing your planning and writing the budget, keep three rules in mind.

First, make the budget realistic. Budgets, like campaign plans, should be based not on the most optimistic assumptions about costs and fundraising, but on reality. In fact, you should do two budgets: a high budget and a midsized budget. The midsized budget is the most realistic estimate of what you think you need to win. The high budget helps you figure out where you would spend money if more comes in. Hopefully you won't have to use a low budget, which would be necessary only if you have very limited success with fundraising.

The second rule we affectionately call DBC. That stands for "Don't buy crap!" You may have seen from your own experiences that many campaigns, for some reason, love to buy things that will never change a single voter's mind or motivate a supporter to go knock on doors. Football schedules with the candidate's picture? Crap. Bobblehead dolls? Crap. A neon sign in the campaign headquarters? Crap. Sweatbands and sponges with the candidate name, can openers, pens, refrigerator magnets? Crap, crap, crap, crap, and crap. Learn to say no. These things might be cute and look nice, but the question is, Do they win voters?

The third rule is to pay the bills and avoid debt. If you stick to your budget and your fundraising meets expectations, you should pay all your bills on time. Debt can be disastrous to candidates; it can take months, sometimes years, to pay off, especially if they don't win. Candidates are personally liable for some of these debts, which hurts them both financially and politically. If the candidate wants to run again, he or she might have difficulty finding a vendor or be forced to pay all bills up front. The candidate also gets stuck with the unpleasant task of having to raise even more money from the people she had been soliciting for funds throughout the campaign. Don't put yourself, your allies, and your family through the pain of having to pay off campaign debt. If the candidate wins, you can often raise funds to pay off debt, but what if you lose? Who will contribute then to pay off the debt? It's very difficult to pay off the debts of a losing campaign.

Writing the Budget

Now you're ready to get started on the budget. If you're a campaign manager, we suggest you sit down with your finance director and the following six items: your campaign plan; a fundraising assessment based on a best-case scenario and a likely scenario; a calendar that contains all relevant dates, including campaign finance report deadlines; a computer with spreadsheet or money management software like Excel or Quicken; a set of detailed budget categories; and estimated costs of all expenditures.

There are four broad budget categories. The first is direct voter contact: field staff, direct mail, and paid advertising. This should constitute 60 to 70 percent of your budget. Next is overhead. Overhead should be kept at 20 percent or less of the overall budget. Overhead includes computers, office, staff salaries (except field staff, which is paid from the direct voter contact category because they are talking directly to voters daily), furniture, travel, office supplies, cell phones, phones, and postage. Twenty percent isn't much money, so it requires minimizing all overhead (another reason to get as much of your office equipment and other overhead supplies donated to the campaign). The third category, fundraising costs, should make up about 10 to 12 percent of your budget. The fourth category is public opinion research, which can include polling, depending on the size of the race. This category should generally take up no more than 10 percent of your budget. Finally, budgets may include a "margin" line item that adds between 3 to 5 percent of your predicted total expenditures. Doing this makes room for critical expenses that come in higher than predicted or help make up the difference if your fundraising is off projections. It also pushes you to raise more than you otherwise might.

Within these categories, there are detailed subcategories:

Direct Voter Contact

▸ Paid advertising. Paid media can be highly effective (see chapter 7), but it costs a lot of money. This category lets you map out the timing of your paid media plan.

▸ Phone banks, direct mail, literature, and paid phones.

▸ Salaries, if applicable, for field organizers.

Overhead

▸ Office, which includes rent, moving costs, phones, and computers.

▸ Supplies, including postage, printing, and office supplies. Don't forget to try to get this stuff donated: ask your volunteers to bring in pens, pencils, paper, and the like. It is important to note that on federal campaigns and in many states and localities, these items must be reported in the campaign's financial report at their fair market value, and they are counted against an individual's contribution limit. Check with the applicable campaign finance or ethical practices board regarding in-kind contributions.

▶ Staff, excluding field staff. This doesn't apply to all campaigns, but larger campaigns will need a line item for staff members.

▶ Technology, which includes your fundraising database (more on this in a moment), Web site, and Internet access. You can also fold these expenses into the office category.

▶ Visibility, including signs, buttons, and bumper stickers.

Research

▶ This includes polling, focus groups, and any opposition and self-research.

Fundraising

▶ It costs money to raise money; fundraising costs include house parties, postage, printing, and fundraising direct mail.

The next step is to estimate costs for these categories. Get as much information about costs as possible. Talk to candidates from the last election and organizers who have worked in the district, look at past spending reports, and consult with party officials. Get several cost estimates before making decisions on big expenditures. Be realistic: it is better to estimate on the high side than lowball a budget and end up cash-strapped.

Once the campaign's expenditures have been categorized, map out when the expenditures will be made, and create a cash flow sheet that provides a month-to-month spending and income guide. The campaign should operate under the assumption that it is going to pay its bills when they are due and should organize its fundraising activities to ensure that the campaign has the necessary cash flow.

Example: Budget for a Legislative Race

Let's use as an example a budget for a legislative race. The next three pages show a sample budget for a campaign that has one paid organizer and a paid fundraiser for the last three months of the campaign and invests heavily in

BUDGET – STATE ASSEMBLY
Wellstone Action

Department	Line Item	Item Totals	January	February	March	April	May	June	July	August	September	October	November	Totals
TV, RADIO & NEWSPAPER ADVERTISING														
	Radio	$ 7,000										$ 5,000	$ 2,000	
	Radio Production	$ 400										$ 200	$ 200	
	Photo Shoot	$ 200			$ 200									
	Print Advertising	$ 5,500										$ 4,000	$ 1,500	
	Unanticipated Costs at 5%	$ 655	$ -	$ -	$ 10	$ -	$ -	$ -	$ -	$ -	$ -	$ 460	$ 185	
	total persuasion	$ 13,755	$ -	$ -	$ 210	$ -	$ -	$ -	$ -	$ -	$ -	$ 9,660	$ 3,885	$ 13,755
														24.1%
POLLING & RESEARCH														
	Polling	$ -												
	total issues development and research expenses	$ -	$ -	$ -	$ -	$ -	$ -	$ -	$ -	$ -	$ -	$ -	$ -	$ -
														0.0%
FIELD - MAJOR EXPENSES														
	Literature	$ 4,750					$ 1,500				$ 2,600		$ 650	
	Direct mail	$ 12,000									$ 3,500	$ 8,500		
	Lawn Signs and Standards	$ 1,250						$ 1,250						
	T-Shirts, Stickers, Buttons	$ 350			$ 250					$ 100				
	Phone ID (Paid)	$ 5,400								$ 5,400				
	Phones (Lease backs/long distance)	$ 750									$ 250	$ 250	$ 250	
	GOTV Telephone	$ 500											$ 500	
	GOTV Mail	$ 4,700											$ 4,700	
	Canvass Expenses	$ 675						$ 75	$ 75	$ 75	$ 75	$ 75	$ 300	
FIELD STAFF														
	Stipended Organizers	$ -												
	Unanticipated Costs at 5%	$ 1,519	$ -	$ -	$ 13	$ -	$ 75	$ 66	$ 4	$ 279	$ 321	$ 441	$ 320	
	total field expenses	$ 31,894	$ -	$ -	$ 263	$ -	$ 1,575	$ 1,391	$ 79	$ 5,854	$ 6,746	$ 9,266	$ 6,720	$ 31,894
														55.8%

TRAVEL - MAJOR EXPENSES (CANDIDATE AND STAFF)

Department / Line Item	Item Totals	January	February	March	April	May	June	July	August	September	October	November	Totals
Gas Reimbursement	$ 450						$ 150	$ 150	$ 150				
Unanticipated Costs at 5%	$ 23	$ -	$ -	$ -	$ -	$ -	$ 8	$ 8	$ 8	$ -	$ -	$ -	
total travel expenses	$ 473	$ -	$ -	$ -	$ -	$ -	$ 158	$ 158	$ 158	$ -	$ -	$ -	$ 473
													0.8%

FUNDRAISING - MAJOR EXPENSES

Line Item	Item Totals	January	February	March	April	May	June	July	August	September	October	November	Totals
Fundraising Event Costs	$ 1,250	$ 50	$ 50	$ 50		$ 50	$ 150	$ 50	$ 50	$ 400	$ 400		
Printing	$ 500	$ 200					$ 100			$ 100	$ 100		
Direct Mail	$ 500	$ 200					$ 100			$ 200			
Postage (non-Direct Mail)	$ 300		$ 50					$ 50	$ 100	$ 100			
Unanticipated Costs at 5%	$ 128	$ 23	$ 5	$ 3		$ 3	$ 18	$ 5	$ 8	$ 40	$ 25	$ -	
total fundraising expenses	$ 2,678	$ 473	$ 105	$ 53		$ 53	$ 368	$ 105	$ 158	$ 840	$ 525	$ -	$ 2,678
													4.7%

COMMUNICATIONS - MAJOR EXPENSES

Line Item	Item Totals	January	February	March	April	May	June	July	August	September	October	November	Totals
Web Site Development / Management	$ 550				$ 300			$ 50	$ 50	$ 50	$ 50	$ 50	
Unanticipated Costs at 5%	$ 28	$ -	$ -	$ -	$ 15	$ -	$ -	$ 3	$ 3	$ 3	$ 3	$ 3	
total communications expenses	$ 578	$ -	$ -	$ -	$ 315	$ -	$ -	$ 53	$ 53	$ 53	$ 53	$ 53	$ 578
													1.0%

ADMINISTRATION - MAJOR EXPENSES

Line Item	Item Totals	January	February	March	April	May	June	July	August	September	October	November	Totals
Office Rent	$ -												
Phones	$ -												
Long Distance	$ 200												
Cell phones	$ 450						$ 75	$ 75	$ 75	$ 75	$ 75	$ 75	
Database	$ -												
Computers	$ -												
Desks, tables chairs and furniture	$ -												
Stationary / Envelopes	$ 500				$ 500								
Photocopier	$ 550									$ 100	$ 100	$ 200	
Postage	$ 200					$ 25	$ 50	$ 50	$ 50	$ 100	$ 25	$ 25	
Supplies	$ 200				$ 25	$ 25	$ 25	$ 25	$ 25	$ 25	$ 25	$ 25	
Overnight Mail	$ -												
Unanticipated Costs at 5%	$ 105	$ -	$ -	$ -	$ 28	$ 3	$ 9	$ 9	$ 11	$ 14	$ 14	$ 19	
total administrative expenses	$ 2,205	$ -	$ -	$ -	$ 578	$ 53	$ 184	$ 184	$ 236	$ 289	$ 289	$ 394	$ 2,205
													3.9%

A sample budget from a state legislative race shows a campaign's budget categories and cash flow. A typical campaign should spend about 70 percent of its budget on direct voter contact and paid media, with the remaining money going to overhead, fundraising and staff salaries.

Department	Line Item	Item Totals	January	February	March	April	May	June	July	August	September	October	November	Totals
PERSONNEL - SALARIES & CONTRACTS															
	Campaign Manager	$ 3,750						$ 500	$ 500	$ 500	$ 1,000	$ 1,000	$ 250	
	Finance Director (salary x # months)	$ 750								$ 250	$ 250	$ 250		
	Unanticipated Costs at 5%	$ 225				$ -	$ -	$ 25	$ 25	$ 38	$ 63	$ 63	$ 13	
	total salaries and contracts	$ 4,725				$ -	$ -	$ 525	$ 525	$ 788	$ 1,313	$ 1,313	$ 263	$ 4,725
														8.3%
PERSONNEL - ADDITIONAL COSTS															
	Payroll Tax @ 8.5% of Payroll	$ 64			$ -	$ -	$ -	$ -	$ -	$ 21	$ 21	$ 21	$ 21	
	Unanticipated Costs at 5%	$ 3			$ -	$ -	$ -	$ -	$ -	$ 1	$ 1	$ 1	$ 1	
	total additional personnel costs	$ 67			$ -	$ -	$ -	$ -	$ -	$ 22	$ 22	$ 22	$ 22	$ 67
														0.1%
OTHER COSTS															
	All other anticipated costs *	$ 700						$ 100	$ 100	$ 100	$ 100	$ 100	$ 200	
	Unanticipated Costs at 5%	$ 35						$ 5	$ 5	$ 5	$ 5	$ 5	$ 10	
	total other costs	$ 735						$ 105	$ 105	$ 105	$ 105	$ 105	$ 210	
	TOTAL COSTS	$ 57,108	$ 473	$ 105	$ 525	$ 893	$ 1,680	$ 2,230	$ 708	$ 6,872	$ 8,367	$ 21,232	$ 11,524	
REVENUES	CASH ON HAND (1/1/2006) =	$ 0	$ 0	$ 828	$ 7,923	$ 10,098	$ 9,705	$ 8,525	$ 14,195	$ 14,388	$ 8,615	$ 17,848	$ 11,416	%TOTAL FR
	Dial for dollars (Candidate Call Time)	$ 13,500	$ 500	$ 500	$ 1,000	$ 500	$ 500	$ 1,000	$ 300	$ 500	$ 4,200	$ 3,500	1000	23.5%
	Direct Mail	$ 12,000	0	$ 5,500	0	0	0	$ 2,000	0	0	$ 1,500	3000	0	20.9%
	Events (mid/high dollar)	$ 9,000	0	0	0	0	0	0	0	0	$ 5,000	$ 4,000	0	15.7%
	Internet/web	$ 4,000	0	0	$ 500	0	0	$ 500	0	0	$ 1,000	$ 1,500	$ 500	7.0%
	PAC contributions	$ 8,000	0	0	0	0	0	$ 2,000	0	0	$ 3,500	$ 1,000	$ 1,500	13.9%
	Houseparties/Events (low dollar)	$ 11,000	800	1,200	1,200	0	0	2,400	600	600	2,400	1,800	0	19.1%
	TOTAL REV	$ 57,500	$ 1,300	$ 7,200	$ 2,700	$ 500	$ 500	$ 7,900	$ 900	$ 1,100	$ 17,600	$ 14,800	$ 3,000	1
	TOTAL COSTS	$ 57,108	$ 473	$ 105	$ 525	$ 893	$ 1,680	$ 2,230	$ 708	$ 6,872	$ 8,367	$ 21,232	$ 11,524	
	CASH ON HAND	$ 392	$ 828	$ 7,923	$ 10,098	$ 9,705	$ 8,525	$ 14,195	$ 14,388	$ 8,615	$ 17,848	$ 11,416	$ 2,892	$ 2,892

direct mail to reach voters. The budget is laid out according to a six-month timeline for our purposes, but of course if the campaign starts early you should create a budget for a longer period of time. In this example, there has been significant fundraising and initial outreach done prior to this budget document, and the campaign has $8,525 on hand on June 1, having already raised money through a very effective first fundraising letter followed by candidate phoning and a series of house parties with key supporters and constituency groups. The strategy of this campaign is to raise money early to scare off potential challengers. The campaign is estimating a total expenditure of $57,500. The race is in a tough swing district with a population of 67,745 and 40,159 eligible voters. You expect a 57.9 percent turnout and your win number is 12,901 (vote deficit is 2,976). Furthermore, while there are no spending limits in the race, there are contribution limits of $500 per person in the election year and an aggregate PAC limit of $8,000. You expect to raise a total budget for the campaign of $57,500.

To understand these numbers, start by looking at the budget categories considered "overhead": administrative, personnel, communications, and travel. The campaign is planning on spending $250 on postage for nondirect mail and fundraising between June and the election. That works out to 365 pieces of first-class mail, or about 60 pieces per month. This number does not include the cost of direct mail, which is calculated separately. Printing costs are estimated at $500 and cover items like office stationery and envelopes (be sure to use union print shops). There is no rent paid in this example. In most low-dollar races, space is either donated or the campaign is run out of the manager's or candidate's house or garage. The remaining few overhead costs come from paying for long distance, cell phone reimbursement, photocopying, and miscellaneous supplies, some gas reimbursement for door-knocking, and Web site development.

Included in the overall overhead costs is a separate category for staff. In this case, the organizer/campaign manager is the primary staff member, and he or she will make a very modest salary of $500 a month starting in June with an increase to $1,000 a month for the last two months of the campaign. This person will be brought in at the start of the summer to coordinate the summer door-knocks and ID calling. A fundraiser will be needed early on in the campaign, and will be a volunteer, but will receive a small stipend of $250. A volunteer field director is brought on in mid-August to run a volunteer persuasion and get-out-the-vote effort.

Smaller campaigns usually can't afford to pay someone to work full-time, so one alternative is to find a good person and at least provide a small stipend to recognize extraordinary effort and to increase accountability. Note that many supplies and office equipment and furniture can be donated or lent to the campaign, although depending on the state it may be counted against the contribution limit of the individual who donates it (again, be sure to learn the applicable laws in your state or locality; in some cases, in-kind contributions count against a campaign's spending limit, so they would need to be categorized as such). Overall, this campaign will spend 14 percent of the budget on these overhead items, which is well within the rule of thumb that you should spend less than 20 percent on overhead. In smaller races the amount of administrative costs should usually be less than 5 percent, and the bulk of overhead costs will usually be for staff.

Under the research category, the campaign has decided not to spend any money on polling and opposition research, relying instead on research from the party and published polling. This decision is up to the discretion of the campaign. Polls are very expensive, and it is easy to spend $10,000 for a bare minimum amount of polling data. Whether it is worth the investment is a judgment call, but a strong case can be made that in a small campaign these precious resources would be better spent on direct mail, and the campaign can rely on party-provided research and the feedback from a summer knocking on doors.

Remember that the bulk of any campaign's budget is allocated to direct voter contact: door-knocking, phoning, direct mail, and broadcast advertising. In this race, direct mail is the main cost. Each targeted voter will receive six pieces of direct mail based on a paid ID program that begins in early September. The campaign plans to spend $5,400 to contract with a vendor of phone services to make professional ID calls to the targeted universes of voters. Paid ID phoning will allow the campaign to quickly and efficiently develop a universe of undecided voters to target (the 2s, 3s, and some 4s, as categorized by voter identification; see chapter 5), so that multiple efforts of mail, candidate contact, and volunteer persuasion can reach exactly the voters you want. This is a wise use of money if the campaign targets the calling well and finds a good vendor. The campaign volunteers can then focus on the important task of beginning persuasion conversations with identified undecided voters.

Direct mail will be the largest single cost for a campaign of this size ($12,000 in this case). The campaign will run radio ads, which will cost $7,400 to produce and air on stations. The amount a campaign can purchase for this amount of money depends on the ad rates for a particular market, but in this case it will provide solid coverage throughout the district for the final three weeks of the campaign. Another $5,500 will be used for print ads in all of the weekly, ethnic, and constituency press in the district. This will pay for significantly sized ads in every weekly for the last four weeks of the campaign. In sum, a total of 79.9 percent of the campaign's budget will be spent on direct voter contact, which is even better than the 65 to 75 percent target.

The campaign will spend its resources over a six-month timeline, and the budget provides a breakdown of that spending. What is not shown on this budget is the early spending that went into an extensive fundraising effort. Most of the resources spent before June went toward covering fundraising costs, postage, and some early printing costs. Every campaign should have a cash flow projection chart, and the chart should be adjusted every month for both income and expense "actuals." Budget adjustments (both up and down) often need to be made late in the campaign, so make sure the budget is constantly reviewed. You will see in this budget that sometimes the costs of a month exceed the revenue taken in. This is normal, especially at the end of a campaign when money is often flowing out much faster than it is coming in. This speaks to the need for good budget planning to ensure that enough resources are on hand, as well as for budget discipline early in the campaign, when there seems to be more money, and close monitoring of the cash flow. The budget and fundraising need to stay closely linked so that fundraising activity and messages to donors get adjusted according to need. At the bottom of the cash flow table, note that the total cash on hand changes as the campaign raises and spends money.

Here are some dos and don'ts to keep in mind as you put together your campaign budget:

Ten Budget Dos

- ▸ Consider every expense in your campaign plan.
- ▸ Save copies of your calculations.
- ▸ Understand that everything costs more than you think.
- ▸ Develop a budget that is as detailed as possible.
- ▸ Set aside funds for your media buy in an interest-bearing account.
- ▸ Involve your candidate in the initial budget discussions and update him or her regularly.

▸ Monitor your budget closely, weekly and daily.

▸ Try to think of all expenses related to an activity.

▸ Understand that your budget is a work in progress and will remain so until Election Day.

▸ Find a form that works for you for keeping track of the budget.

Ten Budget Don'ts

▸ Don't assume that the time period you assign for a particular expense is also the time when you need to pay for it. Often campaigns have to prepay their activities, especially paid advertising.

▸ Don't plan to end with a deficit.

▸ Don't lump expenses together on the same budget line.

▸ Don't rush. The budget is crucial, so take your time and do it right.

▸ Don't just copy your budget from other campaigns; think it through and develop your own model.

▸ Don't hesitate to ask for help in developing your budget.

▸ Don't create your budget without first talking to the candidate, staff, and consultants.

▸ Don't create your budget and never return to it.

▸ Don't make any spending decisions without consulting your budget.

▸ Don't wait until you know exactly what all your expenses will be before beginning your budget.

Fundraising

When Patricia Torres Ray decided to run for state senator in Minneapolis, she knew her biggest challenge would be raising money. She had never run for office before, and the idea of picking up the phone and asking someone to give her money was foreign to her. "Asking for money," she told us, "was excruciating at first." Yet Torres Ray went on to raise enough money to build a strong campaign and win her election. While raising money didn't get easy overnight, Torres Ray created a step-by-step plan for raising money that made the process manageable. Her advice to new candidates is echoed by every experienced campaign fundraiser. "Start with people you really know," she said. "You need to build some confidence and get used to asking for money; it's not something that comes naturally to everyone. It didn't come naturally to me. At first, I would ask those people I knew well to make an investment to get the campaign off the ground, so I could demonstrate my capacity as a candidate and be able to raise even more money. Then I started to tie my organizing pitch to my fundraising pitch. I would say, 'With this money, we will be able to do this together.'" Once Torres Ray started helping people see the connection between her empowering, grassroots message and the need to raise money to get that message to voters, the fundraising really got going.

Lists and Goals

The key to getting those first dollars in the bank, in Patricia Torres Ray's case and in nearly every other grassroots campaign, is starting with those who are closest to you personally, socially, and politically. Like other candidates running for office for the first time, Torres Ray didn't have much experience with fundraising, but had built a lot of relationships with people over the years. "I knew a lot of people, and I knew people who knew other people," she said. Representative Steve Simon, another Minnesota legislator, says new candidates for office should start by making a list and then add to it. "I got a great tip from someone," Simon said. "He told me to make a list of everyone I had ever known. The first hundred people will come tumbling out as you sit down and list them out. Then over the course of a couple weeks, you'll gradually add others. You'll think of a couple names while showering or in the car driving to work. After I came up with the list of names, I sent out letters and on every one, I put a short, personal note."

Building this first fundraising list is a critical first step for every campaign. As Simon describes above, the first hundred names are fairly easy. Start with your holiday card list, Rolodex, or the numbers in your cell phone. Then start thinking of categories of people: parents you have worked with at your kid's school, organizations you belong to, people who attend your place of worship, people you graduated with, major events you have helped work on or coordinated, and so on. One gubernatorial candidate went as far back as childhood friends from grade school and high school some forty-five years earlier. Many of these friends she hadn't touched base with for decades, yet when she called for money the conversation was fun for both the candidate and her old friend and was very productive for raising money. Sometimes it helps to have someone else prompt the candidate to start pulling out names. A target list of three to five hundred names should be your goal. Although this may sound like a huge number, you will be surprised by how many people you know when you sit down and write out the list. As with other aspects of the campaign, be sure to capture every name you come across by putting it into your database. Your list should exist in digital form, like a Microsoft Excel spreadsheet or a Microsoft Access database. Another option for storing your list includes an online database.

Regardless of the type of database you decide to use, you need to be diligent in keeping it updated. This takes time and is often overlooked. Find at least one person to do little else but keeping it updated. As one state legislative candidate said, "It was very problematic for me to keep track of information about the people I met. I was so busy and so consumed by the campaign that I realized early on that we needed one place to collect names. So I made a point to collect business cards from everyone I met, and I would sit down with a volunteer and he would enter all the names into the database, with notes from me about what I remember about the person. That way I could call that person for a donation or the campaign could call him to volunteer, I could personalize the call, like, 'Last time we talked you said your mother was having surgery. How is she feeling?' That personal touch really made a difference, but it would have been impossible without having a place to put that information." Your database is, of course, more than just a fundraising tool. (We cover databases in detail in chapter 12.)

Once you have your database set up (and remember, you will constantly be adding to it throughout the campaign), brainstorm with the campaign manager and finance director to come up with other categories of donors to target. Some of these categories include:

▸ **Your friends' friends.** Friends of the candidate and campaign workers are obvious targets for fundraising appeals, but don't stop there. The way to expand your base and add momentum to your campaign is to continually expand your circle of supporters; the friends of your friends will be far more likely to support a campaign if they have received a personal recommendation from people they know and trust. Ask your friends to help you raise money! One governor's race made this a significant component of its grassroots fundraising effort, even giving it a name—the

Cornerstone Project—and enlisting a super-volunteer staff coordinator who developed a fundraising kit to be sent to supporters and then followed up with surrogate fundraisers to help ensure that money was being raised. Over several months, a hundred people sent out letters to their networks, raising over $75,000 in small contributions. This had the effect of raising real money and at the same time building the base and engaging volunteers in a significant way in the campaign—all through volunteers.

▸ **Personal Rolodexes and holiday card lists** of the candidate or the campaign organizers. Candidates and campaign organizers are often surprised by the number of people they have in their own lists. Similar sources include former college classmates, clients or business associates, and co-workers. One city council candidate, a lawyer with extensive contacts in the legal community, told us she took out her local Bar Association list, identified everyone she knew, and sent them all a letter specifically addressing legal issues in the city. She then followed up that letter with an individual, personalized e-mail to each lawyer on the list.

▸ **Past political contributors.** You can access the giving history of individuals and PACs that have given to candidates or political parties by going to a variety of Web sites, including www.fec.gov and www.opensecrets.org. It is important to note that campaigns are prohibited by federal law from using these lists to do direct fundraising. In other words, it is illegal to download a previous candidate's fundraising list and begin calling those contributors. However, these lists can be used to research a donor's giving history and political preferences. For example, if Cindy Smith is a name on a prospective fundraising list and you want to learn more about her giving history, it is perfectly legal to go to one of these Web sites and find out whom she contributed to and how much she gave.

▸ **Members of supportive groups.** Grassroots campaigns often rely on the support of other like-minded organizations and individuals but frequently neglect to make a fundraising connection to these groups. If a candidate receives an endorsement from an environmental advocacy organization, for example, use that momentum to help the field and press operations, but be sure to explore ways to tap into that organization's fundraising base.

▶ **Political action committees (PACs),** including Leadership PACs, which are established by elected officials interested in supporting like-minded causes. Some campaigns choose not to accept PAC money, which is a political decision that has benefits and drawbacks. If your campaign decides not to accept PAC money, have a plan for making up for this lost income in the budget.

▶ **Local party activists and party officials.** Surprisingly, party officials are often not asked to make individual contributions to campaigns. Yet these are great fundraising sources; they know the issues and have extensive contacts with other potential sources.

In some states, knowing how much you need to raise is a question made easier by the existence of spending limits. These are generally voluntary, but the benefit is that you receive public funding and other subsidies if you agree to the limit. If you are very well financed, you have the option of forgoing these spending limits, but in most states deciding to do so will make it easier for your opponent to raise and spend money as well, because state laws raise or remove spending limits when one candidate forgoes the limits. Spending limits make it simple to define your fundraising goal: you should raise the limit and not any less. The problem is that the limits set by statute are often very restrictive, meaning that hard spending choices have to be made. For example, statewide officeholders in some states are limited to as little as $200,000 in total expenditures. That's an extremely low limit for a state with millions of people, one that immediately restricts your spending decisions. Be sure to know all the campaign finance laws that apply to you, from contribution and spending limits to reporting requirements and important timelines around public financing.

Options for Raising Money

To get a sense of the different choices for how to raise money, take a look at the fundraising pyramid on the next page. A fundraising pyramid helps break down your fundraising goals to manageable segments. This is a fundraising pyramid for a campaign with a goal of raising $40,000. The campaign will work to get 20 individuals to give $500 each, 30 individuals to give $250 each, 125 people to give $100 each, and 200 people to give $50 each, for a total of $40,000. How should you raise that money? For the top two categories, you raise the money through direct solicitations from a phone call from

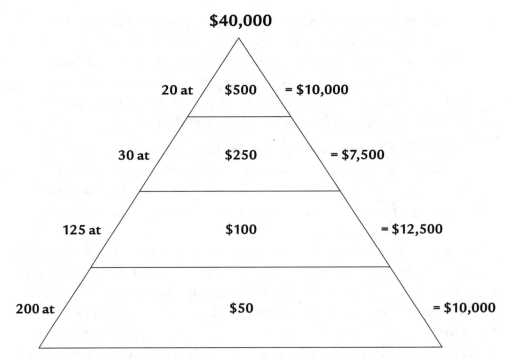

$40,000

20 at / $500 \ = $10,000

30 at / $250 \ = $7,500

125 at / $100 \ = $12,500

200 at / $50 \ = $10,000

A fundraising pyramid can help you prioritize your fundraising and identify tiers of campaign donors. Campaigns want to raise money from a combination of high-dollar and low-dollar donors, with fundraising targets for each category. When it comes to the campaign's bottom line, ten donors giving $100 each is the same as one person giving $1,000 at a time, but there are benefits to finding low-dollar donors that go beyond your fundraising goals; low-dollar donors make up a significant portion of your base of volunteers and can be just as valuable as big donors when it comes to organizing and mobilizing other voters.

the candidate. The amounts at the bottom—from $50 and $100 donors—will come by other means, like house party events, fundraising mail, and Internet donations. This grassroots fundraising work can be woven together with your volunteer organization building. All of your supporters should be asked to give of their time and their money, no matter how small the amount. There is conventional wisdom that large campaigns cannot exist on low-dollar contributions despite evidence to the contrary. Campaigns that are principally financed through low-dollar contributions often attract people who have never given to political campaigns because they don't think their $50 matters compared with $2,000 contributions. These campaigns (think of Howard Dean in 2004) often end up outraising their rivals.

Ultimately, your campaign's solicitation method depends on how well you or the candidate knows the donor and how much the donor is capable of giving. Friends and close supporters of the candidate can do their own fundraising work for the campaign, using the same principle of contacting their friends and asking directly for a contribution. Sometimes the candidate will call together with this person, talking to people who don't know the candidate personally, with the friend making the ask. For example, let's say a candidate, Han Solo, is a partner at a big law firm. His law partners have dozens of friends and colleagues who don't have a personal connection to the candidate. The campaign would ask the law partners to create a list of their personal contacts and to call them with a simple message: "I know Han. I'm a friend and a colleague, and I trust him. I think he'll make a great member of the city council, and I wanted to tell you a little bit about his campaign." They could then go on and make a request for a contribution. If the person needs another nudge, have the candidate follow up in the next few days and repeat the ask. The point is to do everything possible to use the candidate's network of friends and colleagues as a way of making a personal connection to the campaign.

Think of your fundraising resources as parts of a concentric circle. You start in the center and move step by step through the layers of your list, moving from the people you know to potential allies whom you might never have met. It can actually be very difficult for some candidates to start raising money from their friends and family. We have had candidates tell us that they feel embarrassed asking their personal friends for money and that they would prefer to ask strangers. "It was a little weird to ask friends I've known for a long time to give me money," one candidate told us. Mark Ritchie, an experienced fundraiser in the nonprofit sector who recently upset a two-term incumbent to become Minnesota's secretary of state, said, "I had to learn how to ask my friends for help. I had to learn to ask them for their money, their time, their support, to host me at a party, to use their name publicly," he said. Eventually, he grew to actually enjoy asking for help. That's a similar reaction that one of our Camp Wellstone graduates had when the first donations came into his campaign: "Getting those first campaign contributions from friends and family feels like the final scene in *It's a Wonderful Life!*"

While it might not seem easy for every candidate, raising money from people with a personal connection to the candidate with a direct ask is the only way to start from scratch. In that way, raising money is just like getting voters: the more personal the contact, the more likely they will be to support you or give you money. Of course, not every donor at every level can be engaged in a one-on-one conversation. The campaign therefore needs to make strategic choices not just about whom it raises money from, but how.

There are basically four types of donors: personal friends and family, people who share the candidate's ideological positions on the issues and support the candidate because of those positions, people who have an ax to grind with the candidate's opponent and seek to defeat that opponent regardless of who is challenging, and those who donate to secure power, influence, or access. The latter group often donates to both sides. Each of these types of donors can be approached at a different time and with a slightly different message, and the likelihood of their donating depends on the candidate's viability. For example, a candidate's friends don't care about whether the candidate is viable; they donate because they are friends. Power donors, on the other hand, are acutely aware of viability. They will not waste resources on candidates they think have little chance of winning.

As we've discussed, a candidate's friends and family constitute the first circle and should be the first people asked. The message from the candidate is simple: I am running and your contribution is important to me. The second circle consists of ideological donors who share the candidate's values or her advocacy of a cause (like choice groups, organized labor, environmentalists, etc.). These donors can be approached early in the campaign because of shared issues and interests. Their concern is about changing the world, and the candidate's message should convey "Together we can change the world." The third circle consists of folks who are opposed to the other candidate. These donors can be approached earlier in the campaign still, but they may also be looking for viability. Their objective, after all, is to get rid of the other person. The candidate's message to this group of donors is simple: "I am not the other candidate, and I can win." The final circle of donors consists of power donors. These donors are often people who want to protect or advance their economic interests—for example, lobbyists, power players, developers, and lawyers. They often donate later in the campaign when it is clearer who is likely to win and where they might exert their greatest influence. Sometimes these people hedge their bets and give smaller amounts early on to all serious candidates, and follow up with larger contributions later in the campaign with the candidate they think is the winner. It is not at all uncommon to see this group of donors actually donating to a candidate after she has won. The message to this group of donors is almost exclusively about viability and ability to win.

Running a Call Time Program

The best way to manage the task of systematically calling donors is to set up a routine, a physical space, and a process. This is the candidate call time program. Call time is a specifically scheduled period of time on the candidate's schedule, usually two to four hours daily. This is time that the campaign manager and candidate protect at all costs. It is often tempting to avoid call time by cutting into other events, but think of this time as inviolate. Usually another person, a "call time manager," perhaps the finance director or the campaign manager, will sit in the room with the candidate, moving the calls along, taking notes during conversations, and taking care of fulfillment of the contribution pledge. Find a quiet and comfortable place with no distractions. Remember that for most candidates, this is the least fun activity and they will search for distractions. Paul Wellstone came up with some pretty wild excuses not to do call time—he would have "urgent" phone calls to make, desperately "need" to talk campaign strategy, or decide he needed something to eat. As campaign manager, finance director, or call time manager, you have the job of making sure the candidate agrees to a set amount of call time per week and that he delivers on that agreement. And for candidates, just keep in mind that you don't want to lose and look back and say, "If only I had raised a little more money so we could get our message to more voters." Take Kathy Hartman's example in Colorado to heart: "I was almost religious with my call time. I'd call anybody who was a potential donor, anytime, whether I knew them or not."

Make call time as productive as possible for the candidate. A candidate should make calls from "call sheets" that are generated by the fundraising team. These sheets contain everything the campaign knows about the donor: occupation and employer, background, donor history, previous donations, and particular areas of interest. Each potential donor should be assigned an "estimated ask," a specific amount that the candidate should request from the donor. These ask amounts should be aggressive, because in fundraising you often get what you ask for, and many people will be able to give more than you might think. For example, in the case of donors who have a history of consistently giving $200 at a time to candidates, ask for more than $200. They may not give at a higher level, but they certainly won't if they are not asked. They may actually be flattered by the larger request and be more likely to settle at $200, which is fine.

When call time begins, the candidate has reviewed the call sheet, knows at least some background about the potential donor, and understands how much he should ask for. The campaign manager, finance director, or call time manager is in the room with the candidate and has prepared for the call time by double-checking to make sure all the phone numbers on the call sheets are current (it's very frustrating for candidates to call through lists that have wrong numbers). And now comes the essential part: the "ask."

We recently had a guest trainer at a Camp Wellstone session who summarized his presentation on fundraising this way: "There's really only one thing you need to remember when trying to raise money: ask for it." Everything comes down to the ask—if you don't ask and then give the person a chance to respond, you likely won't get a donation. Sounds simple, but it's hard, and it goes against human nature. It's easier, for example, to say something like "I would really appreciate your support and whatever you can give would be great," than it is to say, "I really appreciate your support and I'd like to ask you to make a $500 contribution to my campaign so we can take our message to every voter in this district. Can I count on your $500 contribution?" But that is the more effective approach.

The ask should take place at the end of the fundraising "rap." After engaging with the donor and telling him or her why you are running and how you plan to win, you should move quickly to the ask: "So as you can see, we're putting together a great campaign team and we're gaining momentum every day. To win, though, we believe requires us to raise x amount, and I need your help. You've been a generous donor to past campaigns that we both supported. I know I can win this race. Can I ask you to make a $250 contribution so that I can run the campaign I need to deliver our message to every voter?" After you make the pitch, stop speaking. This is often the hardest part of raising money—waiting through the silence for the response—but it forces an answer from the potential donor. The natural tendency may be to negotiate down or downplay the ask, but good negotiators (and salespeople and reporters) know that silence carries its own weight and power for eliciting responses. One way to stop yourself from the impulse to fill silence is to make the pitch, stop, and then take a drink of water. That forces you to leave your request hanging out there, so the donor is forced to respond. If you fill the silence with small talk, your ask loses its power.

The donor will reply with a variety of responses: "yes," "no," "that's a lot of money," "too rich for my blood," or "I'll think about it." If yes, then collecting that pledge is the next goal. Your campaign should have a way of receiving contributions by credit card, which makes the process much easier and ensures that the contribution is actually made. Ask if the contribution can be made by credit card so it is immediately collected, and explain by saying, "It's cheaper for us and it means you won't have the hassle of writing a check and putting it in the mail." If the answer is yes but the donor prefers not to pay by credit card, the candidate writes or signs a "commitment note" to the donor after the call ends, saying, "It was great talking to you today. It means so much to have your support—thank you for agreeing to make a $300 contribution to my campaign. Enclosed is a self-addressed envelope for your contribution. If you have any questions, please contact me at this number . . ." The call time manager then takes the letter, logs the pledge, and mails the letter (with self-addressed envelope) immediately, so the obligation is fresh in the donor's mind. The longer you wait to send the letter and give the donor an opportunity to put a check in the mail, the less likely it is that you will receive the contribution. Candidates often like to say at the end of call time, "I raised $3,500 today!" Experienced fundraisers know that actually the candidate only received commitments for $3,500 that day, and it's their job now to get the money in the door. Money committed is not money raised until the campaign actually receives the money.

What happens when someone says yes but the campaign doesn't receive a check right away? This occurs quite often, which is why the campaign manager or finance director tracks pledges and fulfillments. One fundraiser we spoke with said she keeps track of all commitments in an online database by marking the date she needs to start following up with the donor. If a donor makes a commitment on May 1, for example, the fundraiser puts a note in the donor's database entry that follow-up is needed starting on May 8. Her database program allows her to run a list that tells her all the people she needs to follow up with on any given day. When, on May 8, she does her daily list of follow-ups, that donor's name will pop up. The best way to follow up is with a phone call. Leave a message if the person isn't available and make note in your database. If you haven't received a check after a couple of days, call again. And so on. You don't want to harass a donor, but if the person made a commitment to donate to your campaign, don't let her off the hook. If she changed her mind, she should be able to tell you that directly.

If you get a "yes" from a donor, follow-up is particularly important when your campaign is approaching a filing deadline. These are the busiest times of year for campaign fundraisers, because you want to show the strongest possible fundraising performance. That becomes part of the candidate's pitch to donors—"In four days we file our campaign finance report and we really need to demonstrate how strong our campaign is"—and you want to do everything you can to get that donation in before the deadline. If that means tracking the money down in person, it's worth it. It's quite common for campaigns to have interns or staff at the ready who can drive to a donor's home or business after the campaign receives a commitment.

Another possible answer is "I'll think about it." This is a tricky answer to interpret. For some donors, it is just a nice way to get the candidate off the phone without having to say "no." For others, it really does mean that a donation is possible but for whatever reason—cash flow, indecision about the race, misgivings about the candidate—the contribution isn't imminent. While you don't want to harass these potential donors, you do need to follow up diligently. The candidate should immediately write a "good to talk to you" note that includes a contribution envelope (just in case). The donor should then receive frequent updates from the campaign—not necessarily hard fundraising asks, but evidence to show the donor that the campaign is worth the investment.

If the donor says no, don't assume that means, "I will never give to your campaign." Maybe the person is trying to hold down on costs for the month or is waiting to make a contribution later in the campaign. The candidate should ask the donor, "I understand this might not be the time for you to make a contribution, but I hope as the campaign moves forward you will reconsider." Another thing you can say is, "Is there anything I can do to change your mind?" Donors who say no should still immediately receive a handwritten note from the candidate, thanking them for taking the time to talk and for considering supporting the campaign.

This brings us to another critical component of fundraising (and many other aspects of a campaign): thanks. It is impossible—impossible!—to thank someone too much. Thanking donors, supporters, volunteers, and anyone who helps the campaign is not only the courteous, right thing to do: it is the best way to guarantee that the money actually comes in, that the supporters stay with the campaign, and that the volunteers keep coming back. Everyone who makes a contribution to the campaign should be quickly thanked within a week. Make this part of your regular routine. Some candidates write thank-you notes or e-mails every night after making phone calls or knocking on doors. Others carve out a specific time every week to write thank yous. Minnesota Secretary of State Mark Ritchie set aside every Monday during the campaign for thank-you notes and calls. Raising money didn't come naturally, but thanking people did. "I was able to link fundraising to something I really love, which is thanking people for helping my campaign," he told us. "I spent every Monday, almost all day, thanking people.

Monday was like our campaign's designated 'Thank You Day.'" The bottom line: don't forget to show your appreciation for the people who are keeping your campaign going. Not thanking a donor will ensure that the donor will not give again, will hurt the campaign's reputation, and will make it more difficult to raise money from others.

Candidate call time should not be confused with paid fundraising calls, which is an option available to larger-scale campaigns and requires hiring a direct marketing firm to raise money or running a paid internal fundraising operation with considerably more flexibility and at a substantially lower cost. A lot of people have reservations about doing fundraising through "telemarketers," but there is a reason telemarketing is so prevalent: it works. For political campaigns, paid phoning—when done right, using the right firm—can be a cost-effective way of reaching potential donors who do not respond to direct mail solicitations or have lapsed in their regular donations. However, unless you are running statewide or for Congress, paid fundraising calls are probably not worth the investment.

Fundraising Events

Events can help you raise money and grow a campaign's base of supporters. In grassroots campaigns, house parties are great organizing events—a chance for the campaign to organize and mobilize its base while also raising money. Candidates usually find it easier to go to fundraising events instead of making phone calls. It is important to note, however, that events are a less efficient method of raising money than direct solicitation and cannot be solely relied on for your fundraising. They usually cost a lot, require staff and volunteer time, and raise smaller individual amounts than call time. But the benefits of fundraising events are often overlooked. Events—even high-dollar events—can also advance a campaign's field plan and should be viewed as both money-raising and base-building activities. They also provide a deadline and a vehicle of giving for people who have pledged money over the phone, and they can get existing donors to give again.

A key concern with fundraising events (and fundraising in general) is keeping overhead costs low. It is not uncommon for campaigns to break even or even lose money on fundraisers because they paid too much for a venue, food, or music and didn't focus on turnout and asking for money. Whenever possible, get event costs donated (be sure to comply with local election laws about in-kind donations). Donors generally don't want their money going to expensive appetizers, wine, or flowers, so don't buy them! The monetary success of a fundraiser is based on what the campaign nets, not on the total dollars raised. The costs of printing and mailing invitations, finding a location, and providing food and beverages can add up very quickly. Many campaigns have gone to the other extreme, proudly providing minimal refreshments to guests. The high-dollar fundraising events sponsored by the Bush campaigns in 2000 and 2004 featured simple meals of hot dogs and potato chips. The campaign explained that donors wanted the campaign to spend money on winning the elections, not treating them to a four-course meal. Whether running events for school board or presidential candidates, the rule of thumb is that fundraising costs should be between 10 and 12 percent of the gross raised, so if you want to raise $100,000, you can spend up to $10,000, but try not to. Too many campaigns try to get around this, but any experienced fundraiser will tell you that the superfluous costs, in the end, do not add anything to the event and only reduce the net cash for the campaign.

Here are ten steps for successful fundraising events:

1. **Recruit multiple hosts for the events,** with each host agreeing to raise a set amount of money and turn out a certain number of people. These hosts can have their names listed on the invitation, which is a way of giving them ownership of the event and highlighting their prominence on the campaign.

2. **Choose a place.** Fundraisers can be held in a wide variety of locations. The most common location is the home of a campaign supporter, since it is convenient and inexpensive. Other good locations include places of business (law firms, for example), union halls, and city parks. Some untraditional but very effective fundraisers have been held in places like museums and theaters. Wherever the campaign chooses to hold an event, you should go to great lengths to avoid spending much, if any, money on the location.

3. **Set targets for money and guests.** Establish a dollar target for the event, and then set a corresponding target for the number of people in attendance. Depending on the size of the campaign, house parties can raise anywhere from $500 to $30,000 and higher, so it is up to the campaign to carefully analyze how much it reasonably expects to raise. For example, if the campaign's goal is to gross $2,000, it can hold a small, personal event with, say, ten

people giving $200, or it could have a grassroots fundraiser with a goal of having fifty people give $40. Of course, while the gross of these two examples is the same, it will probably cost less in overhead—mailing costs, staff time, and so on—to hold the first event, but the second event might be a better way to build a grass-roots base. The key is to mix it up and diversify the types of events and types of donors targeted.

4. **Compile a guest list.** This is similar to the process of gathering names for direct solicitation fundraising. For events held at people's homes, the campaign should rely on that person's neighbors, family, friends, and co-workers to complement the campaign's lists. Make it clear to the hosts that they need to help recruit people to attend the event. The campaign should invite many more people than the targeted goal. Typically, about one in four people invited to a house party will attend. If you use e-mail as the only way of inviting people, it is usually one in ten or fewer. If the goal is to have an event attended by fifty people, the campaign should invite as many as five hundred people or more, depending on the quality of the lists and the amount being asked.

5. **Send invitations.** Once you have set the date, time, and place for your house party, you are ready to send out invitations. Make sure they go out with enough time for busy people to get it on their schedules. Usually two to three weeks is ideal. The invitation can range from the basic (a postcard) to the more formal (a traditional invitation with a reply envelope). There are some general rules for invitations. Without a doubt the more personal they are, the more likely people are to show up (think of which invitations you are most likely to respond to). The most effective approach is to mail invitations and then follow them up with personal phone calls or face-to-face invitations. If you use e-mail, keep in mind that your response rate will be lower, and remember to make it personal. Think of a subject line—"Party?"—that gets people's attention. The idea is that this e-mail is from you personally inviting your friends and family, so although much of the basic information will stay the same, be sure to personalize each message. It will still be important to follow up with a phone call and to include a link for online donations for people who are unable to attend but still

want to help out. Regardless of the presentation, the invitation should contain this information: date, time, place, suggested donation, directions, and RSVP phone number. Reply envelopes are an effective way of reminding the recipient to make a contribution, even if he or she does not plan to attend the event.

6. **Follow up the invitations with phone calls.** One of the best ways to assure a good turnout is to make follow-up phone calls the week before the event. This is a great volunteer opportunity; it gives people a chance to make friendly phone calls and is a proven method of increasing the total number of contributions. Volunteers should be reminded to keep close track of the people who are planning to attend, so the campaign can have a "hard count" of expected guests before the event. Without a hard count, there is no way to know if an event is going to be successful, if it needs to work harder to increase attendance, or if, ideally, the attendance will be larger than expected.

7. **Hold the event.** After all the pre-event details have been taken care of, the event itself should run smoothly and efficiently. At the event, you should have a sign-in table situated as close to the door as possible, with a receptacle for the money clearly visible. The table should also include sign-in sheets, pens, markers, name tags, buttons, bumper stickers, a place for volunteers to sign up, and campaign literature. Refreshments should be a minimal expense, and when possible, left to the host to provide. Some campaign finance laws require that refreshments and food provided by a host for a campaign be counted as in-kind contributions. Be sure you are adhering to whatever reporting requirements exist.

8. **Have a short program for comments and questions.** Fundraisers, in addition to being a financial resource, provide candidates and campaign leaders with a great opportunity to hone a speech and test the campaign's message. The speaker(s) should be introduced by the event's host, and should speak briefly and perhaps take questions from the audience. The program should begin about halfway into the event, which usually runs about two hours. For example, if an event is scheduled from 7:00 to 9:00, the program should start around 7:45 and last for no more than half an hour; twenty minutes is even better.

9. **Collect money.** The campaign should collect contributions from guests as they enter the party, and the host of the fundraiser should make an explicit appeal for money. The best hosts will make the financial appeal at the beginning of the program and at the end, and try to get those who have already contributed to give even more. Good fundraisers are not afraid to make the ask. They demonstrate they want to win by being persistent and aggressive.

10. **Thank the donors and call people who did not attend.** After the event is over, each contributor should receive a written thank you from the campaign. Those who did not attend or send money before the event but are considered good fundraising prospects should receive a phone call from the campaign, with a direct request for a contribution.

Done right, grassroots fundraising events can be huge assets to a campaign. In 1996, Paul Wellstone used this strategy. In one memorable weekend, his campaign held more than five hundred house parties across the state, which raised a surprisingly large amount of money (all in small contributions), were widely attended, and drew great media attention. The campaign also signed up hundreds of volunteers. While events can't replace the cost-efficiency of direct solicitation, they can be a great way to organize your base while also raising money.

Fundraising Mail

In previous chapters we talked about the value of mail as a form of direct voter contact. To persuade voters, mail needs to be eye-catching, succinct, and accessible (you don't want to put persuasion direct mail in an envelope, for example, because most people won't bother to open it). Fundraising direct mail is different. First, mail is good for resoliciting a campaign's existing donors. Second, prospect fundraising mail is aimed at lists of likely political donors, both within and outside the district, who have more time and interest in reading longer messages that exhort them to action. These donors are politically engaged and have likely donated to political campaigns and causes over the years. They are predisposed to support progressive causes and have a history of backing up that support with a financial contribution.

Prospecting for new donors through the mail is difficult. All of us have received direct mail solicitations in our mailboxes, and we've probably thrown a fair number of them away without even opening them. With all the bills, credit card offers, and catalogs that arrive in the mail every day, fundraising letters often seem like just one more thing to clog our mailboxes. So generally only 1 percent of recipients respond to fundraising mail. These people are known as "acquired donors." Since it can be expensive, campaigns can expect to lose money or break even with these mailings but make money later, when the newly acquired donors give for a second, third, or fourth time. When soliciting donors through mail, especially ideologically driven donors and party activists, it is important to consider how mail can be used to communicate the campaign's message to potential supporters and how it interacts with the campaign's field and direct voter contact program as much as it is to think of raising money.

So does prospect fundraising mail make sense? It can if you have the time to resolicit your new donors several more times before Election Day. It gives the campaign an opportunity to boast about its grassroots support: you can talk about how your campaign is fueled by thousands of donors making small contributions. That is particularly effective when your opponent takes money from a small number of donors who write very large checks. Paul Wellstone relied heavily on direct mail solicitations to raise money. On the front end, it was expensive to raise money from a large grassroots network, but ultimately he was able to raise significant amounts in a way that fit with his style and message. If you add grassroots fundraising to your mix, it can became part of a larger campaign theme—that you are raising money the right way, from thousands of people giving small donations.

In addition, it is mostly large campaigns that do prospect fundraising through the mail, because the cost of purchasing lists of potential donors is prohibitive for smaller campaigns. As with everything, look at the costs versus potential return before jumping headlong into this. That said, there are alternatives for smaller campaigns. For instance, the candidate from your party who ran for your seat during the past cycle might have a great list of supporters in his database. Ask him to send a letter to his supporters requesting a contribution to your campaign; this is a cost-effective way to raise money and add names to your own database of supporters because they will be more likely to give money.

Mail can be used as a prelude to your call program. When Elizabeth Glidden first decided to run for city council in Minneapolis, for example, she came up with her initial list of names and decided that rather than call every one of the people on the list, which would have been time-intensive, she wrote a letter that explained her decision to run and asked for people's support. "The first thing I did was send that letter to my personal list," she told us. She then followed up the letter with e-mails and phone calls. The benefit of sending such a letter is that it allows people the candidate might not have had contact with in many years to get reintroduced and to give them a context for a potential donation. As one candidate told us, "There were people on my list I hadn't spoken to since graduate school. If I had just called them up out of the blue it would have been a little awkward and I probably would have spent more time catching up with them than I would talking about my campaign. By sending them a letter, I could get the updates out of the way, so I could then follow up with a phone call." Don't expect to raise a lot of money from these mailings unless you are prepared to follow up with a phone call or possibly an e-mail. Sometimes a powerful letter to a group of friends and family is all that is needed to raise enough money for smaller races. Pam Costain, in her run for Minneapolis school board, sent one fund-raising letter to a group of her friends and family and ended up raising over $22,000 from the one letter, which represented her targeted budget for her race. In this case, a lifetime of working within the community paid off with virtually no time spent raising money.

Some larger campaigns will hire a fundraising mail firm to handle a major portion of the production and mailing of the pieces. If you are serious about investing resources into raising money through the mail, you need to start early and hire a professional. There are direct mail vendors everywhere, and it's important to choose the right one. Mwosi Swenson, a vice president at Mal Warwick and Associates, a top direct mail firm based in California, gave this advice to campaigns looking for a good fundraising mail firm: "It's important to find a direct mail fundraising firm that has experience doing political fundraising. Although there are standard tried-and-true direct response fundraising techniques that cross all markets, political fundraising brings extra challenges and technicalities. From FEC filing deadlines to max-out rules to candidate list exchanges, there are very important things that your direct mail agency must know. In addition to solid experience, look for a firm that knows the power of integration! Your fundraising program will greatly benefit from a coordinated telephone and online strategy that will allow your donors to contribute across a variety of mediums."

Internet

Ever since Howard Dean's presidential campaign shocked political observers by raising millions of dollars in online contributions, Internet fundraising has grown in importance. Take a look at the Web site of any major political campaign, and one of the first things you will notice is a contribution field, which you can click to give money immediately to the campaign. It's a fast, simple, and nearly cost-free way to raise money.

There are some unique aspects to raising money online. First, supporters often consider online contributing a form of activism and a new way to participate. The best way to encourage that participation is by creating a sense of urgency: use upcoming campaign finance filing deadlines and other benchmarks to put a timeframe around fundraising appeals. Set a deadline and set a goal, as when the Dean campaign used the image of a baseball bat that gradually filled up as contributions poured in. Another way to create urgency is to raise money for a specific activity. For example, "We need to raise $10,000 by this Friday at 5:00 p.m. in order to purchase an additional week of radio ads to combat our opponent's negative campaigning."

When establishing an online mechanism for receiving contributions, your first priority is security. Never store credit card information unencrypted. If you don't have a solid knowledge of how online data storage works, be sure you hire someone (or recruit a volunteer) you can trust to help you with this. Most of the vendors that help set up online donation mechanisms will ensure the security of your system. But you must also be sure that whatever system you use gives you the data on your contributors that you are required to collect by the election laws in your district.

We discuss technology more extensively in chapter 12, where we provide a detailed description of what makes for good e-mail appeals and how to use the Internet as an effective organizing and fundraising tool.

CHAPTER 10

Getting to Know Your Candidate and Understanding Your Opponent

In 2006 Martha Rainville, a Republican candidate for Vermont's lone Congressional seat, enlisted a young staffer to research various issues and help her campaign create position papers. The campaign then posted those positions on issues, ranging from energy to health care to transparency in government, on Rainville's Web site. Several weeks later, a citizen activist came across the position papers and thought they looked familiar. She entered a selection of sentences into a simple Google search and discovered that the campaign had lifted almost verbatim the words of other political candidates, including Democrats like Senator Hillary Clinton. The discovery created a firestorm of criticism, leading to the staffer's resignation, embarrassing the candidate, and forcing the Rainville campaign on the defensive, where she stayed for most of the campaign.

The incident is a good example of how basic research—a keyword search in Google—can play a defining role in a campaign and reveal potentially devastating information about a candidate or a campaign. It shows the power of research to set the campaign agenda and determine who controls the message: the last thing Martha Rainville wanted to be talking about was a staffer who plagiarized research material. It also shows the importance of doing research right; cutting corners or making things up usually backfires. Campaigns that fail to thoroughly and ethically research their opponent as well as their own candidate risk giving control of the message to the other side. Knowing every controversial vote, positions on issues, quotes that might be damaging, or personal information like prior arrests are all essential to modern campaigning.

That's not to say that research is all about digging up dirt on the other side. In fact, there are a lot of misconceptions about what research is, and more important, what it's not. It isn't just opposition, or oppo, research. While it's important to know your opponent's record in detail, some of the most important research you do will be on your own candidate. If there is potentially damaging information that will likely come out during the campaign, you can get it out early in a managed, controlled way. Likewise, if there are things in the candidate's past that reinforce the message of the campaign—like evidence of a long-standing commitment to an issue—research can identify it.

Research is not about spying on people. Most large campaigns, regardless of party, send a volunteer or staff member to record the opponent's public events, but they should always identify themselves and be forthcoming about why they are there. There's no reason not to; if the event is public, everyone has a right to be there. But capturing the opponent's public statements is different from misrepresenting yourself or resorting to unethical (or illegal) tactics like recording private phone conversations. Good research tells a story and builds a case for or against a candidate using all the evidence publicly available, and relies on the strength of that evidence—not rumors, speculation, or spying—to make its argument.

Research is knowing everything there is to know about a candidate's public record. It is a focused effort to collect, analyze, and write about that record and define the strengths and weaknesses of the candidate and the opponent. Done properly, research identifies themes and contrasts and will help with nearly every component of the campaign, from message development to polling, debate prep, and positioning on issues. Most important, good research prevents surprises. Unless the candidate says something stupid on the campaign trail, solid self and opposition research lays the foundation for the campaign to be prepared for every possible attack and to think, before the chaos, about potential response and levels of response.

There are four components to research: collection, analysis, writing, and rapid response.

Collection

One of the keys to successful research is finding information that others, including your opposing campaign, miss. That requires using a wide range of sources, not just relying on the Internet. With the growth of online sources, it's easy to assume that any information you want can be found with a little digging on the Internet. While it's true that the Internet contains a vast amount of information and is a primary research source, it is also the first place that your opponent and the press will look. Finding really original research—the type of information that could trip your opponent or your candidate in the heat of a campaign—often requires a little more digging and analysis. You might be surprised at the number of sources you'll find when you turn your computer off and head to a library or county clerk's office, where you can access everything from driving records to the marital history of either candidate in the race.

Another reason it's important to utilize a wide range of information sources is that it helps the campaign look beyond a candidate's positions on issues or public statements. Obviously you want to collect and categorize as many public statements and quotes in newspapers as possible, but you can also find out a lot about a candidate by looking into readily available public information that might contradict or reinforce a candidate's public statements. Research is about the totality of a candidate's record, including both public statements and private actions.

As you begin the process of collecting information about your candidate and your opponent, put each candidate's personal background into a biographical timeline, using the bio on the candidate's Web site or campaign literature as a starting point. Your research will then fill in the details: if the candidate said she was a member of the local city council from 1984 to 1990, your research will show when she ran for election and reelection, who her opponents were, and which issues defined the campaign. If the candidate said she was a member of the state bar association during a certain period, you will be able to find out if the official records reflect those dates. In sum, you want to hold both candidates' official bios up to scrutiny. You might not find anything problematic (or helpful, depending on your point of view), but you're starting the process of really getting to know the candidate, her background, and her personal history.

Once you start to sketch the candidate's biography, you can rely on a variety of sources that fill in the relevant details. These sources include the following:

▸ **Driver's license and motor vehicle records.** Most states make driving records and motor vehicle registration information publicly available. This information will tell you what kinds of cars the candidate owns, whether he has any unpaid traffic tickets, and whether there are any arrests—for speeding, DUI, or other violations—on his record.

▶ **Marital records.** Divorce records are publicly available in every state except New York. If your candidate is divorced, it's important to know what information (financial, child custody arrangements) will be available to your opponents. Similarly, you might be running against a right-wing "family values" candidate, like Louisiana Senator David Vitter (a frequent client of a D.C. madam), whose personal life doesn't square with his political rhetoric. Think of Illinois Republican Jack Ryan, whose divorce records showed that he repeatedly took his former wife, against her wishes, to sex clubs. Divorce records, particularly when they are unsealed, can reveal far more about a candidate than he or she might want.

▶ **Court records.** If you have the time and people to conduct research into court records, you might find a wealth of information about your candidate and her opponent. Criminal and civil court cases are recorded at the courthouse where they are filed, whether the case is at the municipal, state, or federal level. This research can be highly time-intensive, as it requires going in person to a courthouse and working with a court clerk to sift through large volumes of court records. Yet the hard work can be worth it; court records might reveal civil or criminal charges against an opponent or his business, show whether a candidate has been taken to court by the IRS, or expose a bankruptcy filing by one of the candidates.

▶ **Tax records.** A search of a county or federal courthouse can reveal whether a candidate has paid or been delinquent on property taxes, business taxes, or other taxes.

▶ **Voting history.** A surprising number of candidates for public office have spotty records of going to the polls themselves. The voter file can tell you which candidates are registered to vote and how many elections they have voted in.

▶ **Land records.** In 2006, Peggy Lamm, a longtime member of the Colorado legislature, ran in the Democratic primary for Colorado's Seventh Congressional District. Despite the fact that she hadn't been a resident of the district, she changed her official address and entered the race claiming she was a district resident.

Yet some basic research into Lamm's property, voter registration, and motor vehicle registration records revealed that she claimed two Congressional districts as residences. The discrepancy forced Lamm on the defensive, claiming, "I live in both places." Property records can reveal whether candidates are being truthful about their residency, whether they have outstanding property tax assessments (and how much they pay in property taxes), and whether they have sold their homes at fair market value.

▸ **Business and corporation filings,** if the candidate or the opponent are businesspeople. Information about the value of a company or any questionable business practices can be found by reviewing any corporate or business filing documents.

▸ **Campaign donors.** One of the most obvious sources for campaign research is the list of a candidate's donors. Who donates to a campaign and how much they give are common targets for attacks from a candidate's opponents. If a candidate claims to represent the interests of ordinary citizens but accepts a disproportionate amount of money from well-heeled business interests, that's fair game for a campaign researcher. In addition, campaigns can do a lot with information about the average contribution amount and the number of people contributing to a campaign. Basic research into a candidate's campaign finance disclosure forms (Federal Election Commission, or FEC, filings for federal races, and state disclosure filings for state or local races) will reveal how many people donated to a campaign and the average amount of those donations. Grassroots campaigns with a large base of small donors can use this information as a contrast to a campaign that relies on high-dollar donations from a small number of people. Where do you find this information? For federal races (House and Senate seats), all campaigns are required to register and file periodic campaign finance disclosure reports; these are readily available to the public and searchable through the FEC Web site. An even better online resource for searching donors to federal campaigns is Political Money Line (www.tray.com), which allows you to search for contributions by name, employer, occupation, Congressional district, and other keywords. For further analysis of federal donors' backgrounds, you can also access the Center for Responsive Politics Web site, www.opensecrets.org.

▶ **Voting record.** One of the reasons often cited for members of Congress so rarely winning presidential elections is that they have long voting records that have forced them to put their positions on issues on the official record. If your candidate or your opponent has ever held elected office that required him or her to vote on legislation, it is essential to thoroughly research those votes and any potential conflicts or controversies that might arise from the votes. That is particularly true when researching legislators (either state or federal), who are often forced to vote on bills with controversial provisions. For federal candidates, two good sources for voting histories are Project Vote Smart (www.vote-smart.org), which provides voting histories, interest group ratings, and backgrounds of members of Congress; and the Library of Congress's Thomas system of tracking bills (thomas.loc.gov), which includes the *Congressional Record* as well as exhaustive information about bill authors, sponsors, and language. For state candidates, each state has its own system for tracking the legislative record, most of them online. If you are researching a candidate for local office, a city hall or county clerk should have records of past votes, at least in hard copy.

▶ **Public statements.** A candidate's own words can sometimes be all the ammunition an opposing campaign needs. The longer the candidate has been in public life, the more likely it is that at some point he or she said something that is controversial, conflicts with the candidate's current positions, or reveals attitudes or behaviors that cast the candidate in a bad light. In recent years, newspapers, magazines, and other news sources have increasingly archived their articles in searchable databases, making nearly every public utterance by a candidate in the past two decades easily available to the public. LexisNexis is the best source for retrieving these articles; it serves as an online repository for nearly all major American newspapers and magazines. The Web version of LexisNexis is available on a subscription-only basis, but the cost to the campaign is often worth the investment. Be sure that you know which publications from your state or city are available, and take time familiarizing yourself with how to make the most of your searches. You can use LexisNexis not only to research past statements, but also to track any mention of your candidate or the opponent in the print media. Whoever is responsible for research on your campaign should make a LexisNexis (or at least a Google News) search part of the everyday routine.

As you collect your research information, you will want to create a system for filing and categorizing it. Every campaign is different and these systems will vary, but bear in mind a few characteristics of a good research categorization system. First, make sure that everyone who has access to the research data knows how the system works. There will be times when you'll want to access that information quickly, without having to rely on someone who might be unavailable to find the information for you. Whoever needs to have access to research, for example the campaign manager and press secretary, should be trained in how to pull information from your research database. Second, make it available electronically. You might prefer to have hard copies of all documents and file them in cabinets, but also have an online backup. Every research item you have should exist electronically and, if possible, be searchable. Some computers and software have search functions that allow you to find subjects easily with a few keystrokes. The "Spotlight" feature on recent versions of Apple computers, for example, allows you to do Google-like searches of your desktop. And for PCs, you can download Google Desktop, which allows searches of your desktop files. These are good options for smaller-scale campaigns; larger campaigns will want to create an entire research database.

Analysis

Getting started with campaign research is a little like going on a shopping spree. In the first stage you just start throwing anything that looks good into your cart, knowing that after you check out, you can take a closer look at what you've bought. The analysis stage of research is when you begin to put the information you've collected into a narrative. Your research can help tell a story about each of the candidates in the race, creating the foundation of an ongoing case that the campaign makes about each of them.

The primary goal of the analysis stage of research is to identify themes, contrasts, strengths, and weaknesses of each of the candidates. What kinds of patterns do you see in your opponent's voting record? Does he consistently vote on behalf of business interests? Does he moderate his voting as an election year approaches? Is there a connection between his public statements or legislative activities and the individuals or groups who donate to his campaign? What about your candidate? Do her voting history and public statements reinforce the themes of your campaign, or are they inconsistent with her current positions? If you have identified a weakness in your opponent, are you sure your candidate isn't vulnerable on the same issue?

Your analysis of each candidate can be based on both issues and themes. For example, you should be able to go through a succession of issues and identify the candidate's positions: Has the candidate consistently voted against supporting education? Is agriculture big in your state and the candidate has voted against increased aid to farmers? Does she support privatizing Social Security? Does he vote over and over against ethics and lobbying reforms? What about campaign finance reform? Likewise, you can identify themes that don't necessarily relate to issues but are relevant to the campaign. For example, does your opponent have a history of missing votes on key issues? Is there a pattern of rewarding big campaign donors with legislative favors? Are there questionable business dealings that are worthy of making public or are part of a larger pattern of activity? In going through the collected research, it is the researcher's job to identify and record these themes as they emerge.

Writing

The goal of the writing stage of research is to articulate clearly and simply, without using excessive words or rhetoric, the facts that you have collected and analyzed. The most important thing to remember about writing research material for a campaign is this: let the facts speak for themselves. Leave it to others to craft an overall message around the material or come up with sound bites. Research is more powerful, credible, and likely to be read if it allows readers to draw their own conclusions from the facts.

An example from the 2008 Democratic presidential primary illustrates the point. The Barack Obama campaign conducted extensive research into Senator Hillary Clinton's ties to the financial industry in India. They found that Senator Clinton and Bill Clinton had made significant investments in India-based companies and had accepted hundreds of thousands of dollars in speaking fees from a company that had moved U.S. jobs to India. Instead of just laying out the facts, the campaign instead issued a memo with a headline reading, "Hillary Clinton (D-Punjab)," and circulated it to the media, insisting that its source not be revealed. The Clinton campaign got hold of the memo and immediately made it public, and the Obama campaign was forced to acknowledge that it had produced it. A news report about the incident read, "The memo has created a furor in the Indian-American community and raised questions about Obama's claims that he is above attack politics, which are epitomized by secretly distributing opposition research about a rival." Obama quickly apologized for the incident, saying it was "unnecessarily caustic." He was right; it's not necessary to go over the top. If your research is strong enough, it will speak for itself.

As you write your research materials, just as when you develop your message, keep your audience in mind. A research document can be aimed at a wide range of audiences; it might be useful to the candidate for speeches or debate prep, to media consultants who want to back up any claims made in advertisements with citable facts, or to reporters looking for background information on the candidates. Reporters are a particularly important audience for campaign research. Some reporters are especially interested in seeing the research a campaign produces, as a way of both assessing specific charges and countercharges and measuring the strength of the campaign operation. A good research operation is the sign of a good campaign, and reporters take note of it. "I liked to see the research books," says Dane Smith, recalling his three decades as a political reporter in Minnesota. "And I encouraged both sides to just give me their opposition research and let me see everything they had." Ultimately, of course, your audience will be the voters, who may not read the research materials you produce but will be more easily persuaded by arguments backed up by facts and verified by third parties, like reporters.

What do we mean when we talk about "research documents"? There are a variety of documents that researchers prepare:

▸ **Issues documents.** These provide detailed descriptions of candidates' positions on particular issues. At its most comprehensive, an issues document will contain information on every vote a candidate has taken on an issue, every notable public statement, and any other information about the candidate's views on an issue that are relevant to the campaign. Once you have a comprehensive issues document, you can pull selected materials to create shorter, one-page summaries on an issue or certain aspects of it.

▸ **Background documents.** A background document provides a summary of a candidate's voting history, positions or public statements on issues, or other actions that are relevant to the campaign. If the opposing candidate has a long history with a controversial campaign donor, a background document would give a timeline of the relationship between the candidate and the donor, the amounts and dates of campaign contributions, any action that might suggest preferential treatment for the donor,

▲ ▲ ▲

An Example of a Research Document

NORM COLEMAN'S CREDIBILITY GAP

"Coleman will not easily dispel the impression he is an opportunist of the first rank."
—*Stillwater Evening Gazette*, "Coleman Faces Credibility Issue,"
June 23, 1998

Coleman on Bill Clinton and Paul Wellstone

Coleman endorsed Clinton and Wellstone in 1996, and emphasized that they must be reelected. "To those of you who disagree with me I give you an offer you can't refuse. Fight with me next year when I run for mayor. Battle with me in two years if I am a candidate for governor. But join me today in common bond in unity as Democrats to ensure the reelection of President Bill Clinton and Senator Paul Wellstone. . . . I stand before you today to proudly proclaim my support for President Clinton and Senator Paul Wellstone. As the majority party in this state our tent is wide and now is the time, more than ever, to bring together all the voices in that tent to reelect Senator Wellstone and President Clinton."—Norm Coleman on June 8, 1996, at the DFL state convention

COLEMAN: Let us agree that we must reelect Clinton and Wellstone. "Let us unite on that which we agree—on safe streets, on strong families, on vibrant cities, on the opportunity for each and every individual to reach for the brass ring. To make it happen, most of all let us agree that we as Democrats must come together and reelect President Bill Clinton and Senator Paul Wellstone."—Norm Coleman on June 8, 1996, at the DFL state convention

A few months later, as mayor of St. Paul, Coleman claimed he never supported Wellstone and said Wellstone was wrong for his city. Just four months after endorsing Paul Wellstone at the DFL Convention and praising his leadership in helping revive Saint Paul, Norm Coleman claimed he was staying neutral in the U.S. Senate race in Minnesota between Wellstone and Boschwitz. "At the local level, I don't want to stand with people whose vision clearly has been wrong for the city," he said. "Probably Paul [Wellstone] suffers because of that. Politics is local [to me]."—*Minneapolis Star Tribune*, October 26, 1996; Coleman Remarks, DFL State Convention, June 8, 1996

Coleman gave credit to Clinton and Wellstone for safe streets and 100,000 new police. "But without safe streets our economic revitalization stalls and without the commitment to public safety by President Clinton and Senator Wellstone, there would be 100,000 fewer police to keep our urban streets safe."—Norm Coleman on June 8, 1996, at the DFL state convention or any other information that is relevant. These background documents should reinforce the basic message of the campaign, much as this research document from the 2002 Wellstone for Senate campaign reinforced its message that Norm Coleman was more interested in getting elected than in standing up for a set of beliefs.

COLEMAN: Clinton and Wellstone have consistently stood by Saint Paul. "Both President Clinton and Senator Wellstone understand that urban vitality is dependent upon a trained work force. And without summer job programs for youth, worker retraining and support for higher education our progress would be halted. Both President Clinton and Senator Wellstone understand that strong urban centers result in strong state and regional economies and they have consistently stood by Minnesota's capital city."—Norm Coleman on June 8, 1996, at the DFL state convention

COLEMAN: Clinton and Wellstone are important to continue progress toward bright future. "What Paul Wellstone and Bill Clinton have brought to urban centers is hope and opportunity and we must work tirelessly to bring both of them back if we are to continue our progress to a bright future."—Norm Coleman on June 8, 1996, at the DFL state convention

COLEMAN: Clinton, Wellstone, and I share common beliefs. "Friends, Paul Wellstone and I do not agree on all issues, but we share a basic belief that people must be put before politics and that our efforts to keep urban centers safe, clean, and affordable must continue. The fact is that this common belief is shared by 70 percent of the people of Saint Paul, who believe that the city is moving in the right direction for the first time in many years."—Norm Coleman on June 8, 1996, at the DFL state convention

COLEMAN: Paul Wellstone is a Democrat . . . and so am I. "Paul Wellstone is a Democrat and I am a Democrat. And together as Democrats we believe that civility and tolerance must be returned to the Democratic party. Friends, beyond this wall there are three and a half million Minnesotans who are challenging the notions and ideas of this great DFL Party."—Norm Coleman on June 8, 1996, at the DFL state convention

COLEMAN: Wellstone has integrity. "And finally, before I end, a very brief comment about civility, the ability to agree to disagree. It is a very popular word nowadays, but one thing about Paul Wellstone, he was there before it was popular, it defines who he is. It isn't just about issues, my friends, it's about compassion. It is about integrity."—Norm Coleman on June 8, 1996, at the DFL state convention

COLEMAN: Wellstone was there for me as mayor. "One of the most difficult moments for me was when I learned that two of our police officers had been killed in the line of duty. And one of the very first calls I got was from Senator Wellstone who wanted to know how he could contact the families, how he could help. He was with me that day. He was with me the day we buried those officers. Paul Wellstone and I don't always line up, but he has been there as a friend to this mayor. He has been there as a friend to this city, he deserves our support."—Norm Coleman on June 8, 1996, at the DFL state convention

▶ **"Rhetoric vs. reality" documents.** A good way to contrast your opponent's statements with statements of fact, such documents first quote an opponent saying something either false or highly improbable, then cite factual information that contradicts the claim.

▶ **Top ten lists.** An excellent way to summarize key points about your candidate's or your opponent's record, a top ten list can present the positive ("Top ten ways that Candidate Gray has supported veterans") or the negative ("Candidate Pink's top ten votes against our nation's veterans").

▶ **Debate response documents.** A great way to demonstrate the campaign's ability to respond quickly to charges or claims made by the opposition during a debate is to produce response documents. The campaign will likely have a good sense of what charges or attacks the opponent will make and can be ready with general responses, can record specific quotes during the course of the debate, and can then customize the response to the charge. On large campaigns, researchers churn out these responses and send them to reporters while the debate is still occurring.

Rapid Response: Tracking and Media Monitoring

Despite what its name implies, rapid response is less about reacting to an opponent's actions than it is about proactively anticipating when and how your candidate will be attacked. We mentioned earlier that one of the most common questions we get from our training participants is "Should I respond to every charge leveled against my candidate, or does a response simply give legs to a story that otherwise would have been ignored?" Like most questions on a campaign, the answer depends on the situation. There might be times when an attack doesn't merit a response, but generally we suggest that you respond to every substantive charge leveled by your opponent against your campaign. You should also be ready to immediately respond to a gaffe or mistake by your opponent.

Consider an example from Virginia. A highlight of the 2006 midterm elections was the defeat of Senator George Allen. A right-wing conservative with ambitions for the presidency, Allen squandered a huge lead in the polls over his opponent, Democrat Jim Webb. Among the reasons for Allen's loss was a comment he made to a young staffer on Webb's campaign. S. R. Sidarth was a member of the Webb campaign's research operation who attended Allen's public events and recorded his comments on video. Sidarth also happens to be of Indian descent, and when Allen addressed Sidarth during a campaign rally by calling him "macaca," Sidarth captured it on tape. The ensuing firestorm of criticism surrounding Allen's comment and its racial undertones became a dominant theme in the campaign and helped Webb seize the momentum in the weeks leading up to the election. While there were many factors that led to Allen's defeat, it is quite possible that had the Webb campaign not established a system for tracking Allen's public statements, Allen would still be senator today.

One of the best ways to put an opponent on the defensive is to use his words against him. Candidates often misspeak and contradict themselves during the course of a campaign, but those mistakes are caught rarely, and often are not recorded. The most basic function of a campaign research operation is to know and record everything that's being said and written by and about the candidates in the race. With the growth of online news sources, that task is easier than ever, yet it can't be done simply with a daily Google News search. The way to ensure that your campaign isn't missing any public statements or news articles about your opponent is to set up a candidate tracking and media monitoring system. For your tracking system, your campaign should have an intern or staff member attend all your opponent's public events and record them, preferably on video (this is particularly true of Congressional and statewide races). For media monitoring, you can rely on a combination of tracking news stories online, recording television news, and using your network of volunteers to keep track of any news about the campaign they hear in their local communities or on talk radio.

Candidate tracking has evolved significantly in the past decade of political campaigning. Today, most major campaigns employ some system for tracking the public statements of their opponents by finding out the candidate's schedule and showing up for the events. While this tactic can be controversial, it has been widely adapted by both major political parties and is now generally accepted as a legitimate tool for researching an opposing candidate. However, there are unwritten rules about tracking your opponent. First, be respectful. You are simply there to record what happens, not to engage the opposing candidate or his staff in an argument. You are an official representative of the campaign, and your actions speak on behalf of your candidate. Second, never, ever lie. If asked by a member of the opposing campaign who you are, tell the truth. If they refuse you entry into a public event, it will reflect poorly on them. If you lie to get into a public event, it will reflect poorly on you—and more important, your candidate. Third, don't talk to reporters. If asked, be honest about who you are, but leave all press inquiries to the campaign manager or press secretary to handle.

Finding out your opponent's public schedule is relatively easy. Candidates usually post their public events on their campaign Web site or on their party's Web site. The Associated Press has something called the AP Daybook, which is an online listing of all public events on a given day. The Daybook is subscription-only and can be quite expensive, so try to find out if your party or like-minded campaigns can access the Daybook for you. Once you know where and when your opponent is hosting an event, make plans for a member of your campaign team to attend. Campaigns will often assign one person to the full-time job of candidate tracking, which is helpful because that individual will become very familiar with the opponent's standard stump speech and answers to questions and will be alert to any statements that deviate from the norm or could be interpreted as controversial. Your tracker should be equipped with a digital video camera or a digital audio recorder or both, which make uploading faster and easier than using tapes or CDs so the event can be quickly transcribed when the tracker returns to the office.

In addition to candidate tracking, your campaign should have a system for monitoring every mention of your candidate or opponent in the broadcast and print media. There are four main resources for media monitoring: online news sources, subscription-based "clipping" services, daily recordings of the local television news, and local campaign volunteers. The news articles collected through these sources should be compiled in a "daily clips" document that is sent to all campaign staff and close advisers. Ideally, the daily clips will be distributed early in the morning, giving the campaign a head start on crafting a response (or an attack) based on the daily news. When daily clips are done thoroughly, they often become the single news source for the campaign staff and volunteers.

Online sources include any newspaper that produces an online version, which at this point is the vast majority of newspapers. These newspapers are searchable on the Web sites of the papers themselves, through Google News, and through databases like LexisNexis. A simple search of Google News will produce most of the mentions that the candidates get in online newspapers, but not all. Many newspapers now include political blogs, which often contain valuable information not made available in the newspaper itself. These blogs usually do not show up in Google News searches, and there are times when Google misses candidate mentions from news articles. That's a good reason to carefully read every relevant article or blog entry directly on the newspaper's Web site, in case it isn't picked up in other searches. LexisNexis is a great way to track the statements and positions of the candidates over a long period of time. Be careful, however: LexisNexis doesn't archive every major newspaper, and often only goes back a few years, depending on the newspaper. It is more effective as a long-term research tool than as a way of monitoring the daily news, since it often takes several days for articles to appear on its site.

A second way to monitor the media is to use a clipping service. As we mentioned in chapter 8, a clipping service is a private company that flags news articles from a specified district for any mention of a certain word or words. For example, you would hire a clipping service to track every mention of your candidate and your opponent in all print publications in your district (or throughout the state). On a regular (sometimes daily) basis, you will then receive hard copies of the articles in the mail. This is particularly useful when tracking weekly newspapers and other newspapers with small circulations that don't have online versions. A wide range of clipping services are available; check with party officials or other friendly sources to find out if there is a good one available in your area.

Third, your campaign should record—electronically, through a service like TiVo, if possible—the evening broadcasts of all local television stations in your district. Even if you don't think your campaign will get a mention on the local news, it's always a good idea to have electronic files of any local stories that appear on television.

Finally, your campaign's grassroots volunteer network can play an important role as the eyes and ears of the campaign out in their communities. Volunteers are frequently asking for ways they can help, but often they live far from campaign headquarters or areas where the campaign is doing phoning or canvassing work. Assigning trustworthy volunteers to monitor talk radio shows, read their local newspapers for mentions of the campaign, and keep tabs on any local gossip about the candidates is a great way to empower your volunteers.

CHAPTER 11

Maximizing the Candidate's Time with Smart Scheduling

I F YOU ARE A FIRST-TIME CANDIDATE, one of your first challenges is figuring out how to spend your time. You know you need to door-knock, attend community and political events, and raise money in person and on the phones. Soon after the campaign begins, the invitations and opportunities start pouring in. Before long, you find yourself overscheduled: between picnics, candidate forums, and parades, you have less and less time to knock on doors and make fundraising calls. Activity is not necessarily the same things as effectiveness, and a lot of the events are a waste of time. Some are poorly attended or attended only by voters whose minds are already made up, while others might be outside of your target audience or even outside your district. But it's difficult to resist the temptation to say yes to every invitation you receive. "I really wanted to run a grassroots campaign, and not miss any opportunity to talk to voters," one candidate for state legislature told us. "But then I found myself constantly overbooked, going to places day and night. It was exhausting, and most of the time I would have been better off knocking on doors."

Most campaigns quickly learn how important scheduling is for maximizing voter contact and keeping the candidate focused. Scheduling is often the art of saying no—to invitations, suggestions from supporters, and the impulse to agree to everything—and creating strategic opportunities to talk to voters. Many campaigns forget the simple rule about scheduling: go where the voters are. If 30 percent of your targeted voters live in Precinct 2, ideally your candidate will spend 30 percent of her time there. Simple as it sounds, it is actually very difficult to do when a campaign is in full swing. With so many competing demands on the candidate's time, it's hard to map out exactly how the candidate is spending it. That's why you need to agree on a scheduling plan at the beginning of the campaign, one that is incorporated into the campaign plan and is based on strategic choices and data.

The data, of course, are your targeting numbers. Targeting should inform all of your scheduling decisions—where you go, when you go, and how long you stay. Let's use a hypothetical example. You're running for county commission in a largely rural county with two main towns, Jackson (pop. 3,500) and Bolton (pop. 2,000). Your targeting data show you that the western part of the district, Bolton and the surrounding area, is your base. You've concluded that your target audience is made up of working-class families who live near Jackson, which is a blue-collar community in the eastern part of the district. Progressives have fared poorly in the past few elections in Jackson, in part because of the success of conservatives at defining them as tax raisers. You live in Bolton, which is an hour's drive from Jackson. How should you spend your time?

The answer seems easy: do what you can to shore up your base in Bolton, and spend most of your time in the eastern part of the district. While that's correct, it requires a lot of trade-offs that might not seem evident at first. Driving an hour to and from home can wear down the candidate and keep her from other events that would give her a chance to mobilize her base supporters. The campaign might also get invitations to well-attended events in the northern and southern parts of the county. How beneficial is it to go to an event in a rural part of the district, when a well-attended event there might still have fewer people than an event in Jackson or Bolton? Even more difficult is that the campaign will get invitations from base supporters, many of which will have to be declined, with the inevitable disappointment attached to turning down friends. And what about door-knocking? Where should the candidate start, and are there ways to schedule other events in that community at the same time? These decisions are up to you, but you're not alone in making them; you have targeting to guide you. Think of your targeting plan as a how-to manual as you put together your schedule.

The key to making scheduling work is to establish a system and routine for making decisions about the schedule. There are five major schedules to balance: fundraising time, events, direct voter contact time, media time, personal time, and work time (if the candidate has a job outside the campaign). Each of these areas of the campaign will vie for the most limited and precious resource of all: the candidate's time. Making the right decision requires the right people working together to coordinate schedule demands—the campaign manager; a designated volunteer or staff member responsible for scheduling; on larger campaigns the finance, communications, and field directors; and in some cases the candidate—and it requires time to be set aside every week or every few days. To give you a sense of how a scheduling system works, we describe below how a well-run, statewide campaign manages the scheduling process. Keep in mind as you read this that if you are running a smaller campaign with few or no staff, the scale of the scheduling task might be smaller, but the principles still apply. Ultimately, your goal is to use the candidate's schedule to maximize the campaign's scarce resources.

Handling Scheduling Requests

At the beginning of our hypothetical campaign for statewide office, one of the first hires is the scheduler, who will be the point of contact with any organization or individual who has a scheduling request for the candidate (with the exception of the news media, who work through the campaign manager or press secretary, who in turn works with the scheduler). The campaign will receive dozens of invitations to events, some of which are worthwhile and some of which are probably a waste of the candidate's time. And the campaign itself will want to schedule events from door-knocking to fundraising events to rallies to debates to editorial board meetings. The first step in evaluating which of those two categories an event falls into is to get all requests and invitations in written form (which includes e-mail correspondence). Written requests are important for two reasons: they help the scheduler remember all pending requests, and they allow the scheduler to share the requests with other staff members when setting up the schedule. It's a good idea to keep notes on each scheduling request, such as the group making the invitation, location, time, and the results of any conversations with a contact person. These notes can protect the campaign down the road, especially if a group claims that it failed to receive a response to an invitation.

The next step is to make initial decisions about whether to reject a scheduling request or bring it up for discussion in the scheduling meeting. Invitations are rejected at this point when the scheduler feels comfortable denying them without consulting other members of the campaign team—invitations to events that are out of state, poorly organized, or conflict with other things on the schedule. The scheduler should promptly write or call the inviting organization or individual, expressing regrets at not being able to attend. Sometimes there are events that don't work for the candidate's schedule but are worth attending. In those cases, the scheduler should offer to send a surrogate in place of the candidate.

Surrogates

Surrogates are a valuable but often overlooked resource for a campaign. Their time helping the campaign should be systematically managed, much like the candidate's. A surrogate is a person who can represent the candidate or the campaign in the candidate's absence. Surrogates range from prominent supporters to local leaders who can door-knock, hand out literature at festivals, or march in parades. When surrogates fill in for a candidate at speeches, debates, fundraisers, or other events, they will need to be well prepared, with briefing materials and a detailed schedule. A note of caution: with surrogates the campaign should really stress the importance of staying on message. Many surrogates have their own styles, opinions, and personalities that might not be entirely in sync with the candidate's message. Other surrogates may be people who are considering a future run for office, and may be more interested in doing early campaigning for themselves than in getting the candidate's message out. This, however, is rare—good surrogates, regardless of their ambition, provide the campaign with a powerful tool for delivering a message.

Deciding What to Attend

What do you do with the requests that warrant further consideration? The scheduler can't make these decisions alone, which is why the campaign needs to establish a weekly (or more frequent) scheduling meeting. Setting a candidate's schedule is a collaborative process in which the relevant campaign team members—on a large campaign, the scheduler, campaign manager, field director, finance director, and communications director—decide which events the candidate will attend. The scheduler is then responsible for following up and implementing those choices. The candidate does not always attend these meetings (in fact, it's not always a good use of the candidate's time to hash through every scheduling option), but needs to be briefed on the choices and decisions.

At each scheduling meeting, the scheduler presents the invitations and scheduling opportunities, including relevant details about the events. Scheduling needs to look ahead at least two to three weeks, and beyond for some important known events, but the final schedule is often only one or two weeks ahead. To begin, it is important to lock in dates that are not optional. These dates include private time the candidate needs to have: important events with children, anniversaries, even a monthly date with his or her spouse. Work time that is unavoidable needs to be included in these blocked-off times (this is common for smaller races where the candidate is often still working). Then come the events that are a must: debates, major endorsement screenings, and other events that are impossible to miss.

Finally comes the debate over whatever time remains; this will try to balance the time needed for fundraising with the time required for direct voter contact with the need to work with the media. This is no easy task, and scheduling meetings can be long and sometimes tense. What helps is a clear plan that guides the campaign's priorities regarding field and fundraising targets and clear and accurate information about event requests. These details include location, time and date, activities expected of the candidate (if there is a speaking role, etc.), size and demographics of the audience, other candidates or notable people who will also attend, and the host of the event. Do your homework before the scheduling meeting, and utilize your campaign's field operation to get more information. When possible, the scheduler should work with organizers in the relevant communities to find out if certain events are worth attending or not. Don't always take the organizer's word for it—they might tell you that hundreds of people are coming and that the guests include U.S. senators and the governor, but those events don't always work out as planned. It's not uncommon for event organizers to tell you, "If the candidate attends this event, we will have at least three hundred people there!" But a couple phone calls to your key supporters in the community might reveal that seventy-five people typically turn out for this semiannual event.

Once the scheduler has presented information about the request, participants discuss the pros and cons of each scheduling opportunity and make one of three decisions: accept, reject, or defer judgment on an invitation. One approach that has been successful is first to have the debate over key events, including key fundraising events, and make the decision on the most important ones. Then schedule in blocks of time for direct voter contact and fundraising (call time) around these major events and build in earned media opportunities around every trip. Then, if any time remains, lower-priority events can be scheduled if they fit the overall campaign plan and the contour of the rest of the schedule (you don't want to send a candidate across the state for a random event, even if it is in a targeted area, only to have her cross the state back to another event the next day, unless the events are critical). Once you decide to accept an invitation, put it on the candidate's schedule and start pulling together briefing materials (more on that follows), and if you decline the invitation, don't forget to consider a surrogate. In some cases, an invitation is set aside for later consideration. It may be too soon to commit, the campaign may need more information, or you may just want to leave your options open. Accepted invitations are added to the candidate's schedule, which consists of both a long-term, or "block" schedule, as well as a short-term schedule. The block schedule can take the form of a "month at a glance" type calendar that can track the long-term activities of the campaign. This schedule is used for strategic and long-range planning, as it gives the campaign an overview of where the candidate is spending his or her time and whether the schedule is reflecting the campaign's geographic targeting goals. It is also helpful to have a map of the candidate's district or state on a wall to complement the block schedule, with colored tacks or pins that show where the candidate has been.

The Schedule and Briefing Book

The candidate's actual, internal, short-term schedule is highly detailed and includes all the information that a candidate and travel staff need for getting to and from an event and knowing what to do upon arrival. The schedule shows the candidate's arrival and departure time at the event as well as the actual event time. If an event is from 6:00 to 8:00 p.m. but the candidate will only be there from 6:30 to 7:15, note both time periods on the schedule. The schedule should include phone and fax numbers for every location; the campaign needs to be able to be in contact with the candidate at all times without relying solely on cell phones. List all numbers for frequently contacted staff at the top of each daily schedule, and be sure the timing of the events is accurate: a candidate's time needs to be scheduled down to the minute (see "Schedule for Josie Candidate" on page 220 for an example).

An important note about driving instructions: you cannot afford to get the candidate lost. As veterans of Paul Wellstone's campaigns, we can tell you that it's not much fun to get lost with a candidate who hates being late but is running behind for an important event or an opportunity to meet voters. No one likes to get lost, but candidates can be particularly upset about it, with good reason. Thankfully, technology has made campaign navigation infinitely easier. If you have the money, invest in a portable GPS unit, which will save time and make the candidate's (and his driver's) life much less stressful. If you don't have a GPS, driving directions must be clear, concise, and accurate. When possible, the campaign should have a person drive through a route the day before an event, so that the directions are perfect. Be specific: "Drive 2.8 miles on Ridge Road, turn left on Butler Avenue (you will see a sign at the large white house on the corner), go 1.6 miles to Harrison Street." One way to ensure a smooth schedule is to be careful not to overbook the candidate. It is tempting to pack the schedule when there are a lot of great things to do, but be realistic. If the candidate ends up being late or missing half the stops on the schedule because of poor planning or an overzealous scheduler, it reflects poorly on the candidate.

A briefing book is a folder or three-ring binder prepared for the candidate that contains details about the events on the next day's schedule, including a copy of the schedule, memos about the event, and other background material like press clippings and event memos. An event memo is an important way to prepare the candidate. The staff members and organizers responsible for an event usually write these memos, but the scheduler can also write them. Event memos should be clearly written and contain all relevant information: what the event is, who will be there, what the candidate should say. For example, a memo for a fundraising event would be written by the fundraising staff and would contain very specific information about how many people are expected, whom the candidate should thank, how the program will proceed, and what points the candidate should emphasize. Do not leave out any details: "You will be introduced by the host, Mike Jones (see below for background information on Mike and his wife Rebecca); you will speak for 15 minutes and have 15 minutes for questions and answers. You will depart at 7:35 p.m. and proceed to the next event."

The scheduler is responsible for seeing that the briefing book is prepared on time and thoroughly, and delivered to the candidate or a surrogate. The briefing book should also be copied and distributed to all relevant staff. If the candidate wants to speak with the campaign manager and staff members working on the event, they should know the contents of the briefing book. The candidate travels with the briefing book throughout the day's schedule, and it needs to be delivered to the candidate early enough to allow time to study the information. Candidates have their individual preferences about how early they need the briefing book, but it is generally delivered (usually to the candidate at home) as early as possible the night before the day of events.

▲ ▲ ▲

Schedule for Josie Candidate

INTERNAL USE ONLY

[You can list some frequently used staff contact numbers here:]

Marnie Jones, (H) 111-222-3333, (O) 111-222-4444, (C) 111-222-5555, (P) 111-222-6666

[How you list things is important—keep it easy to read:]

February 3, 2007

6:15 p.m.–6:40 p.m.   DEPART from camp office/travel to Cityview Holiday Inn,
                        driver: Aggie Beauchamps, cell: 111-222-7777
    Directions from camp office to Holiday Inn Cityview:
    Right (N) out of parking lot onto Maple St., follow Maple to Elm.
    Left (W) on Elm about 2 miles to entrance for I-90 north.
    North on I-90, 17 miles to second exit for City: "Main St."
    Right (E) at bottom of exit, onto Main St.
    Follow Main St. 6 blocks to HI Cityview.
    Parking available on attached ramp; take elevators to second floor walkway, proceed to Glitzy
      Ballroom A on 2nd floor.
    There will be signs for the ballroom entrance; Jo Smith is expecting you and will take you back-
      stage from there.
    (NOTE: Restrooms off main hallway just before you approach the ballroom)

6:45 p.m.–7:45 p.m.   SPEECH—State Nurses Association Annual Dinner

(6:00 p.m.–9:00 p.m.)   Topic: "What Being a Nurse Means to This Election"
    Speaking time: 20–30 min.
    Briefing/speech: [List name(s) and number(s) of staff who are writing the speech and/or
      preparing a briefing memo on this event.]
    Location: Holiday Inn Cityview
    1111 West Main Street
    City name, ST 55511
    Site phone: 222-333-0000, fax: 222-333-1111
    Event contact: Jo Smith, 222-333-2222, fax: 222-333-3333

Scheduling Smaller Races

Smaller races often do not have the logistical challenges of a larger race or the resources to hire a specific person to schedule. Still, the same guidelines we've given hold true to smaller races as well. Too often in small races the candidate controls his own schedule. This is usually not a productive situation, because

Staff contact: Jamie, pager: 111-222-8888
(O) 111-222-9999, (H) 222-333-4444 [staffer responsible for working with this event]
Travel staffer: [name of staffer who is traveling with candidate]

7:45 p.m.   DEPART for Regent Aviation
Nieve Nunez will drive, cell: 222-333-5555
Directions from HI to Regent Aviation:
Follow Yada Yada St. north to Kellogg Blvd (.9 miles)
Left on Kellogg Blvd to Robert St. bridge (.1 miles)
Right on Robert St. over river to Plato Blvd (.4 miles)
Left on Plato Blvd straight out to Holman Field (.8 miles)
Follow Plato Blvd all the way to Regent Aviation (.2 miles)

8:15 p.m.   Wheels up for Springfield from Regent Aviation
                  212 Clark Street, Springfield
Aboard: [candidate name, travel staff name, and names of anyone else traveling with
    candidate]
Departure from Regent Aviation
Site phone: 222-333-6666, fax: 222-333-7777
Pilot: Peter Pan (Regent's chief pilot)
Tail #: King Air 100, T41BE [Tail # is important if it's a small aircraft and you need to reach
    them urgently. Without tail # you won't be able to radio them.]
Charter contact: Regent Charter, 111-222-0000

9:45 p.m.   Wheels down Springfield, Northcountry Aviation
Northcountry Aviation: 333-555-0000
Joe Upnorth picks everyone up at airport and drives them in his van to the Holiday Inn.
Joe, cell: 333-555-9999, (H) 333-555-1111

OVERNIGHT: Holiday Inn Springfield
Site phone: 444-777-1111, fax: 444-777-1133
Two double bed nonsmoking rooms reserved, one under [candidate name] and one under
    [staff name]
Res. # 111001 and 111002
NOTE: requested quiet rooms away from pool area
[If staff is staying in a different location, just be sure to list all available contact numbers
    for staff and candidate.]

it is extremely difficult for a candidate to say no to someone who asks him to attend an event. Part of successful scheduling is to have a team in place that sets the schedule; that way the candidate has cover and can say, "I'll forward the request to my campaign team." The candidate may even joke about not controlling his schedule, which is a good thing in campaigns.

▲ ▲ ▲

Event Briefing Memo

Thursday, September 14

Tour H & K Manufacturing, Inc.
Meet with H & K workers and representatives of other Jones success stories
10:00–11:00 a.m.
2000 Highlight Road
Kingman
000-000-0000
Contact: Harry Kay

Message

Helping Oregon compete to win. Real-life examples of job-creating success stories and real-life proof of the Jones record.

Purpose

This event is intended to highlight real-life examples of your record of success in delivering jobs and tangible results for Oregon—helping Oregon compete to win. The site was chosen because it speaks to your experience: in this case, helping to win back funding for the Pacific Trade Center. As well, you will be joined at this site not only by the people who work at H & K, but also by a union leader there and others who have been directly helped by your efforts.

Background

- H & K Manufacturing, Inc., has worked with the Pacific Trade Center to improve its operations. There are approximately thirty employees here manufacturing industrial components for machine tool shops. This is a union shop, and the head of the local will join you at this event.
- H & K is moving from the current location because they have outgrown the current space. Business is so good that they are expanding and are looking for a new location. They own the building they are in and won't move until it is leased or sold.
- Senator Boss has visited within the last year, and you can expect the owner to mention that visit.
- You will be joined here by workers from other businesses and organizations you have helped.

Schedulers

It takes a unique person to be a good scheduler. Schedulers are ambassadors of the campaign, yet they need to say no to a lot of requests, many from people who don't like to take no for an answer. Schedulers deal with constantly changing circumstances—events are often added, canceled, or rescheduled at the last minute, programs change, and new developments require changes in strategy.

Following this memo is a list of those expected to send representatives and those who were called and might surprise us by sending someone. You should review this list so that during the discussion you can refer to specific cases.

Participants (see list that follows)

Logistics

- Upon arrival, you will be met by Harry Kay, the president and owner of H & K, and the head of the Local, Sam Allan. They will lead you on a short tour of the manufacturing plant. (Should take about ten minutes.) During the tour, you should shake hands with the workers you meet and ask them about their work. It will be very noisy in there—a good place for brief conversations. NOTE: Kay wanted to give you a much longer tour and briefing. We told him the schedule was too tight. If he tries to get you personally to go for the longer tour, politely beg off.
- Keep in mind: there are picture opportunities during the tour as well as during the meeting to follow. But you must make sure those opportunities exist. The picture we want is you with workers. That means stopping during the plant tour to shake hands and say hello.
- After the tour, Harry and Sam will lead you to an area of the manufacturing floor that will be set up for the discussion. You will be joined by the H & K workers and by your guests from other businesses and organizations. (The machines will be turned off.)
- The discussion site will be informal—some people will be sitting, some will be standing; some people will be close enough to you to be in the picture. The whole idea here is to get a picture of you with workers at a work site to reinforce the message that you will deliver jobs.
- Harry and Sam will introduce you.
- You will speak briefly after Sam. (Your talking points follow here.)
- You should end your remarks by starting the discussion with the workers. There are questions at the end of your talking points that should help.
- This is <u>not</u> a speech—it's a discussion. You should speak briefly, then listen and respond appropriately. Ask them about their experiences. Ask them about whether they are finding the workers they need. Refer to the list of participants and ask, "Who's here from _____?" Then ask a relevant question. ("We made some improvements on Highway 12. What difference have they made?")
- Use your responses to make a point: "You're right. We need more job training and more apprenticeship training. I've supported expanding job training and education and I'm going to . . ."
- Don't be shy about taking credit when people say thanks for your work. Don't overdo it, either.

Schedulers also need to understand the candidate's personality and needs. Candidates are under constant pressure to perform, persuade voters, and raise money. Their reputations and their careers are often at stake. That means that little details matter—how much the candidate needs to sleep, what kind of food she likes, what kind of car she prefers to drive in, whether she's a morning person or not. It's up to the campaign—and it often falls on the scheduler—to pay attention to those details so the schedule moves as smoothly as possible and the candidate can focus on doing her job. Senator Patricia Torres Ray from Minneapolis told us that finding the right person to do the scheduling can make a candidate's life so much easier. "I was very fortunate to have a campaign manager who introduced me to a wonderful student we hired to do all the scheduling," she said. "He really wasn't interested in the other aspects of the campaign, which for me was great—I needed him to keep track of everything related to my schedule, so that I didn't have to worry about it. Keeping him in my campaign was such a high priority that it was reason enough to go out and raise money to pay for his position."

CHAPTER 12

Getting the Most out of Technology

SINCE CAMPAIGNS ARE ABOUT MAXIMIZING scarce resources, it pays to get your technology right. Good technology will save you time by making information readily available and accessible. It can provide a reliable communications infrastructure, a system for managing data, and tools to make the candidate's job easier. Some campaigns will need little more than a single computer and some cell phones to meet their technology needs, while others will require large computer networks, communications systems, and an online organizing structure. We're not going to tell you what will work for your campaign; that's a question only you and your campaign team can answer. But the right technology setup—one that is matched to the size and scale of your race—will make you more efficient and effective at organizing and communications.

Set realistic expectations about your technology infrastructure. Think about what your campaign will actually use, and resist the temptation to add technology for its own sake. A fancy technology setup is useless if the campaign doesn't use it or if you end up spending most of your time trying to figure out how to use it. There are a million different cool things you can do with technology, and it's easy to go overboard—to spend too much time or money for what you get out of it. One good reality check is to think of everything in terms of your goals: does this get me votes, volunteers, or money? If it does none of those things, it is probably not worth the investment. In addition, volunteers and supporters will often approach you with "cool" ideas that might have merit but require time and expertise that you and your campaign team don't have. Rather than dismiss anything out of hand, try to get a commitment out of these volunteers to help implement their ideas. If they suggest setting up a blog, ask them to help create it and do regular postings.

If they suggest podcasts, ask them to help produce them. If they suggest SMS messaging (text messaging) for getting out the vote, ask them to lead it.

Databases

While most of the material in this chapter covers Internet-based technology, the first and most basic decision you will make about technology is deciding how you are going to collect, manipulate, and retrieve your data. Your database, which you might decide to make available online to your campaign team, is the most valuable source of information for your campaign. It contains the names, contact information, and notes about your donors and volunteers and is the collection center for information coming into the campaign. As Senator Patricia Torres Ray of Minneapolis told us, "Keep track of every piece of information you come across on the campaign: phone numbers, cell phone numbers, Web sites, e-mail addresses. I can't emphasize this enough—be very disciplined. If you meet somebody, make sure you collect all their information, and either you or one of your campaign workers should go to the computer every day to type in the information. I have three thousand people in my database. We know who they are, we know their e-mail addresses, and we know how to keep in touch with them."

Ultimately, you want a database that allows you to do two things efficiently and easily: put data in and take data out. Data goes in either through manual entry into a single, off-line database or through an online database. Some campaigns use technology that allows data to go in through personal digital assistants (PDAs), such as PalmPilots. Data comes out of the database in the form of searchable lists.

A range of database software options is available to accomplish these goals. Small campaigns can usually get by with Microsoft Access, which is a relatively simple database program that allows you to both store data and pull lists from the data using a search function. If you are just getting started and are not familiar with Microsoft Access, you can start collecting data in a basic Microsoft Excel spreadsheet. As you learn how to use Access—and we suggest taking the time to learn it, because it is far superior to Excel as a database program—you can then import the data from Excel into Access. Both of these programs allow you to create fields—name, address, phone number, and notes, for example—that can then be used for searches and for printing up lists.

Your database is not the same as the voter file. The voter file contains all the registered voters in your district, while the database contains your donors, volunteers, and other individuals whose names you have collected on the campaign trail. Some of the people in your database will not live in your district (particularly if you have success raising money outside your district), and the voting history information that exists in the voter file might not necessarily be included in the database. Another way to think of it is that every person in your database who is a registered voter in your district is also in the voter file, but not everyone who is in the voter file is in your database. The voter file can be very helpful in enhancing the information in your database; if you have a donor or volunteer in your database and want to know the person's voting history or past ID information, you can look it up in the voter file. Other sources of information can be used to enhance your database, like phone "matches," updated phone number information about the people in your database. You can purchase these records and "match" them to your database in order to ensure that you have the most recent information possible. To find out more information about phone match vendors in your area, talk to party officials or other campaign professionals with experience working in your district.

We recommend that larger campaigns use online vendors to store and maintain your data. The online option has many advantages. Your data is stored on an off-site server, so it is physically protected and always backed up. You can access the data from remote locations. You can password-protect certain parts of your database, allowing volunteers to enter information without jeopardizing the database. The disadvantage of using an online database is cost. Whereas Microsoft Access and Excel are included in Microsoft Office software, you pay online vendors a monthly fee based on the number of records you have in your database. For most campaigns, however, the security and ease of use that accompany an online database are worth the cost.

Database Tips

1. Use Windows Update for Windows 98 and above; use Software Update for Mac OS 9 and OS X.

2. Keep your antivirus software updated! Norton/Symantec has a good program at a cost; a free alternative is AVG Free (http://free.grisoft.com/). For Macs, try Sophos, although viruses are less of a problem with Macs.

3. A firewall is built into Windows XP and OS X. A free alternative is ZoneAlarm (http://www.zonealarm.com/store/content/company/products/znalm/freeDownload.jsp).

4. Follow the instructions in your computer's manual for how to turn on WEP (a form of encryption).

5. Windows Defender, a spyware software, is free (http://www.microsoft.com/athome/security/spyware/software/). Spyware is not usually a problem for Macs.

6. Be sure to take your backups off-site every so often, so that if there's a fire, flood, or theft, you don't lose the backups along with the originals. Test your backups, too! You'll be glad later.

7. Make sure your password is at least eight characters long, is not a word found in the dictionary, and includes nonalphanumeric characters (like % or @).

Online Communications

Technology has come to play a defining role in how many voters perceive and interact with campaigns. Web sites and e-mail are often the first impression that many voters have of a campaign, making it increasingly important to produce crisp and compelling online materials. When it comes to online communication, avoid trying to get too fancy, particularly if you're running a smaller campaign. The attention and excitement that the Dean campaign created online was a sea change for campaigns, but we aren't all running major presidential campaigns, and we can't all raise $40 million on the Internet. There are a number of cost-effective ways of creating a Web site, either by having a tech-savvy volunteer produce it for you, creating it yourself using software like Dreamweaver, or by hiring a company (there are countless Web site developers who create sites for political candidates). As we detail later, a number of good options are also available for sending bulk e-mails at a low cost to your supporters.

Web Sites

As you develop both your Web site and e-mail strategy, think about your audience before you design the product. There are three major audiences for campaign Web sites—supporters, the media, and the opposition. Note that persuadable and undecided voters are not a target audience for the Web site; the Internet remains a largely ineffective tool for moving voters. By far the most important audience for your Web site and e-mail will be your supporters. More than anything else, these online communications resources are organizing and mobilizing tools for your base. Your Web site should have a sign-up field prominently located on the home page, which allows supporters to add their e-mail addresses to the campaign's database. Equally important is having a one-click donation button, allowing supporters to quickly and easily make a contribution to the campaign with a few mouse clicks. In addition to e-mail sign-up and easy donation button, the home page should have a link, preferably "above the fold" (before the viewer has to scroll down), to a volunteer form, issues section, media center, contact information, and biography. To get ideas, look at the Web sites of any of the major candidates for president or statewide offices.

Other features on the Web site could include an events calendar, information on where to vote, photos, and an online store with T-shirts and bumper stickers, yard signs, and of course any other innovative options that give your supporters the tools to support your campaign—from house parties to friend-raising to media monitoring.

Another great online organizing tool for your supporters is a letters-to-the-editor function on your Web site. This tool allows you to write a letter to the editor on the party's homepage, designate which papers you want to send the letter to, and have the letter automatically forwarded to that paper. This is a great example of using technology to make it easy for your supporters to get your message out through the press. It's simple, doesn't require your supporters to look up the e-mail addresses of various newspapers, and allows them to go to the Web site on their own to find out what issues the campaign (or party) is focusing on at the time. While a tool like this requires having a staff person or volunteer with the technical expertise and time to put it together, once it is set up, it requires very little effort to maintain.

While the most important audience for your Web site will be your supporters, you also need to keep in mind undecided voters, your opponents, and the media. For undecided voters who do happen to get to your Web site, be sure to include biographical information, positions on issues, positive press stories about the candidate, photos, and any other information that makes the candidate more "human" (information about family, personal interests, etc.). For opponents, be sure there is nothing on your site that they can use against you, and be careful about using interactive technology (like a comments section of a blog that you don't control) that allows your opponents to post negative things about your campaign. This includes the quality of your photos; if you put a bad picture of the candidate on the Web site, the opposition might download it for use in their direct mail against you! Reporters will also read your Web site, so consider putting a high resolution, downloadable photo of the candidate that the press can use in print or online. Also put contact information for your campaign manager or press secretary, and immediately post to your Web site any press releases the campaign sends out. Never put anything on the Web site, campaign blog, or e-mail that you wouldn't feel comfortable seeing on the front page of the paper the next morning.

An example of a good campaign Web site, reflecting the principles we've described, is the one for Michael Nutter's successful campaign for mayor of Philadelphia. Note the prominent placement of the e-mail sign-up form, the simplicity of the format, and the use of photos.

Michael Nutter's Web site for his successful 2007 Philadelphia mayoral campaign is a good example of a simple site that manages to pack in a lot of information, including the candidate's positions on issues and how to get involved.

Hillary Clinton's 2008 Web site is similarly clear.

Hillary Clinton's 2008 campaign Web site is visually appealing and prominently tells visitors how they can get involved. In addition, the Clinton campaign, like many others in the 2008 cycle, did a good job of using video and frequent updates to the site to keep visitors coming back.

John McCain's 2008 Web site is typical of a growing number of Web sites that simply put a sign-up form with a large photo on the opening page, giving visitors the option of continuing on to the main page but clearly emphasizing the importance of their getting involved in the campaign. This is a good example of a Web site that uses a minimum amount of text and information, but still draws the viewer in.

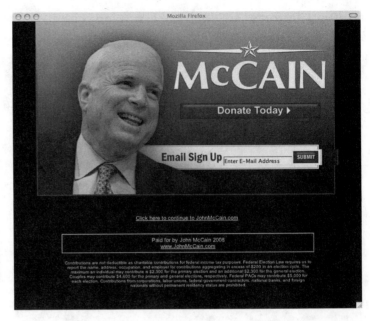

*John McCain's 2008
Web site draws the visitor
in with minimal text and
a clear emphasis on the
importance of grassroots
support for the campaign.*

When finalizing your Web site, consider your district: does it need to be translated into Spanish or other languages of your constituency? Does it look the same on the two major browsers, Internet Explorer and Mozilla Firefox? If you are in a mostly rural district, how will the Web site upload if someone has a dial-up Internet connection (yes, this still happens!)? Consider how graphic heavy your site is, and remember that not everyone has the same broadband capacity as you.

Blogs and Other Web Tools

For campaigns with the resources and technical expertise to pull it off, there are a number of more advanced Web tools that can help you deliver your message, including blogs, podcasts, and social networking communities like MySpace and Facebook. Blogs (short for Web logs) are personal journals on the Web that are continually updated. Blogs have exploded in popularity in recent years and are playing an increasingly influential role not only in mobilizing like-minded individuals to take action on issues, but also in setting local and national political agendas and breaking news stories. You should keep informed of what's being said on blogs in your state, particularly when your campaign is mentioned (see the chapter on earned media for tips on outreach to blogs), and you should consider (if and only if you have the capacity) starting a campaign blog. If you do decide to create a campaign blog, you will need blogging software, of which there are several varieties. If you're new to Web site development and don't know much about blogging technology, you really need to recruit a knowledgeable volunteer or Web developer to help guide you through setting up a blog and understanding its capabilities. If you have a blog, consider the following:

▸ Blogs are not press releases. They must have personal and compelling voices from the campaign, and they must be updated often.

▸ A campaign blog should be everything that a good message is: compelling, interesting, relevant, and timely. If the campaign cannot maintain this, then don't risk doing a blog.

▸ If you open the campaign blog to supporters, you should have a moderated blog, where the campaign approves each posting before it goes live. The campaign blog reflects the tone and message of the campaign, and an unmoderated campaign blog could invite inappropriate and unchecked content that will hurt the campaign.

A blog can be a great addition to a campaign Web site and give it new voice and energy, but it does take time and people to do it right and well.

Social Networking

Large-scale campaigns with the staff and volunteer resources to set up blogs and keep them updated might also consider using podcasts and social networking sites. Podcasts are a great way to deliver a message in a dynamic, interactive way. MySpace and Facebook provide the campaign an opportunity to tie into specific communities of voters and let your supporters link their friends to your campaign. Keep in mind, however, that these cool tools require a lot of time and energy to maintain, and only on larger-scale races do they really meet the needs of the campaign. In addition, if you have thousands of friends on MySpace, what is the next step? What are these friends going to do for the campaign? How can they increase volunteers or the amount of money? Don't use technology for its own sake. These social networking sites are improving their content and options to become more oriented to organize friends toward action, but their potential as campaign mobilization tools has not yet been realized.

YouTube

Finally, a note about YouTube. YouTube is a simple way to put up video of your candidate, campaign events, advertising, and any other visual medium for delivering your message. Not only is it easy to upload videos (of under ten minutes) to YouTube, it's just as simple to embed those videos on your Web site. The site provides the HTML code, which you can simply cut and paste into your Web site administration tool. Take advantage of YouTube's simplicity; it's a great way for both your supporters and undecided voters to get a more complete view of the candidate and the campaign. It's also, of course, a way candidates can get sunk when they say stupid things that are captured on video and immediately uploaded to the site, as happened with Senator George Allen's campaign. YouTube is all the more reason for the candidate to watch what he says and always stay on message.

E-mail

As we discussed in chapter 5, on direct voter contact, e-mail is one more tool available for campaigns to engage supporters in a conversation. While e-mail can be highly effective, particularly as a method of mobilizing supporters for fundraising, campaign events, and volunteer opportunities, it needs to be done right. Boring subject lines, too much text, and too frequent e-mails are guarantees that your e-mail will end up in people's trash without being read. Following are some features of a good e-mail:

- **It's short.** Say what you need to say, and avoid all unnecessary words. If you have more information that people can read, put it up on your Web site and link to it from the e-mail.

- **It's personal.** The best e-mails are written in the first person, from the candidate, a prominent supporter, or a member of the campaign team. People are far more likely to read a personal e-mail than one written in the third person.

- **It's engaging, starting with the subject line.** The subject of your e-mail is extremely important and is often what determines whether someone takes the time to read the message or immediately deletes it.

- **It's action-oriented.** It's fine to occasionally send out general campaign updates, but e-mail is best used when it calls people to take action, whether it's to raise money or sign up for door-knocking. Make it easy for people to take these action steps by providing simple links to contribution pages or sign-up pages for volunteer activities.

▸ **It's easy on the eyes.** Resist the temptation to use a lot of photos and graphics in e-mails. They can take a long time to download and distract from the central message of the e-mail.

▸ **It's sent using bulk e-mail software.** Do not use Microsoft Outlook or other personal e-mail programs to send mass e-mails; such programs do not have the capacity and were not designed for bulk e-mailing. Sending very large quantities of e-mail becomes very time-consuming without dedicated and specialized software.

▸ **It's sent in both plain text and HTML.** Some people have e-mail programs that don't allow them to read HTML images. Bulk e-mail software allows you to send e-mails as both plain text and HTML.

▸ **It's timed.** The best time to send your e-mail is during the middle of the day, when people have already cleared out their junk mail and checked their other e-mail in the morning. Aim for Tuesday through Thursday between 10:00 a.m. and 1:00 p.m.

▸ **It's sent in moderation.** If you send out an e-mail every day, your supporters will quickly grow tired of hearing from you. Save your e-mails for times when you really want people to read them. Once a week is usually the most you want to send out, unless you have some breaking news or are getting closer to Election Day.

▸ **It's well edited.** Bad grammar, misspelled words, and sloppy appearance all suggest an unprofessional campaign. There's really no excuse for sending out an e-mail that hasn't been carefully edited by more than one person.

▸ **It's tested.** Do not send out a bulk e-mail until you have tested it. Macs and PCs read e-mails differently. Yahoo, AOL, and Hotmail read e-mails differently. Internet Explorer and Firefox read e-mails differently. Always test the e-mail and make sure it appears the way you want it to in various programs and hardware.

▸ **It's tracked.** Your e-mail program should have a tool that allows you to track how many people have opened the e-mail and clicked through the links, if there are any. If you don't have this function, Google Analytics is a great program that provides this information and is available on Google's Web site. Keep close track of how well your e-mails do and compare the successful e-mails to the ones that don't get read as much: what did you do differently? It is important to remember that the best metric is the response rate, not the open rate. It's not enough that people open your e-mail and read it; if they don't take the action that you ask them to or at least click to take that action, then it's the proverbial tree falling in the forest when no one's there. Always track the open rate, click-through rate, and finally the actual response rate. For example, if you sent out an e-mail to your supporters asking for a fifty-five-dollar contribution on the candidate's fifty-fifth birthday, how many people actually opened the e-mail? How many people clicked on the donate button but didn't actually give money? How many people opened, clicked, and *gave* money? The final metric is the most valuable.

An example from the *Nation* magazine illustrates how to put all these qualities together into a concise, action-oriented message. It is a fundraising letter from the *Nation*'s Washington editor, David Corn. The subject line of this e-mail is: "I've never done this before." That's a great subject that invites the reader to keep reading. The e-mail then gets right to the point: it's both a way to raise money and a great call to action.

I've never written a fundraising letter—not counting the few notes I sent my parents when I was in college. I'm a journalist. I write articles and books—about politics, national security, and the world around us. And I'm damn lucky; I get paid to do so by *The Nation*. But the magazine has been hit by a fiscal crisis—one caused by the sort of institutional Washington corruption I often cover—and I've been asked by our publishing team to ask you for help. Please click here to pitch in.

The e-mail goes on to detail the nature of the fiscal crisis and what led to it, but even if a reader stops at this paragraph, it is a compelling and straightforward message.

Another example is from a campaign called Fair Wisconsin, which was an effort to fight a proposed civil unions and same-sex marriage ban in Wisconsin. The subject is "I have a confession to make." The e-mail goes on to read:

> Okay, so this is it.
>
> I'm about to make a confession.
>
> I haven't told anyone—not a single one of the staff or volunteers who work at Fair Wisconsin.
>
> I've been working to fight the civil unions and marriage ban since it was first introduced in January 2004. I've done a lot to help—driving around the state to events, writing well over 100 press releases, donating money, organizing large events with very little staff, writing fundraising letters and grant applications, etc.
>
> But I have never canvassed.

This is a great note. It's personal and short and connects with the reader. Most of the people reading this e-mail had never canvassed either, and the tone of the e-mail both lets them off the hook for not having canvassed in the past and gives them a reason to do so now.

Building an E-mail List

Building and growing a campaign's e-mail list is like building the campaign list of supporters. You should be asking for e-mails everywhere the campaign goes—rallies, door-knocking, fundraisers. Using petitions and "tell a friend" campaigns through your Web site, you're likely to collect more and more e-mails if your messaging is exciting and compelling. If you have been endorsed by organizations or individuals with their own e-mail lists, you can either purchase those lists and send an e-mail to them unsolicited or, even better, you can have those organizations and individuals send e-mail to their lists explaining why they support you. Their e-mail message should include a call to action to sign up and become a supporter, with a link to your campaign's sign-up page.

Unless you are on a very large campaign, do not purchase e-mail lists! Some vendors say that they can match your voter file with e-mails for as much as a dollar a name. This is tempting, because it represents the potential to raise a lot of money, but once you buy these e-mails, you are still sending unsolicited e-mails, which have a very poor response rate. Larger campaigns and organizations do buy campaign e-mail lists and send solicitation e-mails, but they have the money to do that for the return. Smaller campaigns do not. Better to have a smaller e-mail list that consists of true and active supporters than a big list of people who never asked to be on your list.

One final note on e-mails: include a privacy policy on your Web site that explains what you will be using e-mails for.

Other Technologies

There are several other new technologies that you can take advantage of. For example, many campaigns use PDAs, like Blackberries and PalmPilots, that allow them to access e-mail and the Internet remotely. Technology that serves the candidate is important, too. How can you make the candidate's job easier? If the candidate is making a lot of phone calls from the road, get her a headset so she can be more comfortable or take notes while on the phone. As we mentioned when discussing scheduling (chapter 11), invest in a GPS system to make sure you don't get lost. Technology that makes the campaign operate more smoothly and the candidate happier is often worth the investment.

CHAPTER 13

The Campaign Manager: What It Takes to Run a Successful Race

Campaigns are difficult challenges for even the experienced manager. They can be intense experiences, with high levels of activity, stress, and public scrutiny. Campaign organizations are imperfect and temporary structures in which very different kinds of people are thrown together and expected to work well as a team. If the campaign has paid staff, they are often young and experiencing their first job, or are older but inexperienced with campaign work. The presence of volunteers adds its own dynamic to the mix. They are passionate about the candidate and causes, may work extremely hard filling important jobs, but are not really accountable in the way a paid staffer is. The unique nature of campaign organizations makes them susceptible to conflict and dysfunction.

Another important point about campaigns is that they cannot be run by committee, and every voice is not equal and not always heard in making decisions. For some progressives this is difficult to embrace, because we believe in democracy and inclusion. Yet campaigns require a vertical decision-making structure for the following reasons:

▸ Unlike most organizations, campaigns operate in an external environment that demands quick action, rapid response, and clear message articulation. You can do that only when you have clear lines of authority. Decisions need to be made quickly and, once they are made, not second-guessed.

▸ Campaigns are time limited. There is too little time to "cross train" or duplicate efforts. Everyone has a job to do, everyone's job needs to be clearly defined, and everyone should be focused on implementing the campaign strategy.

▶ Message discipline: to deliver a message consistently and clearly requires exceptional discipline. Everyone on the campaign (even those who never talk to reporters) needs to be saying the same thing about the campaign and why the candidate is the best choice in the election.

▶ Electoral campaigns are unique among organizations because they are all organizations focused around one individual. Therefore, there is ultimately one point of accountability on every campaign, and that lies with the candidate. The organization naturally flows from the candidate to the campaign manager and all the way down to the volunteers.

Having said that, the best campaigns have both a nimble and an efficient management structure, while also being inclusive. They have highly engaged and motivated staff and volunteers who feel a sense of ownership and stake in the campaign. Winning progressive campaigns invite large numbers of people to take an active role in the effort. The best managers actively seek input from volunteers and other campaign staff, and your campaign can gain valuable feedback from those working most directly with actual voters. Invite advice and input, but make it clear also (by setting expectations up front) that once decisions are made, the time for debate and discussion is over. This is an important way to build solidarity and common purpose and to minimize infighting and turf wars. The key to striking a successful balance is to clearly delineate roles and responsibilities up front and as your operation expands.

Other than the candidate, nobody's responsibilities are greater than the campaign manager's. The campaign manager has several jobs: keeping everyone from the candidate to the campaign team motivated and focused, managing down to the staff and key volunteers and up to the candidate and candidate's spouse, managing the campaign's consultants, making sure income and expenses stay aligned, and seeing that the plan is implemented and that the campaign is making progress toward victory. We do not equip people very well for the important and difficult job of helping good candidates run the kinds of campaigns they need to win. But there are some behaviors and best practices—some art and some science—that campaign managers should consider to help them get the most out of all involved in the campaign.

Survival Tips for Campaign Managers

An essential skill of any skilled manager is the ability to listen well to the people you manage. When dealing with people from whom you are seeking strong and dedicated work performance, find out how they respond to different forms of management, and understand the strengths of an individual. You get the added benefit of good feelings from other people when they know they've been heard. You want to be open to hearing comments about the campaign, the work, and how to make improvements. Listening well doesn't mean you have to agree with others; instead, it better informs your ability to manage and get the most out of them. The importance of listening extends to volunteers. Actively seek and receive input from your volunteers. Not only is this invaluable feedback on what is working with actual voters, but it is also a way to develop solidarity and volunteer leaders who take more ownership of the campaign. Schedule time to sit down with your volunteers and field staff and listen to what they are hearing from voters.

Use your campaign plan. As we discussed in earlier chapters, the campaign plan should be widely known to everyone on the campaign and should serve as your primary management and accountability tool. The best plans are written with lots of detail, all the way down to quantifiable goals on specific timelines. The plan becomes the basis of people's work plans, and then management of an individual becomes about direct accountability through numerical goals established in the plan.

Establish office and work norms right away. Get clarity early on about the expectations of staff and key volunteers relating to work hours, standing meetings, ways to deal with problems, and other basic office rules. Then it is your job to make sure that you and everyone else sticks to them. Getting everyone to agree up front to norms is a tool to hold people accountable if the norms break down. For an example of such norms, check out the following Campaign Code of Conduct:

1. Be serious but have fun. Energy and excitement are infectious. Politics is serious business, but if you are not having any fun or getting something out of the campaign, get out, because chances are that the folks you are trying to get on board will also "get it" and get out.

2. Take care of yourself—physically and emotionally. Working on a campaign means too little sleep and too much stress. Take care of yourself. Yes, this is your mother: eat vegetables, drink

in moderation, stay focused, exercise, and make the time to stay healthy emotionally and physically.

3. You are part of a team, and the team is why you are here. You win campaigns by working as a team, not by trying to be the superstar. If you badmouth a co-worker, you hurt the team. If you badmouth the candidate, you hurt the team. If you badmouth the campaign, you hurt the team.

4. If you have a problem, address it with the appropriate person in an appropriate way. Frustration and aggravation are normal. Being pissed off is normal. Wanting to scream is normal. But yelling and swearing in front of the office (or in front of volunteers) is unprofessional, demoralizing, and annoying. Problems with supervisors, co-workers, the campaign, or a volunteer should be dealt with privately with the appropriate person or people.

5. Find one close friend as a "vent partner." In World War II it was "Loose lips sink ships." In politics, loose lips—indiscriminate complaining and venting—sink campaigns. Gossip is fun . . . only if it's about the opponent's campaign. But since everyone also needs to vent, find that one confidant to "tell all" to, one you can trust not to "tell all" to anyone else.

6. Do not leave campaign papers or plans lying around. Not to be too Alberto Gonzalez, but you need to assume that other campaigns are paying attention to your desk, your trash, and your regular campaign "haunts." Too many campaigns have been undermined by carelessness with confidential inside information.

7. If you think you are being paid too little, ask for more, but don't complain about it. If you went into politics primarily to make money, get out. You won't be happy, you won't be any good, and you won't make any money. It's OK to be interested in what everyone else makes, but if knowing this makes you crazy, don't ask. There are plenty of other things to focus on.

8. Sexual harassment is a crime. Period.

9. Remember you are always an ambassador for the candidate. For most voters, you will be as close as they get to the candidate. How you act, what you say, what you do, what you wear reflects back on the campaign and candidate.

10. Clean up. Moldy rotten food, old pizza boxes, half-filled cups of coffee, and crushed beer cans may make for an interesting "campaign atmosphere" (or frat house), but most people and volunteers just find such things disgusting.

As campaign manager, you are an important model for other staff and volunteers about work habits and the office culture. Always remember that as campaign manager, you set the tone in a powerful way for the office.

While you don't want to share campaign secrets with the outside, don't be afraid to share appropriate information with people and allow for input. This is important as a way of eliciting important feedback, generating creative ideas, and keeping people feeling fully part of the campaign. Information can be shared in staff meetings when there is an understanding that things don't leave the room. You can do little things like give people an advance peek at ads, literature pieces, and other campaign material. Volunteers should hear the general components of the plan and strategy to win. The importance of a campaign having a clear, efficient decision-making structure does not mean that your campaign can't also be open and inclusive of large numbers of people.

A good campaign manager is someone who does not take the ups and downs of the campaign and the candidate personally. Campaigns are emotional roller coasters, particularly for candidates. The campaign manager often is the one person the candidate can blow off steam with. Campaign stress will often make candidates overreact to little things that go wrong. The campaign manager needs to be the calm in the storm for the candidate and for other staff and volunteers. The best thing a campaign manager can do in these cases is to understand his or her role as a shoulder for the candidate and try not to take it too seriously when the candidate overreacts to little mistakes. Instead, put these interactions into the context of the overall stress a candidate is probably feeling.

Encourage all staff and volunteers to be in constant problem-solving mode. When issues, problems, or conflicts emerge, don't let them fester. Instead, figure out how you can get this problem solved so you can move on to the work at hand. That means providing people the opportunity to surface things so they can get fixed. It is also important to forecast for people that problems and conflicts will arise, and that it's everyone's job to work quickly to solve them. Use evaluation of staff (working from the plan) to head off future problems. When in problem-solving mode, use one-on-one conversations and the original work plan to get people back on track.

Be comfortable not knowing everything and not having all the answers. Know what you don't know and go out and surround yourself with those who do know. Behind every good campaign manager is a skilled team of specialists. Often the manager's job is to make sure everyone else is working at his or her best. Also behind every manager is a set of mentors who give counsel and advice when a manager faces a difficult problem.

Avoid the paid-staff-versus-volunteer culture split. Key volunteers should be as much a part of the team as paid staff. Too often, volunteers, even those who are critical to the campaign's success, sit outside closed doors when decisions are made. Volunteers are gold and are one of the campaign's most valuable resources; they should be treated as such. In campaigns that have only volunteer labor, supervolunteers should be identified and named and treated as though they were paid staff.

Manage up to the candidate. Early on, set the operating norms that will work between you and the candidate. The candidate and manager should decide when to talk regularly, how they will handle problems, and how they like to work. The candidate should respect the manager's line of authority, and if that is not happening, the manager needs to raise it with the candidate.

Managing the Campaign outside Your Campaign

One of the most common frustrations we hear voiced by first-time campaign managers is the lack of control they have over the campaign that is occurring outside your campaign, ostensibly aimed at helping it to win. A wide range of organizations, some of which are prohibited by law from coordinating with your campaign, may be engaging in activities like direct mail, phoning, and paid advertising that complement, or in some cases contradict, your campaign's hard work. Here is what a few of our advanced campaign training participants told us about some of their unpleasant experiences working with the campaign outside their campaign:

> ▶ "The single biggest issue that I faced on the campaign was learning to navigate the bureaucracies of a statewide coordinated campaign and finding a way to make my smaller campaign a part of their efforts."

> ▶ "Eventually, the party began to give more resources and attention to [my candidate], even maxing out on contributions, but the campaign staff considered the party a Johnny-come-lately. This

led to a tense relationship between the campaign's staff and the party's staff. . . . It is an unfortunate example of how infighting can destroy a progressive cause."

▸ "Because the race was targeted as a pick-up seat, and possibly the race that would make the difference between a Democratic majority and a Republican majority in the state Senate, it garnered a great deal of attention from the Senate Democratic Caucus. This was both a blessing and a curse. On the one hand, the resources provided to the campaign were invaluable and allowed for many options not otherwise available. . . . On the other hand, having invested so much in the race, they understandably exerted an uncommon level of influence in all aspects of the campaign. . . . Tension between the campaign manager and the caucus liaison was palpable and resulted in a lack of clarity as to who was the primary source of leadership on the campaign."

These problems occur often on campaigns, and while there are limits on what you can do about it, it is important to understand and properly relate to all the other entities that may be involved in your campaign in one way or another.

There are four major categories of groups and outside activity in the orbit of a campaign: the political party and its related committees, political action committees (PACs), issue advocacy organizations and 527s, and labor organizations. One key piece that must happen before you launch your campaign and as you write your plan is to know all the laws that affect your race and affect how you can or cannot interact with outside entities. This is extremely important since laws vary widely from state to state.

Parties and Their Committees

The state party, of course, is one of the first places to turn for essential resources to run your campaign. The formal connection to the party starts with an endorsement and/or nomination through winning a primary. Parties then use their unique status in campaign finance laws to assist their candidates' campaigns in various ways depending on the type of race (federal, state, or local) and different state laws. Party committees that may be involved in your campaign include the local level (the city, county, legislative or senate district party committees), the statewide level (the state party and its coordinated campaign), the legislative level (the state House and Senate party caucus campaign efforts), and the national level (the Congressional and Senate campaign committees and the party's governor and state legislative committees).

An enhanced voter file is often the most important single campaign asset maintained by most state parties, and you will want to gain access to this file and start using it as soon as you can. Most parties run a coordinated campaign to work on behalf of multiple campaigns and the entire party ticket. This means that the party campaign runs "in coordination" with individual campaigns and works from a plan that draws input from campaigns and shares resources and strategy to elect all candidates of that party. The coordinated campaign follows a plan that the major races agree to and then usually help fund.

Coordinated campaigns work specifically for multiple candidates at a time—usually at least three candidates in most major races—and work generally to support the whole ticket by making sure faithful party voters know who the party's candidates are and then making sure party supporters get out and vote on Election Day. This can be a huge asset, or for smaller campaigns it can be frustrating if it is not clearly understood from the beginning what resources are realistically available to the campaign from the coordinated campaign. The campaigns that get the most attention and voice at the table during coordinated campaigns are often determined by the importance of the race and how much money the campaign has raised to support the coordinated campaign. These are usually the major statewide or federal races and the legislative caucuses on behalf of all of the legislative candidates. But as in life, the squeaky wheel often gets the grease, so make sure your campaign takes full advantage of coordinated campaign activities and never stops asking for the help you think you need. Make sure you get and understand the coordinated campaign plan. The rules governing coordinated campaigns are a complicated mix of federal, state, and sometimes local laws. It is important to fully know what the state and federal laws say about how a party may contribute to your campaign and how you can interact with it.

Another way that the coordinated campaign can be helpful is in providing polling and other research data, especially for campaigns in which polling and a professional research operation might otherwise be out of reach. Voter ID information through a paid or volunteer phone bank is another important resource. Multicandidate voter identification is a very helpful way to target specific slices of undecided voters based on other candidate's IDs. This can also be matched with polling information. Note, though, that if you are running a campaign for county commissioner or sheriff, you may not be included in a multicandidate ID script. Once a script identifies more than three candidates, it becomes very cumbersome and less effective. Think creatively how your campaign might use this information even if you are not included on the script. Finally, a party's coordinated campaign can be very helpful in providing office space, volunteers for rallies and other candidate events, and key visibility locations for lawn signs. Depending on the race and the party, party lists can be lucrative fundraising opportunities as well. The party's coordinated campaign is less useful in other areas: issue persuasion (because it often has to be for multiple candidates), candidate scheduling, specific campaign media and spokespeople (although an effective coordinated media strategy is a very useful role for the party's coordinated campaign), campaign message development, and campaign literature (since, again, it often has to be for multiple candidates).

The House and Senate state legislative caucuses can play a major role in legislative races, particularly those that are deemed priority races. Legislative political caucus campaigns can be robust efforts—from recruiting candidates; to training; to campaign support in the form of a voter file, targeting, polling, field staff, and other services; to running its own direct voter contact programs and even making independent expenditures on behalf of its candidates. Make sure you stay in close conversation with the legislators and staff in charge of the caucus campaign efforts. Take full advantage of what is offered by these caucuses, and if necessary, be prepared to make the case that your race should be considered a priority. Caucuses can also help you hook up with legislator campaign mentors, who share their experiences as successful candidates as you run your race.

The national equivalent to the legislative caucus campaigns are the Congressional and U.S. Senate campaign committees. Learn what these committees can do for you, and be a strong advocate for your candidacy with these committees.

Community Organizing and Issue Advocacy Organizations, Federal and State PACS, and 527s

Organizations that are working to make change on issues and in communities that you care about can be important players in your campaign. These organizations come in various organizational flavors: 501(c)(3), 501(c)(4), PACs, and 527s. A 501(c)(3) is a tax-exempt charitable and educational organization that can work in the civic engagement realm but cannot try to influence the outcome of elections. The key here is to know clearly what each type of organization can and cannot do and with whom you can and cannot coordinate. Again, the rules vary according to your state, especially regarding local and state races. Campaigns cannot coordinate with 501(c)(3)s. Campaigns can typically coordinate with a PAC. Rules for 501(c)(4)s vary for local and state races according to state law. And the laws regarding 527s are changing as this book is being written. Again, any coordination with any of these groups should be checked out by competent legal counsel, for the rules are changing constantly.

Although campaigns cannot coordinate with a 501(c)(3), the latter are playing an increasingly important role in electoral politics. They focus on efforts to increase election participation through voter registration, voter education, and election protection at polling places. They must be strictly nonpartisan, but 501(c)(3)s may find out and publicize the positions that candidates take on their issues. It must be done in an evenhanded way without creating any preference for one candidate over another. 501(c)(3)s hold candidate forums to help voters understand where they stand on issues.

A 501(c)(4) is an organization that can engage in more direct political activity, including endorsing candidates and encouraging its membership to vote according to those endorsements. A 501(c)(4) can also work in certain ways on a candidate's behalf outside its membership, as well. Many (c)(4) organizations have political action committees that also endorse candidates and make direct or in-kind contributions to their endorsees. PACs are official committees set up in campaign finance law and subject to contribution limits that often are the only way organized groups can make contributions to candidates that share their issues and interests. 527 organizations are part of the IRS code that includes any political organizations that are not 501(c)(4)s or PACs.

The first step in interacting with the organizational political sector is to seek endorsements. Endorsements can help validate your campaign with particular constituencies and lead to resources such as campaign contributions and volunteers. The laws governing the different organizations and what they can and cannot do in elections are complex because they are a combination of state and federal campaign laws and IRS tax law. For instance, a (c)(4) organization can endorse federal candidates and communicate with its membership about those endorsements without that activity counting as a contribution to the candidates. But some states don't allow (c)(4)s to communicate with their members about state and local races without it being considered a direct contribution. And if a (c)(4) or PAC wants to talk to voters outside its membership, then the rules about independent expenditures may kick in. This is another area where knowing the law and how your campaign fits in is important so you can take maximum advantage of these other organized groups to help win your election.

Labor Organizations

For most progressive campaigns, organized labor will play an important role. Often labor provides extensive funding and volunteers for campaigns. Labor unions are increasingly creating their own electoral programs around their endorsed candidates, often called a member-to-member program. This has proved to be one of the most significant ways to turn out union members and their households for endorsed candidates. This is generally a bonus for those campaigns that have been endorsed and are priorities for involved unions. It can, however, mean that unions are recruiting volunteers for their own efforts rather than for the campaigns they support. Be respectful of this and at the same time be clear about what your campaign can use the most from labor supporters.

Most unions have endorsement and screening processes that allow candidates for an office to screen before members or an elected board to determine whether the union will support them or not. Prepare your candidate for this screening process beforehand. Sit down with labor supporters and leadership from a variety of unions. Once endorsed, there are several specific ways that unions can help. First is through a financial contribution if the union has a PAC. There are also ways that unions can host fundraisers for endorsed candidates. Most unions also have their own internal communication tools—Web sites, newsletters, newspapers, and so on. Make sure that your campaign knows the deadlines and provides relevant information to the editor in charge of the publication in time. Almost all unions have general membership meetings that provide a good way to meet rank-and-file activists in the union. These folks often make excellent volunteers (and sometimes paid staff). Finally, as we discussed in base building, candidates perceived as "one-month labor supporters" (the month leading up to the election or right before the endorsement) leave most union members and leaders feeling used and angry. Build real relationships, and show up for rallies, picket lines, and other labor events when you are not asking for their support. Unions can generally coordinate their activities with a political campaign, although there are again specific laws that govern this coordination and limit it. Many campaigns create a specific labor coordinator who works with the unions to coordinate efforts and create visibility and opportunities for interaction. As with everything else in this section, rely on competent legal advice before engaging in coordinated activity.

CHAPTER 14

Turning Out Our Voters: Getting Out the Vote

WHEN MOST CANDIDATES AND CAMPAIGN WORKERS start a campaign, Election Day seems so far away. By the middle of the campaign, the days can feel endless, the parades and picnics start blending into one, and the summer months drag into fall. Then suddenly you find yourself in the closing weeks of the campaign, not knowing where all the time went, and you need a strategy for getting your voters to the polls. This happens on campaigns all the time, and too often the candidate and the campaign team are so engrossed with the day-to-day of the campaign that they forget to start planning for getting out the vote until it's too late. It is not enough to deliver a compelling message and have a well-run campaign; the true test of a campaign comes when it translates support into votes by mobilizing its supporters on Election Day. The campaign's get-out-the-vote (GOTV) operation is a big effort that has its origins at the beginning of a campaign and requires careful planning, well-coordinated work with other campaigns and within your own campaign, and sufficient lead time.

But GOTV activities can be exciting and fun. There's nothing quite like the energy at the end of the campaign, when everything is on the line, emotions are running high, and people understand that their hard work is coming to an end. "One of the things I love about the last few days of the campaign is that everyone—from the campaign manager to the volunteers—is doing the same work, side by side," a campaign veteran told us. "The hours are long and the work is exhausting, but you're running on pure adrenaline. There's always time to sleep after the election is over!" Getting out the vote is also a time when you should be able to count on large numbers of volunteers. Volunteer recruitment for getting out the vote is often easier than normal volunteer recruitment, in part because it's the end of the campaign but also because GOTV work is pretty straightforward: the phoning and canvassing message is very simple, and there are easy activities, like lit drops, to offer volunteers. The key, of course, is to make sure you ask volunteers early in the campaign to help with GOTV efforts. For example, on Paul Wellstone's campaign we asked our supporters to do three things: volunteer, donate money, and take Election Day off from work to help us turn out voters. In this final stage, everyone needs to work as if there is no tomorrow—because when it comes to the campaign, there is no tomorrow!

Everyone agrees on the importance of turning out voters, but organizing all the work that goes into getting out the vote can seem like a monumental task, and it's hard to know where to start. Remember, you've done this before when the campaign started. As before, you need a plan, but now instead of planning for a months-long campaign, you're planning for a much shorter period of time, the final three to five days before the election, and then Election Day itself. And as before, you should start with identifying your audience: Who are you trying to turn out at the polls, and how can you reach them? The good news is that you already have answers to these questions. Through early base building, voter ID, and persuasion, you've made countless phone calls, knocked on the doors of your district repeatedly, and learned a lot about the voters in your district. The people you are targeting for GOTV efforts are your supporters—the 1s and 2s in your voter file (see chapter 5), the new voters you have registered during the campaign, and the people who live in high progressive-performance precincts, whom you need to turn out if you have any chance of winning.

The goal of getting out the vote is the same as it has been throughout the campaign: to engage these voters in multiple conversations. But this time the conversations aren't to identify which candidate they support, nor is it to persuade them to support your candidate. That work is over. These are people who you know support you, and the message to them is very simple: unless you go to the polls and vote, we won't win, and we won't have the opportunity to work on the agenda that we share in common. These multiple conversations take place at the door, through phones and mail, and with lit drops, and they are layered over the final few weeks of the campaign, with a particular emphasis on the last five days.

Like everything else on a campaign, successful GOTV work starts with a plan. The plan should be written early—the basic outline should be part of the starting campaign plan—and the details finalized no later than one month out from Election Day. As you put your GOTV plan together, keep in mind three principles.

First, there are four time periods covered by the GOTV plan: the early voting period (which varies by state), the transition period, the five days before the election, and Election Day itself. While planning starts on day one, the campaign moves into GOTV mode beginning thirty to forty-five days out from Election Day (unless early voting or voting by mail changes your deadlines). This is one of the most difficult times in a campaign. Just at the time when most voters are beginning to make up their minds and direct voter contact persuasion needs to be at its height, the campaign also needs to shift its focus toward planning for mobilizing its supporters. Rarely can both of these crucial tasks be done by a single individual, so many successful campaigns, especially larger campaigns, assign a dedicated person to thinking through and putting together the GOTV plan and preparations. As Election Day moves closer, increasingly more attention and resources are dedicated toward the GOTV effort. In the last week, the campaign switches into full GOTV mode, and everyone is working on compiling lists and making the final preparations for the last five days. This means that one night (usually about a week out) the persuasion phone banks stop. A day later, all of the data from phoning and canvassing need to be processed and the first mailings and new lists prepared for starting the effort on the last five days. Campaigns that can manage this difficult logistical and operational switch are often successful, but it requires extensive planning and preparation.

The second important principle of a successful GOTV program is repeated, personal, and layered contacts. We have said throughout this book that the most effective way of connecting with voters is through repetition and personal contact. That equally holds for getting out the vote.

The third principle is the need to plan for a major volunteer operation, so recruiting for the final days of the campaign should start early and be managed by a GOTV coordinator. After all the work you have put into training, motivating, and empowering volunteers, you now rely on them to finish the campaign strong.

Absentee and Early Voting

In the past decade, a number of states have enacted laws to make voting easier for their residents. To date, twenty-eight states allow "no-excuse absentee voting," which means that any eligible voter can request an absentee ballot, without having to have an excuse (such as being out of town or otherwise unable to vote on Election Day). Some states, like California, have a system of permanent absentee voting (PAV), which allows any eligible voter to be permanently registered as an absentee voter. This practice now accounts for up to 30 to 40 percent of voters in some locations in California, and it is growing. Fifteen states allow no-excuse early voting, which means that in a defined period of time before the election (usually the last month), any voter can go to a designated voting site (often a county clerk or city hall) and cast a ballot without needing an excuse. In 1988, Oregon became the first (and remains the only) state to adopt a vote-by-mail system for all its elections, eliminating traditional Election Day voting and mandating that all votes be cast by mail. However, many states have modified vote-by-mail programs so that whole districts or parts of districts (often rural and remote districts) have vote-by-mail balloting. Some have a centralized polling location if a ballot is not mailed in; some do not. Increasingly, many states are moving toward voting by mail, which makes voting more convenient (and saves money; Oregon has saved millions of dollars in administrative costs) and presents both opportunities and challenges that campaigns have been increasingly addressing in recent elections. Most state party organizations and statewide campaigns have early vote plans, sometimes with their own budgets, that complement the broader GOTV effort.

It's easy to see why early voting can give your campaign manager and GOTV coordinator heartburn. After all, your campaign plan relies on a linear timeline that culminates on a single day—Election Day—and all your campaign activities revolve around an established end date. But what if Election Day rolls around and 10, 20, or even 40 percent or more of voters have already voted? Early voting complicates the traditional arc of a campaign as it relates to timing. Campaigns that wait too long to seize campaign momentum or break through to voters with an important announcement or attack on an opponent run the risk of missing voters who have already cast their ballot. If a campaign is like standing in front of a room full of the members of your intended audience, early voting allows audience members to start filing out of the room before you have made your closing argument.

On the other hand, early voting creates great opportunities. Your base supporters can take care of voting early and free themselves up to devote their entire Election Day to helping turn out other voters. More important, your campaign can focus on a group of voters that can turn the election in your favor but who traditionally are difficult to turn out: sporadic voters. By the final weeks of your campaign, you should have a significant number of voters in your database whom you have identified as 1s and 2s—people you can reasonably expect will vote for you—but who have sporadic voting histories. They tend not to vote in off-year elections, haven't voted for several election cycles, or only recently started voting. These voters are notoriously difficult to get to the polls, and they require a lot of resources from your GOTV efforts. Early voting offers these voters a quick and simple way of voting without having to go through the "hassle" of showing up at a polling place on Election Day, and it allows the campaign to start "banking" votes. Most states that have absentee or mail ballot options require voters to apply for their ballot. This allows a campaign to target these voters early on in the campaign. For example, absentee ballots can go out many weeks (even months) before the election, but the campaign also knows exactly to whom the ballots go and when. Additionally, many states, including Oregon, track the return of mail or absentee ballots. This allows you to determine which of your supporters have actually voted and then to direct more resources to those who have not.

So how do you put together an early, mail, or absentee vote plan? First, you might not need to. Such plans are often created and implemented by political parties, particularly "coordinated campaigns" that serve a slate of candidates. If you are endorsed by a party and are part of that party's coordinated effort to turn out voters, it's likely that the party will have its own early, mail, or absentee vote program. Find out who is being targeted, how they are being contacted, and how often. Don't be afraid to ask questions; if you are part of your party's slate of endorsed campaigns, this work is being done in part in your name, and you should know what's being done on your behalf.

But let's assume you're on your own to put together an early, mail, or absentee vote plan, or you target supporters who do not necessarily support the rest of the party slate, an increasingly likely circumstance. Who is it that you're targeting? Certainly you want to target sporadic voters, making the case to them that voting is simple and easy, just a matter of sending in an absentee ballot or showing up at a designated voting location any time during the final few weeks of the campaign. But you don't need to stop at sporadic voters for your early vote universe. What about your consistent voters—is it worth having them vote early, so you can recruit them to volunteer on Election Day? What about seniors or people with disabilities, for whom you want to make voting as easy as possible? These decisions are up to each campaign, and these questions should be part of your internal discussion about how best to target your early, mail, or absentee vote plan. Ultimately, the decision will be made according to the type and frequency of contacts you plan to make, and how much money you have to do it. Make sure that your field program is geared around key early, absentee, or vote-by-mail dates. For example, your campaign's field canvass might target absentee voters in key precincts (or likely supporters based on your targeting) to door-knock in the few days after absentee ballots are mailed. Canvassers can be trained not only to persuade voters, but also to direct voters toward filling out and sending the absentee ballot.

To give you a sense of how to target early voters and contact them through the mail and by phones, let's use an example from the state of Vermont, which allows no-excuse absentee voting during the final four weeks of a campaign. The Vermont Democratic Party's Coordinated Campaign—an umbrella campaign that worked on behalf of all the Democratic nominees on the ticket—decided in 2006 to make early voting a key part of its GOTV strategy for that year's midterm elections. Months before the election, the coordinated campaign created a separate budget line item for early voting and began to plan a voter contact program specifically targeted to potential early voters. Using targeting information from previous elections, combined with the results of volunteer and paid phoning, the campaign knew that a small universe of sporadic voters could make a pivotal difference in several races. After internal discussion and debate, the campaign settled on a universe of roughly 30,000 voters who were solidly supporting the Democratic ticket but had inconsistently voted in previous elections, particularly in non-presidential years like 2006.

Once the universe was set, the next challenge was coming up with a voter contact plan. The campaign decided to contact these voters at least three times, using both mail and phone calls. Direct mail was key to the plan. Under Vermont state law, voters can request an absentee ballot directly from their county clerk, but they can also authorize a third party to request the ballot for them. That means the voter could tell the Vermont Democratic Party to request an absentee ballot on his or her behalf. That, in turn, would give the party valuable information: they would know who requested ballots and be able to follow up with each voter to see that the ballot was actually sent in. A good mail piece would not only inform voters of their right to request an absentee ballot and vote early, but would also provide a way for voters to request a ballot through the party. So the first thing the piece would include was a perforated card that voters could tear off, containing name and address information and a request from the voter to receive an absentee ballot in the mail. The voter would then mail the piece (which was self-addressed and postage paid) back to the party, which would then request the ballot from the secretary of state's office, which would then mail the ballot to the voter. In short, the party was serving as a middleman between the voter and the secretary of state's office, making it easier for the voter and collecting valuable information for the voter file.

In addition to providing voters with an easy method of requesting a ballot, the mail piece also had to convince voters—many, if not most, of whom did not realize how easy it is to request an absentee ballot and vote from home—to take advantage of early voting. Of course, the standard rules of direct mail applied: the piece had to be visually appealing, short on text, heavy on graphics, and easy to understand. The campaign then brainstormed various messages that might resonate with voters. They knew they wanted to emphasize the ease of voting absentee, but should they focus on how easy it is to forget to vote, given how busy people's lives are, or should they focus on unexpected events that might come up that could prevent people from voting on Election Day? In the end, the campaign settled on a message that was specific to Vermont. The final mail piece had a simple photograph of a "Vote Today" sign buried in snow. When a voter opened the piece, she would see an appealing image of cozy slippers in front of a warm fire, with a simple headline on top: "Or Not." Underneath the headline was a description of how easy it is to vote—no need to wait in lines or rearrange a busy schedule to go to the polls on Election Day—along with a tear-off card to send back to the party to request an absentee ballot.

It was a good mail piece but it wouldn't be effective unless voters actually read the subsequent text and took the time to send in the request. So the campaign recorded an automated phone call—a "robo-call"—that would be placed to these voters on or close to the day they received the mailing. We discussed robo-calls in chapter 5 and warned you of their limitations as a way of persuading voters, but robo-calls can often be used as organizing tools when layered with other contacts. A prominent political leader in Vermont recorded the call and delivered a succinct message: "I just wanted you to know that you will be receiving an absentee vote request in the mail. All you have to do is fill out the attached card, mail it in, and within a week you will receive a ballot in your mailbox that you can complete at home and drop in the mail. It's that simple."

Next, the campaign used volunteers to make follow-up phone calls to this same universe, asking voters if they received the mailing, if they had sent in the absentee ballot request, and if they had any questions. Through these volunteer calls, the campaign was able to track who had actually requested a ballot and who had not, and could follow up systematically with those who hadn't. What made it even easier for the party was that the names of anyone who requests an absentee ballot in Vermont is public information. So every day, the campaign would call the county clerks throughout the state and request a list of people who had sent in a completed absentee ballot. They were then able to look those names up in the database and track their progress. This way, they could find out not only whether their targeted audience was sending in absentee ballots, but whether their opponents were successfully turning out their supporters. It turned out that by matching the names of absentee ballot requesters with the campaign's voter file, the campaign knew going into Election Day that it had turned out four times the number of voters than the other side did.

Clearly, this is a complicated process that requires a lot of staff time and attention to detail. To review, there are eight steps to this process:

1. A direct mail piece is designed and a "drop" date is set.

2. A robo-call is placed to recipients of the mail piece within a day or two of their receiving the mail.

3. The voter fills in the early ballot request form and mails it back to the campaign (or party).

4. The campaign receives the request and sends it to the secretary of state's office.

5. The secretary of state's office mails a ballot to the voter.

6. The voter completes the ballot and mails it back to the secretary of state's office (or to local election officials, depending on the state).

7. The campaign places daily calls to the secretary of state's office or local election officials, getting a report of all the people who sent in ballots the previous day.

8. The campaign calls voters on their early vote list who have not yet sent in their ballot.

Obviously, this requires close attention to detail and significant staff and volunteer resources. That's a main reason why political parties or coordinated campaigns often handle the early voting process. But in the absence of a party infrastructure, and if your campaign has the volunteer and financial resources to pull off such an aggressive early vote operation, there's no reason why you can't do it yourself.

The Final Days and Election Day

As hard as it is for those of us who like working on campaigns to believe, a lot of our supporters don't give much thought to an election until the final few days of a campaign. It's up to you to remind them, as many times and in as personal a way as possible, of the stakes in the election and the importance of their voice. The last few days is when the campaign puts into action a GOTV plan that includes canvassing, phoning, lit drops, mail, and campaign events. These tools should help you contact a lot of voters and to keep contacting them over the course of five days. During this period, your goal should be to contact consistent voters one to three times with a GOTV message, and to contact sporadic voters and new registrants between three to seven times. That may sound like a lot, and it is, but our experiences—as well as empirical evidence—show that voters need multiple contacts (just as in voter persuasion) to break through the clutter and actually hear the GOTV message. While you might run the risk of annoying a voter or two because you've made a lot of phone calls or knocked on their doors a few times, the benefits of motivating more voters to go to the polls outweigh the risk, as slight as it is, of a voter not going to the polls simply because the campaign contacted her too many times. In fact, we doubt that there has ever been someone who refused to vote simply because he was contacted too many times. Remember, this is the culmination of thousands of phone calls and door-knocks and should reflect the aggressive, well-organized field operation you have created.

Perhaps the biggest mistake that campaigns make in their GOTV messaging is the assumption that getting out the vote is about reminding people to vote. This assumes that the reason most people do not vote is because they forget. So often GOTV scripts read something like this: "I'm just calling tonight to remind you that tomorrow is Election Day and we hope we can count on your vote." Perhaps in some very small or obscure elections that occur at odd times (like many township elections), voters don't know that there is an election going on. Most do, and most voters who don't vote do so not because they forgot it was Election Day or didn't know there was an election, but because they are not motivated to vote or think that it isn't that important or are intimidated by the process. This fundamentally changes the GOTV contacts we make. They are not reminder contacts so much as persuasion contacts—not to persuade the voter to support our candidate—but to go to the polls. They should be motivating, inject urgency and importance to the race, and connect (just as in any good persuasion) with what a voter actually cares about. This again is a lesson in good lists and record keeping.

Canvassing

The best way to motivate people to vote is to knock on their doors and speak to them in person. GOTV canvassing is simpler than ID or persuasion canvassing. The point is not to persuade them to vote for you (because you've already done that and identified them as a supporter in some way), but to motivate them and convince them of the importance of voting, provide the necessary information to vote (polling location, times, identification if necessary, etc.), and make it easier for them to get to the polls. It makes sense, then, that you want to start in the neighborhoods where your support is strongest and, depending on how many volunteers you can recruit, move out from there. If a precinct is particularly strong, with a 65 percent progressive performance or above, the campaign should do what's called a "blind pull"—knock on every door in the district. This is more efficient, easier, and hits a broader number of people than working from targeted supporter lists. The logic is that even if you knock on the door of an opponent, the odds are high that you will end up turning out nearly two people or more to that one opponent if you knock on every door. In swing precincts, you want to be careful not to turn out your opponents. Here you will use walk lists taken from the most current information in the voter file, and knock on the doors of your supporters (your identified 1s and 2s).

In the days leading up to the election, hit as many doors as possible with a simple message: Tuesday is Election Day, here's the one-sentence message about the candidate and why your vote is important, and here's literature (if the voter isn't home, leave the literature at the door). You also want to tell people—and include on the literature if possible—the location of their polling station and the hours during which they can vote. Then go on to the next door. On Election Day, you want to repeat this door-knock program, but all in one day. Ideally, the campaign will have a list of its identified supporters in each precinct. Each voter should receive, in addition to a phone call, a knock on the door from the campaign during the day. Depending on the state, poll watching may factor into your door-knocking. Some states allow official observers for the party or for the campaign to "watch" the polls and record who has voted and who has not. Some states even post the sign-in sheets at regular times. Then the monitor relays the names of supporters who have not voted to a canvassing team that can be dispatched to the doors of people who haven't yet voted. This is affectionately known as "knock and drag," and it's usually done later on Election Day, as the campaign gets more lists of people who haven't voted yet. Be clear before setting up a poll-watching operation about the laws in your state. Simply having people hang around the polls watching without being able to efficiently collect and send information is a waste of precious volunteer resources. GOTV canvassing can also have a general visibility benefit for the campaign. Door-knockers in T-shirts, cars with signs, and door hangers on every door serve as a reminder of the candidate's grassroots strength.

Phoning

Although less personal and therefore less effective than canvassing, phoning plays an important role in layering contacts during GOTV work. Phoning allows for a large volume of contacts and reaches those outside your door-knocking areas. Some larger campaigns will use paid callers for this, although data show that paid calls, unless very personalized and conducted by well-briefed and trained phoners, are not nearly as effective as volunteer calls and are rather costly. The effectiveness of a trained volunteer call is about 1 out of every 30 calls resulting in voters coming out who would not have otherwise, while vended calls without good training specific to the district and race is only 1 out of every 100 or more calls. Robo-calls, while cheap and often used, have little or no effect on voter turnout. They are best used to highlight other types of contact or to provide last-minute information on a changing race or on polling locations.

Other campaigns will run volunteer phone banks. The GOTV phone call is simple, consisting of four parts: a reminder of how urgent it is to vote, information on polling locations and times, asking if the voter has questions or needs assistance getting to the polls, and a thank you. For example:

I'm calling from the Miller for Congress campaign. We're calling voters who are concerned about health care because the race is *very* close, and if we are going to win we need every vote. Can we count on your vote for Miller to fight for health care we can all count on this Tuesday, November 6? *[Wait for a response; if the answer is yes, provide them with the following information.]* Polls are open from 7:00 a.m. to 8:00 p.m., and your polling place is St. Martin's Church on Main Street. Do you know where that is? Do you need a ride to the polling place? Thank you so much for your time and once again, please don't forget to vote on Tuesday, November 6.

If a voter needs a ride to the poll, verify the name, address, and phone number. You want to continue calling through your lists, maximizing your connect rate. On Election Day, you keep calling until the polls close: the key to victory is calling people until they say they have voted. The campaign may have reminded someone to vote in the morning, but it never hurts to remind him or her again. Keep calling people until they say they have voted.

The other benefit of phoning is that it's less resource intensive. Rather than pulling together walk lists and leading teams of volunteers through neighborhoods, your volunteer phoners can move through lists of targeted voters quickly and easily. If resources allow, the campaign should consider using volunteers to make calls leading up to Election Day and then rely on paid calls on Election Day so volunteers can be directed to door-knocking.

Literature Drops

Normally when you send volunteers to people's doors, you want to engage people in a conversation. Lit dropping isn't one of those occasions. Lit dropping is done when people are not home and in some areas at night on election eve or early morning on Election Day. Some campaigns call this Midnight Madness. Although it usually starts before midnight, Midnight Madness is the start of the campaign's final twenty-four hours; it involves sending teams of volunteers (for security reasons, you should go in teams of two or more people) throughout the district to "drop" literature in doorways and on car windshields. Midnight Madness lit drops often happen after a final GOTV rally on election eve. Your campaign will likely be working in collaboration with other campaigns or through a coordinated campaign, and usually volunteers meet at a designated time at a location with plenty of space for canvassers to pick up literature, meet up with other members of their canvass teams, and if possible, hear the candidate or a group of candidates fire up the crowd. Union halls, campaign headquarters, and other centrally located venues with plenty of parking make good places to kick off a Midnight Madness lit drop.

Targeted Mail

Depending on your budget, you may add GOTV mail into the mix as well. Especially with sporadic voters, mail is one more contact layered onto your phoning and canvassing work. These pieces should follow the same principles as good direct mail. They have a message of urgency, contain information on polling location and hours, and should hit mailboxes no later than the day before the election. By itself, GOTV mail doesn't have much effect, but combined with phone calls and knocks on the door, it's one more contact with a voter, one more reminder about the importance of voting, and a way to provide in writing important information about polling locations, identification requirements, and contact numbers for assistance.

GOTV Broadcast Advertising and Online Reminders

If your budget allows, you might also decide to run short ads on local radio stations or in community newspapers, in particular ethnic and constituency-based radio and newspaper outlets. Sending e-mails and text messages to your supporters is a cheap and simple way of adding one more layer of GOTV contact. Like other GOTV materials, these are simple, clear reminders of the urgency of voting.

Rallies and Visibility

Visibility plays an especially important role at the end of the campaign. You want to build momentum going into Election Day, and standing on street corners with signs, holding banners from highway overpasses, and waving to cars in busy neighborhoods are all ways to build that energy and momentum. Rallies are another way, particularly if they receive press coverage. Be sure, however, that if you are putting effort into turning out numbers of people for a rally, you combine the rally with door-knocking, phoning, or lit dropping. Use it as a volunteer mobilization tool in addition to getting press attention and firing up your base.

Election Protection

Unfortunately, protecting the ability of all voters to exercise their voting rights is an important component of getting out the vote. An election protection program (which many civic engagement organizations also create and implement on Election Day) starts with equipping people with all the information about their rights as voters. Knowing who can vote, how to vote, where to vote, when to vote, and why voting is important is critical information, especially for those who are not currently participating in the political process. Your campaign can play an important role in getting this information out to your voters. Know the laws and rules governing polling places. Communicate early with election officials and iron out any expected problems, and educate voters about their voting rights. Establish an election protection legal rapid-response team, with lawyers stationed in or prepared to go to polling places where problems are likely to arise. If possible, establish a toll-free election protection hotline, staffed by lawyers, and broadcast the number widely so people know they have recourse if they are denied the right to vote. This intentional disenfranchisement happens with shameful frequency, particularly among historically oppressed groups. Widespread voter suppression in African American and Native American communities has been witnessed in recent elections. Also, pay particular attention to the needs of communities that have special barriers to voting: people with disabilities or with language difficulties (be sure to have multilingual volunteers or staff available to help), people experiencing homelessness, victims of abuse, ex-felons, and those who are very transient. Great work has been done in recent years to address the needs of these constituencies, such as efforts to preserve the confidentiality of victims of domestic violence when they register to vote; help homeless individuals find ways to establish residency; help those with disabilities know their rights; and help individuals who served time and are off paper to reestablish their right to vote. Public education, combined with organizing with vulnerable constituencies, can really make a difference in opening up the electoral process.

Earned media plays a role in election protection. One of the tactics of voter suppression is to create anxiety in voters before Election Day by pushing press stories with predictions of "chaos," "massive problems," "long lines," and "widespread voter fraud," and efforts to vigilantly "watch the polls" to protect against irregularities. These so-called predictions can turn voters away from the polls even before Election Day. We must counter these efforts with a message of encouragement to exercise the right to vote and participate in our democracy. We should never buy into these doom-and-gloom scenarios, but should instead use earned media to inform people of their rights.

The campaign should also enlist well-trained, knowledgeable supporters to observe polling activities. While state laws vary about who can witness polling activities, most states allow one representative of each major political party to observe the voting process. Your campaign can play a role in this effort by helping to identify, recruit, and train these poll watchers. With the right training, ordinary citizens become the eyes and ears of democracy, watching for problems at the polls, assisting other voters, and reporting irregularities if they do arise. Election law is usually not complicated, but it is essential that advocates know the rules and hold election officials accountable. A simple training program can give people the knowledge they need to be advocates at the polls.

In addition to training citizen advocates, it is also important to create a well-trained legal team of lawyers, law students, and paraprofessionals who have particular knowledge of election law. These individuals then become available to staff a toll-free helpline that the campaign could establish (hopefully in coordination with other campaigns or the party), to be deployed as necessary to problem precincts, to communicate with local election officials, and to document any irregularities.

If problems at the polls come up, respond immediately. Dispatch legal assistance to the polling location, and inform election officials of the names and full contact information of those whose rights may have been violated, thorough descriptions of the incidents, and names and contact information of witnesses. This information should be forwarded to whichever governmental bodies are responsible for guaranteeing the election. If, as in the case of some states, the problem resides in those bodies themselves, then it is essential to report violations to independent legal entities whose role is to guarantee civil rights of citizens. It is also important to keep good records of any complaints or improprieties that you hear about or are reported to you in the case of a recount.

Sample GOTV Program

To give you an idea of how to layer multiple GOTV contacts and prioritize voters, here is an example of a GOTV program for the final weekend and

Election Day. It starts with a direct mail piece that hits on the Friday before Election Day and ends when the polls have closed and everyone has voted.

Friday

▶ Mail piece to the entire GOTV universe. The piece has the closing message of the campaign, a sense of urgency about voting, an "ask" for votes, and information about where to vote and when the polls are open. GOTV radio spots start running on stations that are likely to be listened to by base voters. A midday earned media GOTV event, timed to get press coverage and get into the weekend election story, should have a good visual image of the excitement and energy of the campaign.

▶ Because the campaign won't be doing volunteer phoning to consistent voters (because you want to focus on sporadic voters), you can do a robo-call to consistent voters from a prominent campaign supporter urging them to vote.

▶ Hold visibility events like sign-waving on busy street corners in targeted neighborhoods during rush hours.

Saturday

▶ Canvass high-progressive-performance but low-turnout precincts with a GOTV message. Canvassers should give out polling location information at the doors or leave it on a GOTV lit piece at the door.

▶ Run phone banks all day to GOTV targets in noncanvassable areas and to all sporadic voters.

▶ Make use of visibility with the candidate in places where crowds gather (sporting events, etc.).

Sunday

▶ Phone banks continue all day to sporadic and noncanvassable GOTV targets.

▶ Canvassing in high-performance/low-turnout precincts continues.

▶ Continue visibilities with candidate in places where crowds gather.

Monday

▸ Make second round of calls to sporadic voters.

▸ Visibility continues throughout the day, during rush hour and in areas like food courts and other high-traffic areas.

▸ Hold final GOTV rally for *all* volunteers at 9:00 p.m., after phoning ends.

▸ Rally attendees go out afterward for Midnight Madness lit drops in high-progressive-performance precincts.

Election Day

4:30 a.m.

▸ Make wake-up call to the staff and volunteer leaders!

6:00 a.m.

▸ Legal team assembles and election protection volunteers head to their polling locations.

▸ Visibility: GOTV volunteers go to bus stops, holding signs and encouraging people to vote.

▸ Send e-mail blast to all supporters urging them to vote early, with an invitation to the election night victory party.

▸ Continue to run radio ads on Election Day, if allowed by law.

7:00–9:00 a.m.

▸ The polls open, and morning voting rush starts. This is a good time for the candidate to vote.

▸ Visibility moves to key polling places (be sure to know the laws regarding how close you can be to the actual polling location).

▸ Door-knocking teams gather at a staging area before they go out into neighborhoods.

10:00 a.m.

▸ Canvassers hit the streets for first round of canvass, targeting high-performance/low-turnout precincts.

▸ Rides to polls begin.

▸ Paid phone banks begin GOTV calls to entire universe and continue until polls close. In this case, the campaign chooses these calls over volunteer calls, preferring to send volunteers door-knocking instead.

Noon

▸ Provide lunch for canvassers.

▸ Receive thorough updates from checkers at polling locations. You should adjust the canvass and phoning programs according to where turnout is lower than expected. For example, if one of your targeted precincts is reporting low turnout numbers, send more canvassers to that precinct to turn people out.

▸ Phone calls continue.

▸ Visibility for lunch crowd: send volunteers to highly trafficked lunch areas, like downtown office buildings and food courts.

2:00 p.m.

▸ Second shift of door-knocking begins.

▸ Phone calls continue.

▸ Get second turnout report and make adjustments in canvassers' target locations.

3:00–7:00 p.m.

▸ Afternoon voting rush begins.

▸ Visibility continues during rush hour.

▸ Phoning continues.

▸ Third shift of door-knocking begins.

7:00–8:00 p.m.

▸ Make final door-knocking sweep.

▸ All hands to phone banks, calling until polls close.

▸ Poll watchers remain at polling locations until polls close; watch for long lines and encourage voters not to leave.

▸ Victory party begins!

Case Study: Minnesota Democrats in 2004

In 2004, a year with hotly contested presidential and state legislative races, the Minnesota Democratic-Farmer-Labor Party knew that its fortunes rested on a massive GOTV program to increase turnout among its base voters. To get the job done, the party used a two-pronged strategy. In low-turnout base areas (those that traditionally support Democratic candidates at least 65 percent of the time), the campaign ran massive "blind" canvasses (knocking on every door in a neighborhood) on the weekend leading up to Election Day and then again on Election Day itself. In nonbase areas, the campaign ran targeted volunteer canvasses and a phone program to talk only to identified supporters. Traditionally these nonbase areas would have been ignored in a GOTV program, but by targeting to specific voters, the campaign was able to maximize its turnout throughout the state, even in places where it was not winning a majority of the votes.

On Election Day, volunteers canvassed each door in low-turnout base areas up to three times throughout the day until they had confirmation that every eligible voter in the household had voted. To maximize efficiency of the operation, volunteers hung on doors a piece of literature that had a different color on each side, something that was first experimented with in the 2002 Wellstone election. One color facing the street meant everyone in the house had voted, while the other indicated that people hadn't been home or hadn't yet voted. This way, the second and third waves of volunteers knew if they needed to go to a house again. Volunteers walked and drove eligible voters they met on the doorstep to the polls. Rather than just remind people to vote, the canvassers were well trained with a script that emphasized the importance of the election and motivated people to vote. The "knock and drag" operation went to over 800,000 doors on Election Day and personally escorted to the polls 30,000 people who otherwise likely would not have voted. This represented more than 1 percent of the final electorate.

To make this huge volunteer operation work, GOTV centers were set up throughout the state. To move large numbers of people in and out of these centers and maximize the amount of time talking to voters, volunteers were efficiently greeted, signed in to make sure there was contact information, assembled into a team of four by a "shepherd," given a highlighted map of the streets they would be canvassing and driving directions to the area, fed and given hot drinks, and then trained on the objectives and process for persuading people to go to the polls. At some centers, as many as 4,000 volunteers moved seamlessly through on Election Day, and as the day progressed, volunteers were funneled to areas that were reporting lower voter turnout.

Added to this canvassing operation were (1) a targeted, volunteer-based phoning program that made more than 500,000 calls in the final four days to likely supporters without strong voting history, (2) an election protection program that put trained lawyers in more than five hundred precincts throughout the state, and (3) a thousand volunteers engaged in visibility activities leading up to and on Election Day. Although the scale of this effort was bigger than some, the principles were the same as those we've discussed in this chapter regardless of the size of the election: repeated, personal contacts with targeted voters; clear communication about the urgency of participating in the election; and ensuring that people's civil rights are upheld. When put together, this GOTV program was one of the main reasons that Minnesota led the nation in voter turnout at 77 percent and the Democratic-Farmer-Labor Party enjoyed an incredibly successful election.

CHAPTER 15

You Won. Now What?

In the classic film *The Candidate,* Robert Redford plays an unlikely candidate for U.S. Senate who stages a stunning upset victory against an entrenched incumbent. In the final scene, Redford's character, dazed from his victory, looks at his campaign manager and says, "What do we do now?" It's an apt ending to the film, since this scene often plays itself out, one way or another, on campaigns all the time. For months, sometimes years, candidates are engaged in a contest with a definite end: Election Day. But what happens after Election Day? If you win, you go on to serve in office and deliver all your campaign promises, right? And if you lose, you pack up the office and call it a day? It would be nice if it were that simple, but it's not. Serving effectively and delivering on your campaign agenda requires a concerted and deliberate effort to stay in touch with the groups that helped get you elected. And moving on after a defeat, even if a future run is not on the horizon, requires a systematic cataloging of campaign materials, databases, lists, and other information that will be helpful to future progressive candidates.

One of the most important things to remember, and easiest to forget, is that the days immediately following an election are important opportunities to archive all relevant campaign documents and materials. It's easy to forget because everyone on the campaign, including the candidate, is in a state of complete exhaustion, and the last thing people want to do is go back to the campaign office and archive materials. That's completely understandable; the campaign staff and volunteers should take a day or two off to rest and decompress. But soon after the election, they should be back in the office, taking the time to systematically organize all the campaign materials that could potentially be useful for another run by the candidate or another candidate down the road. Before campaign workers head off for vacations or their next jobs, it's imperative that they take part in this crucial work.

It is also important to get together with campaign supporters and workers and celebrate, regardless of whether you win or lose. Part of this celebration is to acknowledge the work that was done. At a separate meeting, campaign workers and key volunteers should get together to debrief the campaign—win or lose—to determine what worked, what could have been improved on, what should never be done again. This debrief should be systematic and should result in a written document that can be part of the archived materials.

Beyond archiving materials and sending thank-you notes to all campaign supporters via snail mail and to your e-mail list, there's still a lot of work ahead. If you lost your race, the end of the campaign can also mark a beginning of sorts. We mentioned in chapter 5 the example of Newark mayor Cory Booker, who came back from a close defeat to win an election four years later after a deliberate strategy of staying in touch with his supporters and broadening his base in the interim. Booker is hardly unique in rebounding from an electoral defeat to go on to win elected office. In fact, we would estimate that most members of Congress or statewide officeholders have lost at least one election in their careers. The key to rebounding from a defeat is to learn from your mistakes, but also to build on the networks of supporters and volunteers that you established in the first campaign.

If you won on Election Day and find yourself asking "What do we do now?" the short answer is, "Keep it up." The most effective elected officials keep their campaign infrastructure alive to maintain contact with their supporters and constituents and to prepare for reelection. This infrastructure provides the "scaffolding" on which to build a meaningful constituent contact plan. Following are some suggestions for any newly elected public official for being an effective advocate on the inside while still maintaining a connection to groups and individuals on the outside of the political process. (Be sure that you understand and follow all the relevant laws regarding official and campaign work separation when it comes to the campaign database and other activities. Some of these things can be done with official money, some cannot, so know your local laws and follow them.)

> ▶ **Plan your constituency contact.** Just as the campaign had a plan, complete with specific tasks, you also need a postelection plan for constituent contact and ongoing relationships with the community. Within this plan there will be distinct jobs or roles for staff

and volunteers to play, as well as specific tasks related to constituent engagement. Elected officials should take time at the front end to think through what they want to accomplish, what the timeline is, and who will get the work done.

▸ **Maintain your database.** One of the most basic political tasks of any elected official is to create and maintain an effective database of constituents. This means ensuring that the names you collected while running for office are continually updated and enhanced with the issues of concern to them as individuals and groups. Never underestimate the power of a clean, well-maintained list of names. As you serve your constituents, these people become part of your ongoing database. Take the time to set up your database right from the beginning and commit your staff to maintaining it well.

▸ **Map your relationships.** As a candidate, you developed many relationships with community leaders and concerned citizens during your campaign. These key relationships are the foundation for your infrastructure of constituent contact and engagement. However, now that you are an elected official, many more people will be willing to engage with you. Begin by thinking about specific individuals or organizations that are influential in your communities and whether or not you already have a relationship with them. Once you have mapped your existing relationships and those that you want to build and strengthen, you will need to decide how you will communicate with each group. This requires a commitment to meeting with leaders, learning about their issues and concerns, and asking for their help in finding solutions to their challenges. This also requires a comprehensive constituent contact plan. Here is a list to help you think about who should be in your universe of contacts:

- ▴ cultural, religious, or ethnic affinity groups
- ▴ professional associations
- ▴ organized labor
- ▴ life stage groups such as seniors, students, and parent associations
- ▴ issue leaders
- ▴ neighborhood/block club leaders

> ► **Assign staff or volunteers to each constituency.** Despite the best intentions, many groups do not get the attention they deserve because no one is assigned to build and maintain the relationship with them. Be deliberate about this by assigning a staff person, a key volunteer, or a member of your family (or yourself) to be a liaison with each community you consider important to your agenda.

Constituent Contact Plan Outline

Let's look in greater detail at your constituent contact plan. As you know, regular, ongoing contact with your constituents is key to remaining accountable to your district, increasing transparency in government, and keeping voters happy with the job you're doing. This requires multiple, varied forms of communication that should be planned out to maximize impact and ensure you are accessible to all constituents. Here is a sample constituent contact plan template with suggested communication strategies that can help you craft your own plan tailored to your community.

Literature and Letters

How will you communicate with your constituents through the mail, given your budget? Think about the following options:

- ► **Questionnaire.** Many elected officials send an issue questionnaire to constituents at the beginning of a legislative session or beginning of their term. In general, this does more to make the elected official appear to be accessible to constituents than it does to actually gauge constituent attitudes. Use a questionnaire in conjunction with other means of follow-up and outreach.

- ► **Targeted mailings.** Elected officials may send issue-specific literature to constituents who have expressed an interest in that issue through the course of the campaign season and through contact with your office.

- ► **New resident welcome letter.** Elected officials may frequently obtain lists of new residents to the district from city/town halls. Send a welcome letter to these new constituents welcoming them to the community and providing a brief introduction to your office and an invitation to contact you at any time. This can also be paired with a personal phone call. If you have a database of all residents in the district, like your voter file, be sure to update it to reflect these new constituents.

▸ **Follow-up letter.** Any constituents who contact your office on a particular issue should receive a note alerting them to progress on that issue, thanking them for their thoughts, and asking them for help if appropriate by shoring up more community support.

▸ **Congratulatory letters.** When you learn of any significant achievement by individuals or organizations in your district, send a note to acknowledge it. Monitor local papers and gather information from key constituent leaders for this information. If you have ever received a congratulatory letter from an elected official on the occasion of a birth of a child, a graduation, or an anniversary, you know how much this personal attention matters.

▸ **Responses to constituent contact.** All constituent letters, e-mails, and phone calls should be acknowledged and responded to appropriately.

▸ **Door-knocking and event handouts.** For face-to-face contact with constituents, you may door-knock from time to time. Prepare a small (quarter-page) piece with basic contact information, your issue priorities, and an invitation to contact your office.

Forums

Forums are an excellent way to make yourself accessible and learn more about what issues are of concern to your community. There are a variety of forums available to you:

▸ **General.** These are free-form events to hear constituent concerns and take questions on whatever is on people's minds.

▸ **Issue focused.** Particularly relevant or pressing issues to the district may demand a forum focused specifically on that issue. Do these in collaboration with organizations or active constituents who are leaders on the issue, and be sure to time them in advance of key committee hearings or votes on relevant legislation.

▶ **Constituency focused.** Target forums to specific constituencies as part of a broad effort to engage people from key communities in your district, particularly underrepresented constituencies, and engage them in the political process. Be sure when planning these forums to pay attention to accessibility to the targeted constituency—geographically (where do people congregate?), culturally (do you need an interpreter?), and logistically (at what time of day are people available?).

Media

It is much easier to get earned media as an elected official than as a candidate. Use it to influence the public debate.

▶ **Newspapers.** Newspapers are great ways to communicate with your constituents. Public opinion pieces, letters to the editor from your supporters, press releases, and press events are all critical to keeping in touch with your constituents.

▶ **Public access television.** Many elected officials host their own public access TV shows. While it might not seem like these shows get a broad audience, they attract more viewers than many people think, and they particularly attract seniors, a demographic that turns out to vote in large numbers.

All the rules about earned media in campaigns apply to elected officials: create relationships and target media outreach to all types of media from TV, radio, print, and specialty press.

Community Outreach

Use your office to build your base of supporters and reach out to those not typically involved in the political process.

▶ **Community events.** Have a presence at important community events and identify constituents who can be leaders on issues you are working on.

▶ **Community group meetings.** In addition to special events, community groups have regular meetings. Ask leaders of these groups if you can sit in on a meeting and have a brief opportunity to say a few words. These groups include neighborhood associations, PTAs, the American Legion, student groups, and so on.

▶ **Advisory committees.** Meet with leaders from those communities that you dealt with on your campaign to get input and advice on issues important to the community and to hear their thoughts on issues coming up before you on a daily basis.

Door-Knocking

As you know, door-knocking is the most effective way of communicating with voters. If you have the time, door-knock in the off-season, when your constituents least expect it. It's a great way to stay in touch, but it's also a way to send a signal to any potential opponent that you are an aggressive and constant presence in the community. You might also consider door-knocking in an area in advance of public events or before major legislative or policy decisions. Track these conversations in your database.

Web Site and E-mail

It is critical to have an online presence and to be able to get information to constituents quickly and cheaply.

▶ **E-mail newsletter.** Regularly update constituents via e-mail on recent/upcoming votes, key issues up for debate, and your positions on those issues. Promote your e-mail list and collect e-mail addresses at community events. Maintain a supporter and campaign worker e-mail list. This is a way to keep in touch with campaign workers and supporters in a more intimate way and keep them involved.

▶ **Web site.** Provide key contact information, position statements, news, and updates. Keeping your campaign Web site updated and operational is essential.

Databases

Just as you would for a campaign, figure out how you will track and manage different types of constituent contact. Maintain your campaign volunteer database, keeping it current with volunteers from your constituent base. Also maintain your campaign voter file; keep it up to date and use it to target mailings based on issue interest.

You should also keep a current list of all new residents, including the basic biographical information available from city or town hall, the month they were added to the list, the date a welcome letter was sent, and any notes.

Develop and Organize for Your Agenda

The next step in constituent engagement is finding solutions to the problems faced by your community. Depending on the office you hold, you may have access to teams of researchers and constituent contact staff that can continually give you information about the concerns of your district, or you may be fielding calls from constituents on your cell phone. Either way, here are some tips on how to take an idea, be it your own or from a constituent, and make it public policy.

- ▶ Consult policy experts in the given field, including academic researchers, legislative assistants, nonprofit and opinion leaders.

- ▶ Get a sense of the recent history of the issue. Ask if anyone has tried this idea before in the state. If so, what were the results?

- ▶ After getting a handle on the historical information, seek out the political information. Which fellow elected officials may be allies? Will any be adversaries? How much political will or power does each have?

- ▶ Draft the legislation, with assistance from staff if available. Be sure that any final version that is submitted is something you have confidence in. Even if the policy will be altered later, do not introduce legislation that is poorly crafted.

- ▶ Create advisory groups. Draw on the relationships developed with your constituents to create citizen advisory groups that offer guidance on the attitudes of your district. These groups can be created along demographic or issue-focused lines and can meet regularly or be called in only when you face a decision on a policy or action related to the members of that group. These groups can act as critical backup when you're faced with an unpopular or difficult decision and can offer a sounding board on how your decisions affect their lives and the lives of their neighbors.

▶ Engage volunteers and supporters. As an elected official, you can play a key role in developing new leadership among your constituents by asking them to take on the tasks of organizing behind your agenda. By engaging volunteers and supporters in these tasks, you accomplish two goals: getting the message about your priorities and your issues out to a wider audience and building the skills of your allies to engage in issue advocacy work. Examples of tasks that you can ask volunteers to do include writing letters to the editor in support of your agenda or an issue you are working on, recruiting constituents to attend a town hall forum, or mobilizing constituents to give testimony at a hearing. Be intentional about organizing behind your issue. Not only will this ensure success, but it will also engage constituents and build their skills.

Stand by Your Convictions

We spent a lot of time in this book talking about the importance of authenticity and standing up for your core values. Sometimes that is easier to do as a candidate than as an elected official. For elected officials, the process of creating policy solutions to the problems of the district is a balancing act; you need to weigh the attitudes of your constituents with your own priorities and values. How do you decide what policies to support? This is something that only you can decide. However, authenticity is a characteristic that not only is proving to resonate with voters during election time, but also engenders a leadership of moral clarity that most people in this country—left, right, or center—are hungry for.

Minnesota State Representative Steve Simon tells us that he believes it is crucial that elected officials look to their values when making policy decisions. "I think that public officials owe their very best judgment to their constituents," explains Simon. "Sometimes, that judgment may lead to unpopular decisions. Exercising independent judgment also means being courageous." By making clear to constituents and your fellow elected officials where you stand on the issues, you communicate integrity and authenticity to your constituents. What is most important is that a conversation happens with the affected constituencies and parties before the decisions are made.

This shows respect for people's opinions and a willingness to listen (and maybe even hear new information). It is also something that is too often overlooked, because it is uncomfortable for an elected official to tell supporters that he or she will not be with them on an issue. That is why we keep coming back to the courage of one's convictions. Having these respectful conversations is perhaps the single most important thing elected officials can do to continue building and expanding their base and building a community around a progressive agenda.

Acknowledgments

Lᴉᴋᴇ ᴏᴜʀ ᴛʀᴀɪɴɪɴɢ ᴘʀᴏɢʀᴀᴍs, this book draws deeply on the specific experiences and wisdom of many successful and committed campaign professionals, candidates, and grassroots organizers. We would particularly like to thank the candidates and others who agreed to be interviewed for the book: Andrew Gillum, Celestine Jeffries, Elizabeth Glidden, Gloria Totten, John McCoy, Kathy Hartman, Mark Ritchie, Matt Filner, Patricia Torres Ray, Peggy Levesque, Peggy Flanagan, Ralph Remington, Rebecca Otto, and Steve Simon.

We also want to thank the extraordinary group of individuals who make up the Wellstone Action staff: Jane Austin, Adriana Barboza, Fawn Bernhardt-Norvell, Jeff Blodgett, Pam Costain, Kim Couch, Camille Cyprian, Stephanie Dodge, Peggy Flanagan, Ben Goldfarb, Jennifer Haut, Laura Keys, Erik Peterson, Lonna Stevens, DawnMarie Vihrachoff, Mattie Weiss, Tracey Wells-Stewart, and Elana Wolowitz, and our devoted volunteer, Marge Boyle.

Todd Orjala from the University of Minnesota Press is a great editor who pushed us to do this project, and we are grateful to the Press for its commitment to advancing the Wellstone legacy.

Index

JEFF BLODGETT is executive director of Wellstone Action and has twenty-five years of community organizing, issue advocacy, and political management experience. He spent thirteen years as a senior aide, adviser, and campaign manager to the late Senator Paul Wellstone, running all three of his election campaigns. Blodgett has worked on dozens of other election campaigns and issue advocacy efforts, including Amy Klobuchar's successful election to the U.S. Senate in 2006.

BILL LOFY is a senior trainer for Wellstone Action's national training programs. In addition to working for Wellstone for six years as a press aide and campaign organizer, he has worked on campaigns at the local, state, and presidential levels, including managing the 2006 coordinated campaign for the Vermont Democratic Party and the 2000 Minnesota Bradley for President campaign. He is the editor of *Politics the Wellstone Way: How to Elect Progressive Candidates and Win on Issues* (Minnesota, 2005) and the author of *Paul Wellstone: The Life of a Passionate Progressive.*

BEN GOLDFARB is director of training programs at Wellstone Action. In 2006, he was campaign manager for Senator Amy Klobuchar, and most recently he served as strategic research and communications consultant for the main opposition party in the 2007 Irish Parliamentary Elections. In 2004, he was the get-out-the-vote director for the Kerry–Edwards campaign in Minnesota. He also served as executive director of Progressive Minnesota, managed the Benanav for Saint Paul Mayor campaign in 2001, and helped lead a public employee union's electoral program in 2002.

ERIK PETERSON is director of education and labor programs with Wellstone Action. He has more than twenty-five years of experience in grassroots community, labor, and electoral organizing and twenty years as a trainer and teacher. He served as a field consultant on the 1996 and 2002 Wellstone for

Senate campaigns and has helped build several labor-community-political coalitions, including the Duluth Living Wage Coalition and Duluth's Community Religion Labor Network. Most recently he has served as the lead consultant for Mark Ritchie's 2006 secretary of state race and as the northern Minnesota get-out-the-vote director for America Votes.

SUJATA TEJWANI is a senior trainer for Wellstone Action's national training programs with fifteen years of electoral and issue campaign experience in communications and management at the Congressional, senatorial, and presidential levels, including for Senator Paul Wellstone (1996), the Democratic National Committee (1997–99), Maryanne Connelly for Congress (2000), Louis Lucas for Congress (2001), Senator Max Cleland (2002), Kerry/Edwards–Democratic National Committee (2004), Cover the Uninsured (2003, 2004, 2007), and Give Kids Good Schools (2006). She also develops and coordinates trainings for Democratic GAIN and EMILY's List.

Educate.

Advocate.   Organize.

Wellstone Action!

WELLSTONE ACTION (WWW.WELLSTONE.ORG) is a national center for training and leader development for people and organizations involved in politics and public life. Founded in January 2003, Wellstone Action honors the legacy of Paul and Sheila Wellstone by helping thousands of others to continue their support and advocacy for the progressive cause.

Through Camp Wellstone, our Advanced Campaign Management School, and other training programs, Wellstone Action teaches candidates, campaign workers, and volunteers across the country the basics of grassroots political action, drawing from Paul Wellstone's successful approach that integrates grassroots organizing, electoral strategizing, progressive public policy, and ethical leadership. We train candidates and organizers working on campaigns at all levels, from local offices to major statewide and Congressional races.

Much of the material in this book is based on the curriculum of Wellstone Action's Advanced Campaign Management School. This intensive training teaches the fundamentals of winning campaigns, building the skills of a new generation of campaign managers, and developing leaders and professionals for long-term involvement in campaigns and the progressive movement. We do this work because there is a need for large-scale, broad training that infuses the progressive movement with organizers, candidates, and volunteers equipped with the skills to recruit and elect a new wave of progressive candidates so that we can ultimately win on the issues we care about.

More than fourteen thousand people have attended our training programs in thirty-nine states.

To learn more about the Advanced Campaign Management School, Wellstone Action, and our other work, contact us at:

Wellstone Action
2446 University Ave. West
Suite 170
St. Paul, MN 55114
(651) 645-3939

www.wellstone.org